THREE

PILLARS

of

MODERN

WESTERN

CULTURE

Richard Wagner's Impact on James Joyce's *Ulysses*
and Marcel Proust's *In Search of Lost Time*:
Leitmotifs, Endless Melody, and *Gesamtkunstwerk*

William H. Pastor

Published through Opus Self-Publishing
Politics and Prose Bookstore
5015 Connecticut Avenue NW
Washington, DC 20008
www.politics-prose.com // (202) 364-1919

Cover Art: Left Image: *Marcel Proust, Photograph (1895),* Museum of Letters and Manuscripts, accessed on September 10, 2020, Wikimedia Commons, https://commons.wikimedia.org/wiki/File:Otto_Wegener_Proust_vers_1895_bis.jpg.
Middle Image: *Richard Wagner, Photograph (circa 1860),* accessed on September 10, 2020, Wikimedia Commons, https://commons.wikimedia.org/wiki/File:Richard_Wagner_2.jpg.
Right Image: *James Joyce, Photograph (1904),* accessed on September 10, 2020, *Wikipedia,* https://de.wikipedia.org/wiki/Datei:JamesJoyce1904.jpg.

To Cathy, my wife and lifetime companion, who is better in every way than the composite of Brünnhilde, Isolde, Gilberte, the Duchesse de Guermantes, Albertine, and Molly.

Walter: So it might be not dream, but poetry?
Sachs: The two are friends, gladly standing by each other.
Walter: How do I begin according to the rule?
Sachs: **You make it yourself, and then you follow it.**

—Richard Wagner, *Die Meistersinger von Nürnberg*,
Act 3, scene i, emphasis added

There are sins . . . evil memories which are hidden away. . . . **Yet a chance word will call them forth** suddenly and they will rise up to confront him in the most various circumstances. . . .

—James Joyce, *Ulysses*, episode 14: Oxen on the Sun,
14.1344–50, emphasis added

But a new writer had recently begun to publish work in which the relation between things were so different from those that connected them for me that I could understand hardly anything of what he wrote. He would say, for instance: "The hose-pipes admired the smart upkeep of the roads" (and so far it was simple, I followed him smoothly along the roads) "which started every five minutes from Briand and Claudel." At that point I ceased to understand, because I had expected the name of a place and was given that of a person instead. **Only I felt that it was not the sentence that was badly constructed but I myself that lacked the strength and ability necessary to reach the end.**

—Marcel Proust, *In Search of Lost Time*,
The Guermantes Way, vol. 1, p. 950, emphasis added

CONTENTS

Preface to the Second Edition

My initial goal was to write *Three Pillars of Modern Western Culture* during the COVID 19 summer "quarantine" of 2020. While I met that goal, the delta variant during the summer of 2021 provided the opportunity to address comments and questions raised by readers of the first edition. It also provided me the opportunity to make corrections and incorporate additional information.

This second edition includes, among other topics, a clarification of the difference between a theme and a leitmotif, how the term "*Gesamtkunstwerk*" can apply to art forms beyond opera, and an elucidation of Pater's dictum: "All art constantly aspires towards the condition of music." For non-Wagnerians, I added an appendix with a glossary of Wagner operas and characters. For philosophically-minded readers, I added an appendix on the philosophers who influenced Wagner, Joyce, and Proust. In total, I enhanced the first edition with nearly twenty additions, as either footnotes, paragraphs, or appendices.

I would like to thank all those who provided me with comments and suggestions. Special recognition goes to Jean Arnold, Thomas Stanley and Mark Golden for their insights that improved the writing and thereby the reading of *Three Pillars of Modern Western Culture*. My wife, Cathy, deserves a special shout-out beyond her recognition in the Dedication for her insights, edits, and support in our creating the first and second editions of *Three Pillars of Modern Western Culture*.

ILLUSTRATIONS

Cover:

Left: Marcel Proust, 1895

Middle: Richard Wagner, circa 1860

Right: James Joyce, 1904

Acknowledgments

This book would not have been possible, in fact, it would not have been conceived without the Wagner Society of DC (WSWDC). I must acknowledge Aurelius Fernandez, president emeritus of the WSWDC, for introducing me to the WSWDC. Their monthly lectures and their annual weekend retreat to rural West Virginia, aptly called Wildnis, provided the aesthetic and intellectual foundation for this book.

Lectures by Jim Holman, chairman of the WSWDC, and Saul Lilienstein were invaluable to my appreciation of all things Wagner. Wildnis deserves its own shout out. Beginning in 2001, during our three-day retreat, we would discuss the music, libretti, and cultural milieu of Wagner's operas. Lectures were provided by Jeffrey Swann and Simon Williams. Many of their lectures are found on the WSWDC's website and are a "must see" for anyone interested in Richard Wagner's music dramas.

Nearly fifteen years ago, a group of WSWDC members formed a Wagner Book Group (WBG). We continue to meet every two or three months in someone's home (by Zoom during the 2020 COVID pandemic) to discuss a Wagner-related book. Each meeting is an intellectual salon and our *Gesamtkunstwerk*: we talk, we eat, we drink, sometimes we play music, and we talk some more.

The WBG meetings served as a springboard for me to make connections with political, social, philosophical, and aesthetic areas of nineteenth-, twentieth-, and now twenty-first-century art, music, literature, philosophy, and culture in general. In particular, the WBG exposed me to the influence that Wagner had on the symbolists, as well as modernist writers, such as James Joyce and Marcel Proust.

Christopher Griffin, an instructor with the bookstore Politics and Prose, in Washington, DC, deserves special mention. He opened the door for me into the world of James Joyce and, in particular, to *Ulysses*. Often one does not know who is speaking or thinking in *Ulysses*. Mr. Griffin directed us to the public domain audiobook which, when listening to while reading the text, makes

Ulysses much more accessible than only reading the text. That site is: https://archive.org/details/Ulysses-Audiobook. Somewhat ironically, I do not remember how I first became interested in Marcel Proust. That memory remains in lost time.

I also must acknowledge my very good friends, Al Navidi and Emily Armstrong. We have shared countless fantastic dinners paired with fine wines. Although we closed out many dinners with Wagner excerpts, we never discussed a word of Wagner's impact on Joyce and Proust. The same cannot be said of my cycling buddies, Andy Lees and Don Silverstein. They gracefully put up with my discourse on Wagner, Joyce, and Proust, but I did notice that their pace picked up whenever I began talking about the content of this book. Gil Herrera, my good friend and probably the most intelligent person I know, has yet to come over to Wagner (or Joyce or Proust). He is more of a Mozart person, but I will keep trying to bring him into the fold. And my first book sale, while still in draft form and undoubtedly bought under Dionysus's influence, goes to Allan Ingenito. Whether he will read my book is another question, but a sale is a sale.

Lindsey Reinstrom, my copy editor, and Gareth Bentall, my publishing manager, deserve credit for helping me to turn my manuscript into a book.

Last, although she should be first, is Cathy, my wonderful wife. How she persevered through my endless chatter about Bloom and M. de Charlus and Wagnerian *leitmotifs* is a mystery to me. She must have been paying attention since she always had contributions, insights, and clarifications that are dispersed throughout this book.

Although I am indebted to all those mentioned above, any mischaracterizations, misunderstandings, and errors are mine alone.

Introduction

Leitmotifs, endless melody, and *Gesamtkunstwerk* are three terms intrinsic to Richard Wagner's music dramas. Wagner discussed these terms in his theoretical writings[1] and constructed his operas around them. James Joyce and Marcel Proust knew Wagner's operas and theoretical writings. Moreover, Joyce and Proust consciously incorporated the literary analogs of *leitmotifs*, endless melody, and *Gesamtkunstwerk* into their groundbreaking modernist novels: *Ulysses* and *In Search of Lost Time*,[2] respectively. The purpose of this book is to illustrate how these two novelists used Wagner's nineteenth-century musical techniques in their twentieth-century novels.[3]

A *leitmotif*, in the simplest and rudimentary definition, is a musical theme[4] associated with a character, emotion, or object. It is a short passage of music that functions to remind the listener of past events and foreshadow future events.

---

[1] For scholars and Wagnerites, see *Art and Revolution* (1849), *Music of the Future* (1849), and *Opera and Drama* (1852), in English translations by William Ashton Ellis.

[2] *In Search of Lost Time* is the accepted English translation of the title of the French novel *À la recherche du temps perdu*. Hereinafter, *À la recherche du temps perdu* will be referred to as *In Search of* unless the context requires the French title. See note 62 for a more complete explanation of the various translated titles.

[3] Many writers used characters from Wagner's libretti in their literary works. Examples of such usage include George Moore's *Evelyn Innes*, nearly all of Thomas Mann's works, but most conspicuously in *Blood of the Walsungs*, Paul Verlaine's *Parsifal, and* T. S. Eliot's *The Waste Land*. The Wagnerian formal structures of *leitmotif*, endless melody, and *Gesamtkunstwerk*, not the content of the libretti, are the focus of this manuscript.

[4] Themes are different from *leitmotifs*. Themes communicate the main idea of a work, whereas *leitmotifs* function like a signpost pointing to different sections of the work. A musical *leitmotif* differs from a musical theme insofar as a musical *leitmotif* is associated with a particular character, object, emotion, or idea; themes do not carry this level of specificity. For example, while Beethoven's sixth symphony includes sections that sound like birds and thunderstorms, these nature sounds do not depict a particular bird or thunderstorm. In contrast, Siegfried's funeral march in Wagner's opera *Götterdämmerung*, is not a generic funeral march. It is Siegfried's funeral march. Literary *leitmotifs* function in a similar manner as musical *leitmotifs* by their association with other literary characters, objects, emotions, or ideas. For example, compassion is one literary theme of *Ulysses*. The word "jingle" is a *leitmotif* in *Ulysses*. When Leopold Bloom hears his and Molly's bed jingle by Molly's stirring shortly after 8:00 a.m., it is significant that it is their bed jingling and not some other bed, since that "jingle" is associated with Molly's tryst with Blazes Boylan in that bed.

Through various musical techniques, a *leitmotif* can be transformed to acquire new associations and new sounds, thereby generating new emotional responses; yet this new *leitmotif* is audibly related to the original *leitmotif*.

Strictly speaking, an "endless melody" is neither endless nor a melody in the ordinary sense of the word. It is a long passage of music that is woven together with *leitmotifs*. This linking of *leitmotifs* and their permutations functions to create coherence within an extended passage of music.

Gesamtkunstwerk is the integration of many individual arts into one work. This concept is aspirational in nature with the goal of enriching a work of art. Opera is particularly well-suited for employing this concept because it intrinsically involves many art forms.[5] These arts include music (composition and orchestration), literature (libretto), voice (spoken and sung words), acting (dramatic or comic), architecture (sets and props), dance (choreography), and design (lighting).

The ideas of *leitmotif*, endless melody, and *Gesamtkunstwerk* are the organic framework of this book as they apply to Wagner's influence on James Joyce's *Ulysses* and Marcel Proust's *In Search of Lost Time* (hereinafter *In Search of*). Employing an organic metaphor, *leitmotifs* are the vertebra, endless melody is the skeleton, and *Gesamtkunstwerk* is the entire body. These ideas will be briefly discussed in this Introduction and further developed in chapter 1.

The main purpose of this book is to show how these ideas are employed by Joyce and Proust in their literary masterpieces.[6] My approach is straightforward. First, I show that Joyce and Proust were well-acquainted with Wagner's works, including his operas. Second, I provide references to Wagner and his works in *Ulysses* and *In Search of*. Third, and most important, using textual examples, I illustrate how Joyce and Proust used *leitmotifs*, endless melody, and *Gesamtkunstwerk* in the structure of these two literary works.

While my method is straightforward, my goals are lofty. These goals are to stimulate interest among Wagnerians who are primarily music lovers, in the novels *Ulysses* and *In Search of*, and to stimulate interest among Joyce and Proust lovers who are primarily literature lovers, in the music of Wagner. For those

---

[5] The concept of *Gesamtkunstwerk* also applies to non-operatic works of art. An example of *Gesamtkunstwerk* in interior design is the dining room in the Palais Stoclet in Brussels, and an example in architecture is The Red House in Bexleyheath, England. In literature, *Gesamtkunstwerk* can be illustrated in a work by the use of varying writing styles, allusions to different time periods, depictions of distinct geographic places, or descriptions of diverse emotional states.

[6] Joyce wrote several other major works including *Dubliners* (1914), *Portrait of the Artist as a Young Man* (1916), and *Finnagans Wake* (1939). I am restricting my analysis to *Ulysses* (1922).

who are in both camps, I hope to deepen their understanding of the historic and artistic connection among these three pillars of Western aesthetics and culture. For those not in any of these groups, this is an opportunity for a trifecta.

The story of how I came to write this book is oddly appropriate to the three protagonists, i.e., Wagner, Joyce, and Proust. It is a story of a memory, a reminiscence, and a journey back in time. I was in the waiting area of the Kansas City airport on my way to see the 2016 production of Wagner's *Tristan and Isolde* at the Metropolitan Opera. On my lap sat a hardcover book. In response to a question from the person on my left, I answered that I was reading Marcel Proust's *Remembrance of Things Past*. To my right I heard a deep piercing groan, like Kundry being unwillingly yanked into consciousness in act 2 of Wagner's *Parsifal*. That cry of despair, followed with profanities, emanated from a middle-aged woman.

I learned that this unnamed woman had been a French major in college. She told me, in language heavily sprinkled with profanities, that, at the direction of her French professor, she had written her senior thesis on Marcel Proust's *À la recherche du temps perdu*. We talked about her Proustian-related experiences until we boarded the plane and our talk soon receded into my memory. Like a *leitmotif*, this memory would resurface whenever I heard the name "Proust."

If I could relive that moment, I would have quoted Frank, the unemployed English professor speaking with his nephew Dwayne, from the 2006 movie *Little Miss Sunshine*:[7]

> Frank: "Do you know who Marcel Proust is?"
> Dwayne: "He's the guy you teach."
> Frank: "Yeah. French writer. Total loser. Never had a real job. Unrequited love affairs. Gay. Spent 20 years writing a book almost no one reads. But he's also probably the greatest writer since Shakespeare. Anyway, he uh . . . he gets down to the end of his life, and he looks back and decides that all those years he suffered, those were the best years of his life, 'cause they made him who he was. All those years he was happy? You know, total waste. Didn't learn a thing."

---

[7] *Little Miss Sunshine* (4/5) movie CLIP-Remembrance of Things (2006) HD", YouTube, 2:17, 7/29/2015, https://www.youtube.com/watch?v=7VbYokM9dY4; for the text, "*Little Miss Sunshine* (2006) – Steve Carell as Frank – IMDb, accessed on 10/26/2020, https://www.imdb.com/title/tt0449059/characters/nm0136797.

I wish I had recited that clip to her. I suspect she would have laughed with the realization that hearing the name "Proust" was her madeleine cake. That bite of "Proust" vividly resurrected her senior semester in France, the town of Illiers (Combray), M. de Charlus, Albertine, and a plethora of memorable characters and events. I wonder if, like the Narrator in *In Search of*, it might have caused her to consciously analyze her memories. Her analysis might have been far and wide as with a telescope or narrow and focused as with a microscope. In contrast, like Joyce's protagonist in *Ulysses*, Leopold Bloom, her memories might have emerged from her semi-consciousness, going from place to place, in a seemingly random fashion. Would she better *understand* her world like Proust's Narrator or better *feel* her world like Bloom? Or would she pick up an airplane magazine and look at the pictures for the next two hours? Sadly, we will never know.

In 1989, I purchased the two volume Moncrieff translation of *Remembrance of Things Past*. It took me longer to get to page three than it took Wagner to complete *The Ring of the Nibelung* (hereinafter *The Ring*). Around 2017, I learned that Wagner is mentioned a lot in Proust. Being a Wagner enthusiast, but far from being a perfect Wagnerite, that motivated me to retrace my steps back twenty-eight years and turn all the way back to page one. I was inspired to catalog every reference to Wagner, whether to Wagner directly or to one of his operatic characters. With that motivation I was off to the races—or at least past page three.[8]

The first Wagnerian reference came relatively early in the novel, on page 137. This might not sound all that "early," but the novel is nearly twenty-three hundred pages, so page 137 barely gets you out of the starting blocks. The Narrator is in a church at a wedding. For brevity's sake I quote just a fragment of the sentence with the Wagnerian reference bolded: ". . . a bloom of light giving it that sort of tenderness, of solemn sweetness in the pomp of a joyful celebration, which characterizes certain pages of **Lohengrin**, certain paintings by Carpaccio. . . ." The Wagner references kept coming, so I kept reading. While reading Proust I reached retirement age and retired.

Upon retiring in 2018, I decided it was time to tackle another book that "everyone should have read" and that book was James Joyce's *Ulysses*. I started with a five-session course at a local bookstore and became fascinated with the wanderings of that alienated, but kind fellow, Leopold Bloom. The instructor never mentioned Wagner, but I saw several not-so-opaque references to Wagner. For example, in the Circe episode (15.4235–44), during a

---

[8] A description of Wagner characters and operas mentioned in this book are found in Appendix E.

hallucinatory Walpurgis Nightfest in a brothel, Stephen shouts: "'No! No! No! Break my spirit, all of you, if you can! I'll bring you all to heel! **Nothung**!' (He lifts his **ashplant** high with both hands and smashes the chandelier. . . .)" (emphasis added). This scene clearly refers to act 1, scene i of *Die Walküre*. In this scene in Hunding's hut, Siegmund pulls the sword from the tree into which Wotan had previously thrust it. Siegmund names the sword Nothung.

Now I was confronted with the Newtonian three-body problem, but my three bodies were not three physical objects circling each other and trying to come up with a set of equations describing their motion. My three-body problem was how to relate these three pillars of Western culture: Wagner's operas, Joyce's *Ulysses*, and Proust's *In Search of*. A reasonable first question to ask is whether there were significant relationships between Wagner and Joyce and between Wagner and Proust? Is there anything about these three artists that provides a meaningful link between the music composer and the novelists?

On first blush, these three artists could not be more different from each other. Of the three, Richard Wagner (1813–1883) had the most colorful life. There are dozens of biographies describing Wagner's turbulent life. Perhaps the most exhaustive, and the foundation on which other biographies are based, is Earnest Newman's four-volume opus *The Life of Richard Wagner*. In brief, Wagner gave up a lifetime tenure job as *Kapellmeister* of the Dresden Opera to actively participate on the politically liberal side in the failed 1848–49 revolution in Dresden. As a result, with a death sentence hanging over him, he fled to Switzerland. He was not to return to Germany until 1862, when the ban was lifted. During his exile in Zurich, he wrote many of his theoretical opuses describing his revolutionary operatic style, as well as several of his major operas.[9] He was a perennial debtor and often on the run from his creditors. In 1864, he was financially rescued by his future patron, King Ludwig II of Bavaria.

Wagner married Franz Liszt's daughter, Cosima, but not before having three children with her while she was married to his friend, the conductor and Wagner disciple, Hans von Bülow. In 1876, in Bayreuth, Germany, he opened the Bayreuth Festival in his *Festspielhaus*, an opera house he designed and built. The annual Bayreuth Festival in the Festspielhaus continues to this day. Among his ten mature operas, Wagner is most famous for the four-part, sixteen-hour-long *Ring* cycle and the desire-themed opera *Tristan and Isolde*. He died a national, in fact, an international acclaimed composer. Moreover, his works

---

[9] See Appendix D.

spawned a level of cultural enthusiasm that came to be identified as Wagnerism, and in certain instances, tended towards Wagnermania[10] during the late nineteenth century and early twentieth century.

James Joyce (1882–1941) saw his family's wealth disappear due to his father's alcoholism, and Joyce struggled financially for much of his life. In the voice of Stephen Dedalus, Joyce viewed Irish culture as beaten down by usurpers (England), religion (Catholics), alcohol, and poverty. *Ulysses* describes this culture. The novel takes place in Dublin, on June 16, 1904, among the lower middle class where men spend a lot of time drinking and happiness seems to be found at the bottom of a bottle. This is the Dublin where Leopold Bloom and Stephen Dedalus spend June 16, 1904.

The Irish were not happy with their portrayal in *Ulysses*. The *Dublin Review* panned it as "spiritually offensive" and "physically unclean." *Ulysses* was not even permitted to rise to the level of being banned in Ireland—it simply was never imported during Joyce's lifetime. When Joyce died in 1941, the Irish consul was conspicuously absent from Joyce's funeral.

Marcel Proust (1871–1922) came from an upper class and highly cultured family surrounded by music, art, and theater. Due to his family's wealth, he never had to work for money. He was supported by his parents until their death, his father in 1903 and his mother in 1905. At age 35, following his mother's death, Proust inherited, in late twentieth-century currency, $4.6 million.[11] Unlike Wagner and Joyce, Proust wanted to be liked and was generous, both with his time and money.

---

[10] I am using the term "Wagnermania" to mean a devotion to, or passion for, all things Wagner, particularly Wagner operas. Beginning with Baudelaire, through the Symbolists, into the 1920's, and arguably even today, Wagner devotees tend toward an almost cult-like focus on Wagner. Joseph Horowitz, *Wagner Nights: An American History*, does not shy away from the word cult: "All this [Wagnerism] forms the context for America's Wagner cult" (Horowitz, p. 7); and "Wagnerism as a necessary crusade—a cultural movement, empowered...to see and judge the whole world in the light of Bayreuth...." (Horowitz, p. 2) Jed Rasula, *History of a Shiver*, makes a similar claim: "The personality, opinions, theories, music, and proselytizing of the composer were magnified through the lens of Wagnerism—a formidable device, ranging in capacity from telescopic to microscopic and acquiring the aspect of a distorting lens along the way. Wagnerism was a force unto itself." (Rasula, p. 77) Rasula further asserts that Wagner's music inspired religious devotion. (Rasula, p. 89) Wagner's *Festspielhaus* and his home, *Villa Wahnfried*, (including his grave) are treated as sacred shrines by many Wagner devotees or Wagnerites. Even today, Wagnerites do not appreciate it when Wagner's operas are treated in a light-hearted or satirical fashion.

[11] William C. Carter, *Marcel Proust: A Life*, p. 402.

In Search of describes the upper crust of Parisian society (Society) around the *Belle Époque*.[12] The Narrator describes a culture comprised of offensive superficiality, hypocrisy, and deceit. It is a culture in transition, soon to pass into irrelevance after World War I. Proust could not find a publisher for the first volume, *Swann's Way*, and had to pay for the costs out of his own pocket. *Swann's Way* was an immediate success, and thereafter Proust did not have to pay for the publishing expenses for the remaining six books of *In Search of*. During his lifetime Proust was awarded the Prix Goncourt, France's most prestigious literary prize.

Wagner's works are written in operatic language, i.e., music and German libretti. *Ulysses* is written in English; *In Search of* is written in French. Each of Wagner's ten major operas tells a different story, has its own sound, and aside from *Die Meistersinger*, primarily resides in mythical realms. Wagner's operas are very "serious," some would say "heavy," and many of the characters are strange beings, functioning as archetypes rather than as normal human beings. From *The Flying Dutchman's* Senta through *Parsifal's* Kundry, I dare say that no one would want most Wagnerian characters as one's neighbor.

In contrast, the characters in *Ulysses* and *In Search of* are all too human. Stephen Dedalus is a bit obnoxious and at times irritating, but for the most part, he is a very bright kid who has not found his place in the world. Leopold Bloom is harder to pin down as a personality type. He has a lot of pluses and minuses, but they balance out to the median line on a bell curve. The Narrator in *In Search of* is a social climber but probably no more so than many people we have encountered in the workplace. While liked and respected by his colleagues, the Narrator has his problems: his love life is in shambles and he is obsessed with his mother's kiss.

Joyce and Proust have very different writing styles. Leopold Bloom, the predominant voice of *Ulysses*, expresses himself in fragments of thought using the literary method of stream of consciousness. The Narrator of *In Search of* expresses himself in long thoughtful sentences using the literary method of interior monologue. As a result, the pages of *Ulysses* have lots of whitespace, whereas the pages of *In Search of* are almost all print.

If I could spend an afternoon in a pub or cafe with either Joyce's Bloom or Proust's Narrator, Bloom would drink water or perhaps a glass of cheap

---

[12] Belle Époque, literally means "Beautiful Age" and is a term commonly used to refer to the period in Parisian history between 1871 and the beginning of World War I in 1914.

Burgundy wine, whereas Proust's Narrator would have a glass of Dom Perignon or Château d'Yquem. Perhaps neither would want to spend an afternoon with me, but they would express their reluctance very differently. Bloom would internalize that he wants to get away: "Get rid of him quickly. Take me out of my way. Hate company when you." The Narrator would paraphrase Madame de Sévigné's comment by saying that I was depriving him of solitude without affording him company.[13] In contrast, Wagner would hold court the entire afternoon and well into the evening.

Wagner, Joyce, and Proust were very well read, including in philosophy. Each of these artists was significantly influenced by specific philosophers, and this influence impacted their respective artistic works. Wagner was influenced by Ludwig Feuerbach (1804-1872) and Arthur Schopenhauer (1788-1860). Joyce was influenced by Plato (428-348 BCE), Aristotle (384-322 BCE), Thomas Aquinas (1225-1274), Giambattista Vico (1668-1744) and George Berkeley (1685-1753). Marcel Proust was influenced by Henri Bergson (1859-1941). For more information on these philosophers and their impact on Wagner, Joyce, and Proust, see Appendix F.

While differences abound between *Ulysses* and *In Search of*, there are significant similarities. Both books are "modern." The authors' primary focus is not what happens in the objective world. Rather, their primary focus is what occurs within a character's subjective psychological reaction to the world, i.e., a character's consciousness. The significant action of both novels occurs in the mind.

The objective or physical time of both novels is linear. *Ulysses* takes place on June 16, 1904, from 8:00 a.m. to around 3:00 a.m. the following day. *In Search of* traverses about sixty years. It begins around 1860 and continues until a few years after World War I. Within this objective time, like the stories in *The Arabian Nights*, we travel through a labyrinth of realities, bringing in countless time periods, history, the arts, politics, humor, sciences, psychology, sexuality, adultery, jealousy, memory, imagination, sleep, death, love, desire, hatred, and just about every human emotion. In other words, these books show us the world; each one is a literary *Gesamtkunstwerk*.

In both novels, subjective or psychological time, as manifested in the psychological life of the characters, is a spiral that moves both forward and

---

[13] James Joyce, *Ulysses*, episode 5, Lotus Eaters: 5.22; Marcel Proust, *In Search of*, vol. 2, *The Captive*, p. 388. Orlando, in Shakespeare's *As You Like It*, captures their sentiment succinctly: I do desire we may be better strangers. (3.1.347)

backward in time. This subjective time folds in on itself and is forever encroaching and interrupting the characters' objective time. Events of the present keep pulling Bloom and the Narrator back to their respective pasts. For the reader, this means that the past acquires greater significance as the present unfolds, and we better understand the present as we recollect and remember their past. This time-shifting technique is similar to a Wagnerian *leitmotif*. But how was the connection made between Wagner's musical technique of *leitmotifs* and Modernism as expressed in these two novels of the early twentieth century?

Wagner's influence on modernism was the focus of the Wagner Society of Washington DC 2019 Wildnis retreat, which touched briefly on Wagner's influence on Joyce's *Ulysses* and Proust's *In Search of*. Following the retreat, I was stimulated to dig deeper into Wagner's impact on these two literary masterpieces. Wagner, and his music, was a common element to three major "isms": Romanticism, symbolism, and modernism. In fact, Wagner's influence was so powerful that it led to a cultural phenomenon called Wagnerism, and at its extreme, Wagnermania. Wagnermania was just as it sounds, a passion for all things Wagner. However, Wagner and his music meant different things to different people, but it all was identified as Wagnerism.

Three Wagnerian artistic innovations, *leitmotifs*, endless melody, and *Gesamtkunstwerk*,[14] played a major role in the cultural phenomenon of Wagnerism. Wagnerian scholars have identified these three formal Wagnerian innovations as having enormous impact on Joyce's *Ulysses* and Proust's *In Search of*. I found, however, that scholars did not support their claims with many actual illustrations. In other words, I found more assertion than demonstration. I wanted to find more illustrations to better understand the assertion. As is often said, the devil is in the details.

Appreciating a work of art does not require an analysis of the work in terms of its formal properties, any more than appreciating a poem requires recognizing it as a Shakespearian sonnet, or appreciating a work of architecture requires knowing the number of nails or crossbeams used to hold it up. The pleasure experienced when embracing works of art does not require knowledge of their composition. However, knowledge does not diminish that appreciation. In fact, I would argue that understanding the craft that goes into a work of art, or really any activity, increases one's sense of wonder. To use Proustian imagery, the more

---

[14] Wagner did not invent musical *leitmotifs*, but he developed them to a new level of sophistication. The term *Gesamtkunstwerk* was coined by K.F.E. Trahndorf in 1827. Wagner used this term to describe one of his operatic aspirations. See section 1c below for a more detailed explanation.

time we spend studying something, the broader our memory reservoir and the richer and deeper our appreciation. Knowledge is not a slayer or destroyer of experience, but rather, it is the soil in which experience is nourished.

For example, in *Ulysses*, it is a bit past 8:00 a.m., and Bloom is bringing Molly some tea and toast in bed. She asks him the meaning of a word in a book she is reading.

> - Show here, she said. I put a mark in it. There's a word I wanted to ask you. She swallowed a draught of tea from her cup held by a nothandle and, having wiped her fingertips smartly on the blanket, began to search the text with the hairpin till she reached the word.
> - Met him what? He asked.
> - Here, she said. What does that mean? He leaned downward and read near her polished thumbnail.
> - Metempsychosis?
> - Yes. Who's he when he's at home.
> - Metempsychosis, he said, frowning. It's Greek: from the Greek. That means the transmigration of souls. (episode 4, Calypso: 4.331–42)[15]

We learn later that Molly phonetically sounds out the word as "Met him pike hoses." Taken by itself, the above exchange is hilarious: "Met him what"; "Yes. Who's he when he's at home." Throughout *Ulysses*, Bloom refers to "met him pike hoses," metempsychosis, and related terms many times, but if we do not recognize these repetitive references as reminiscences that create a literary *leitmotif*, then we have, at best, a superficial understanding and a mere surface pleasure. Recognizing "met him pike hoses" and its related terms should lead our awareness back to Molly in bed and all that Molly and their bed signifies to Bloom, including where the usurper, Blazes Boylan, will soon be visiting. Taking the reader both back in time and into the future is the function of a literary *leitmotif*.

William Blissett asserted that there are more than 150 *leitmotifs* in *Ulysses*.[16] I do not know if anyone has identified the number of *leitmotifs* in *In*

---

[15] Joyce's humor continues. Molly responds: "'O rocks!' She said. 'Tell us in plain words.'" In episode 18, Penelope, Molly reflecting on the origin of the phrase "tea off flypaper" recalls her earlier exchange with Bloom: "'. . . if I asked him he'd say it's from the Greek leave us as wise as we were before. . . .'" (18.240–41)

[16] Blissett, "James Joyce in the Smithy of His Soul," p. 115.

Search of. This brings us to the problem of identifying *leitmotifs* in literature, as well as naming them.

Identifying *leitmotifs* in music and in literature can be quite difficult. Both have a notation and a structure that is taught and can be analyzed. Musical notation is fixed; and therefore, given certain technical musical skills, one can "see" the motif and follow its transformations. Literature uses grammatical rules that are embedded in ordinary language. Given a certain degree of literacy, one can "hear" the motif and follow its development.

Creating literary *leitmotifs* from ordinary language is difficult for the writer and can be very difficult for the reader to recognize. For example, the simple word "chair" can stand alone or be part of a family of "chairs." It can refer to the electric chair, a royal chair, i.e., a throne, a dollhouse chair, a wheelchair, a highchair for a baby, the chair (person) of a department, a rocking chair, a stool, another word for a sofa, and the Platonic Chair, to name but a few uses of the word "chair."[17] Is "chair" a *leitmotif*? It is impossible to determine out of context.

Ordinary language also contains synonyms which complicates the problem of identifying literary *leitmotifs*. Even more confusing for identifying literary *leitmotifs*, are descriptions that *prima facie* do not appear to refer to the same concept. For example, "she transfers jobs to be with him," "she buys him presents," "they argue but she but does not leave," can all express the *leitmotif* "love" or "psychological dependence" or "enabler." Ordinary language is as ambiguous, if not more so, than musical language.

In *Ulysses*, Stephen often quotes Latin texts. Latin is in some sense identified with Stephen. Therefore, Latin can be identified as a literary *leitmotif* for Stephen. For example, when Malachi Mulligan quotes Latin, we know that he is mocking Stephen. Latin also is identified with the Catholic Church and Stephen's Jesuit education. The Church, and Stephen's Jesuit education also function as literary *leitmotifs* in *Ulysses*. Latin, which was the language of the Catholic Church, is one of the bondages that Stephen identifies as keeping Ireland in poverty and keeping him psychologically trapped in the past. When we hear Stephen quoting something in Latin, we are reminded of Stephen, Ireland, the Church, oppression, and psychological repression. If Latin sentences or phrases do not trigger these memories and associations, then we are missing, and I would say not appreciating, a major component of *Ulysses*.

---

[17] The Narrator in *In Search of* is subject to verbal abuse from M. de Charlus for sitting in the wrong chair. The Narrator failed to identify the Louis XIV chair in Charlus's room. (*GW*, vol. 1, p. 1111)

Recognizing literary *leitmotifs* in *Ulysses* is a crucial first step for enjoying the novel. Giving them names comes later, if at all. The same analysis applies to *In Search of.*

Love and jealousy are two major *leitmotifs* in *In Search of.* They are so tightly interwoven for the Narrator that the experience of one is the experience of the other. Are they one or two *leitmotifs*, or are they sub-*leitmotifs* of the *leitmotif* "self," i.e., the Narrator in his solipsistic world?[18] The Narrator has a propensity for self-gratification. Is this character trait one motif, or does it fall under the broader motif of the Narrator's inability to form meaningful personal relationships?

Even seemingly simple examples of identifying and naming *leitmotifs* are not that simple. For example, in Book 4, *Cities of the Plain* (also known as *Sodom and Gomorrah*), the Narrator casually mentions that Albertine was "fond of riding, a pair of saddle-horses." (*Cities of the Plain*, vol. 2, p. 304.) Then in Book 5, *The Captive*, vol. 2, page 463, he fantasizes that "with her horse she should take it into her head to ride off somewhere, wherever she chose, and never to return again to my house. . . ." In Book 6, *The Sweet Cheat Gone*, page 716, we learn that Albertine was thrown from her horse and died. If we read the fact that she was killed by her horse (the horse that the Narrator gave her) in isolation from its history, it does not stimulate our memory and, as a result, we will have missed much of the significance of the event. Albertine is dead. But her death is linked to the Narrator both materially—he gave her the horse—and psychologically in that he fantasized about her death. The difficulty is how to speak of this collective bundle of moments in the novel. The horse motif? Albertine's death motif? The Narrator's "Albertine death fantasy" motif? It is not easy to solve this problem to everyone's satisfaction. Fortunately, naming *leitmotifs* is not the purpose of this book. In chapters 3 and 4, I discuss a handful of *leitmotifs* in each work. While I have given them names, the reader is free to give these *leitmotifs* different names. The connection, not the name, is the point.

Ulysses and *In Search of* pushed the structural boundaries of literature. Joyce created fragments of sentences for Bloom's stream of consciousness. Proust created exceptionally long sentences for his Narrator's interior

---

[18] The Narrator thinking of the dead Albertine: "It is the tragedy of other people that they are to us merely showcases for the very perishable collections of our own mind." (*The Captive*, vol. 2, p. 773) "Only by art can we get outside ourselves, know what another sees of his universe, which is not the same as ours and the different views of which would otherwise have remained as unknown to us as those there may be on the moon." (*The Past Recaptured*, vol. 2, p. 1013)

monologues. These new structures take the form of a Wagnerian endless melody. Just as Wagnerian musical endless melodies are constructed from musical *leitmotifs*, literary endless melodies are constructed from literary *leitmotifs*.

A Wagnerian endless melody has two characteristics. First, while long, it is not endless. More important, it consists of *leitmotifs* that create coherence within a non-traditional melody line. For example, Siegfried's "Funeral March" at the end of act 3, scene ii of *Götterdämmerung*, is an eight-minute segment of music comprised of at least ten motifs.[19] These *leitmotifs* relate to Siegfried's history and include: Death Chords, Walsung, Sieglinde, Love, Love Longing, Sword, Siegfried, Hero, and Brünnhilde motif. Siegfried's "Funeral March" either ends with, or segues into, Alberich's Curse and the Tyranny *leitmotifs*.

Joyce and Proust create their literary endless melodies by connecting their strings of thought (Joyce) or long sentences and paragraphs (Proust) with snapshots of their past, present, and potentially future experiences. A sample of Bloom's thoughts illustrates this point: "I too. Last of my race. Milly young student. Well, my fault perhaps. No son. Rudy Too late now. Or if not? If not? If still?" (episode 11, Sirens: 11.1064–65) This run-on thought is incoherent at the objective level, but coherent at the subjective level. The context is Bloom listening to the song "The Croppy Boy" which ends with the boy's death by hanging. Bloom, an only child who converted from Judaism to Christianity, is the last of his race. He has a daughter, Milly. His son, Rudy, died eleven years ago when Rudy was eleven days old. Bloom and Molly have not had sex since Rudy's death. Throughout the novel Bloom and Molly individually ponder whether they will once again develop a sexual relationship that could result in a male heir.

Much of the action in Proust's *In Search of* and Joyce's *Ulysses* occurs in their characters' minds. The two authors, however, explore the workings of consciousness differently. Joyce primarily uses stream of consciousness whereas Proust primarily uses its cousin, interior monologue. These two literary devices are discussed in chapters 3 and 4, but they can be illustrated with a hypothetical example.

Let's suppose that earlier in the day my friend, Mary, says to me: "Let's meet at 3:00 p.m. and go to the store to buy some apples." Later, when I recall that conversation, à la Joyce, the thought might stream through my consciousness as "me 3 fru" or as "Oh! 3 damn." A reader may find it difficult to

---

[19] See Monte Stone, The Ring *Disc: An Interactive Guide to Wagner's* Ring Cycle, 1999.

understand the meaning or reference of "Oh! 3 fru", particularly if that thought was joined with several other fragmented thoughts. Per Proust, as interior monologue, the thought could appear as follows: "What do I have to do tomorrow afternoon? Oh yes. I'm meeting Mary at three o'clock, after my dentist appointment, to buy some fruit. Apples, yes, just like my Adam's apple. Adam and Eve. Who would have thought they would regret shopping for apples?"

Stream of consciousness writing does not follow grammatical rules and can be difficult to decipher. Interior monologue follows grammatical rules but can be equally difficult to follow, especially if the monologue goes on for a long time. In the below example, Proust's Narrator describes his feelings toward the recently deceased Albertine:

> For if it was not in itself anything real, if it depended upon the successive form of the hours in which it has appeared to me, a form which remained that of my memory as the curve of the projections of my magic lantern depended upon the curve of the coloured slides, did it not represent in its own manner a truth, a thoroughly objective truth too, **to wit that each of one of us is not a single person, but contains many persons who have not all the same moral value and that if a vicious Albertine had existed, it did not mean that there had not been others,** she who enjoyed talking to me about Saint-Simon in her room, she who on the night when I had told her that we must part had said so sadly: "That pianola, this room, to think that I shall never see any of these thing again" and, when she saw the emotion which my lie had finally communicated to myself, had exclaimed with a sincere pity: "oh, no, anything rather than make you unhappy, I promise that I will never try to see you again." (*The Sweet Cheat Gone*, vol. 2, p. 754, emphasis added)

This nearly two hundred-word sentence is grammatically correct. However, unless the reader realizes that the Narrator is reacting emotionally to several distinct memories of Albertine, the reader will be completely lost. The Narrator imagines a person's history as comprising thousands of pictures. Each picture represents a memory that evokes a different emotional response in the Narrator. This theoretical exposition of the nature of the self is embedded in the Narrator's allusions to Albertine. The reader will recognize the Narrator's allusions to many different "Albertines" and the emotions that each "Albertine" evokes in the Narrator. In one moment, the Narrator feels hatred toward Albertine when he remembers that she lied to him on a specific occasion. The next moment he feels desire when he recalls the time she told him he could visit her in her room. A moment later he feels profound loathing when he pictured her with Lea. Then, he feels a nostalgic fondness when contemplating never seeing her again. Finally, he feels hate once again when he remembers another occasion when Albertine lied to him. This cornucopia of emotions can drive the reader crazy in at least two ways: trying to follow the Narrator's train of thought and to pin down the Narrator's feelings toward Albertine. Each of these emotions is a constituent part of the endless melody that Proust uses to express the Narrator's conflicting reservoir of emotions.

Recognizing literary *leitmotifs* and endless melody in *Ulysses* and *In Search of* enriches one's experience of the novels. One can read the words "Tap Tap" without associating it with Bloom's intrinsic kindness or his theory of music. One can also observe the Narrator's obsessive jealousy without recognizing the parallel obsessions of Swann, Charlus, and Saint-Loup, but then the reader misses half the story and ninety percent of the pleasure. Identifying the Wagnerian techniques of *leitmotif* and endless melody that Joyce and Proust use will make the novels more accessible and more enjoyable. Finally, one is left with a sense of wonder at the multi-temporal, multi-spatial universes Joyce and Proust allow us to enter. These two authors provide us with a kaleidoscopic view into art, science, philosophy, history, literature, psychology, and life. Experiencing *Ulysses* and *In Search of* is experiencing a literary *Gesamtkunstwerk*, a complete work of art.

Chapter 1 includes a brief discussion of the transition from Wagner's Romanticism to twentieth-century modernism. Chapter 1 also contains an overview of Wagner's development of *leitmotifs*, endless melody, and *Gesamtkunstwerk*. This is followed by a discussion of the artistic movement between Romanticism and modernism, known as symbolism. Chapter 2 provides a summary of *Ulysses* and *In Search of*. Chapters 3 and 4, the heart of this book, are parallel in design. Chapter 3 focuses on Wagner and Joyce and Chapter 4 on Wagner and Proust. Each of these chapters includes biographical evidence of the Wagnerian connection, textual references to Wagner, and textual illustrations of *leitmotifs*, endless melody, and *Gesamtkunstwerk*. Chapter 5 discusses the role of time in both works. Chapter 5 also includes my assertion that time functions, not as a *leitmotif*, but as a framing concept in which *leitmotifs* exist. Appendix A provides a table of Wagnerian references in *Ulysses*. Appendix B discusses different ways Romantics and Moderns, as expressed by Wagner, Joyce and Proust, approach the hero, humor, and eroticism. Appendix C is a table that illustrates the structure of Joyce's *Ulysses*. Appendix D lists the dates of composition and publication of Wagner's ten major operas, the sections or episodes of Joyce's *Ulysses*, and the seven books that make up *In Search of*. Appendix E is a glossary of Wagner operas and characters discussed in this book. Appendix F discusses the philosophers influencing Wagner, Joyce, and Proust.

The two primary sources I used were James Joyce's *Ulysses* edited by Hans Walter Gabler and Marcel Proust's two-volume *Remembrance of Things Past* translated by C. K. Scott Moncrieff. *Remembrance of Things Past* is now commonly referred to as *In Search of Lost Time*. In the text, I abbreviate *In Search of Lost Time* as *In Search of*. Although in Book 5, *The Captive*, we learn that the Narrator's name is "Marcel," I chose to use the nomenclature "the Narrator." This avoids the temptation to read *In Search of* as an autobiography.

Citations for *Ulysses* and *In Search of* are placed within the text. Citations for *Ulysses* are by episode number, episode name, and line(s). For example, episode 4, Calypso: 4.332, refers to episode 4, also known as Calypso, line 332. Citations for *In Search of* are by the book name abbreviation, volume number, and page number. For example, *SW*, vol. 1, p. 33, refers to *Swann's Way*, volume 1, p. 33. Book names are abbreviated as follows:

SW: *Swann's Way*
WBG: *Within a Budding Grove*
GW: *The Guermantes Way*
CP: *Cities of the Plain*; also known as *Sodom and Gomorrah*
C: *The Captive*
SCG: *The Sweet Cheat Gone*; also known as *The Fugitive*
PR: *The Past Recaptured*

Throughout the text I use the commonly used English titles of Wagner's operas, some of which retain their German names.

One final note on the spelling and grammar within quotations from *Ulysses*. *Ulysses* is the mid-point between Joyce's readable *A Portrait of the Artist as a Young Man* and his, without a library full of secondary sources, very unreadable *Finnegans Wake* (*FW*). Therefore, the reader should be prepared for many quotes from *Ulysses* that appear to contain gross typographical errors. They are not.

CHAPTER 1
Background: From Romanticism to Modernism

Both Joyce and Proust admired and knew in detail Wagner's music. In 1903, when visiting Paris, Joyce wrote to his mother: "Tell Stannie to send me at once ... my copy of Wagner's operas."[20] At a concert in 1909, as an amateur tenor, Joyce sang a part in the quintet from *Die Meistersinger*. Referencing Richard Ellmann's definitive biography on Joyce,[21] Timothy Martin notes that Joyce began acquiring Wagnerian material as early as 1899, and by 1920 Joyce's library "included fifteen books by or about Wagner and many others in which Wagner figures importantly. Only Shakespeare occupied more space on Joyce's shelves."[22]

---

[20] Timothy Martin, *Joyce and Wagner: A Study of Influence*, p. 16.

[21] Richard Ellmann, *James Joyce*.

[22] T. Martin, *Joyce and Wagner*, p. 18. Also see William Blissett, "James Joyce in the Smithy of His Soul." Blissett discusses Joyce's "Wagnerism" in Joyce's early works, including his book of poems *Chamber Music* (1907) and play *Exiles* (1918). Blissett's essay also discusses the symbolists' influence on the intellectual and artistic foundation of Wagnermania that dominated art straddling the turn of the twentieth century. Although now almost a cliché but still a complex and multi-layered phenomenon, Wagnermania is encapsulated in Walter Pater's statement that all art should strive toward the condition of music. See Pater, Walter, "The School of Giorgione," *The Renaissance: Studies in Art and Poetry*, (Start Publishing, LLC, 2013, originally published in 1873; 3rd edition 1877). Pater's dictum means that art should communicate in purely abstract terms and not through representative symbols. This idea of abstraction in art was identified with the emotionally transcendent states induced by Wagner's music. Pater's contention, while not without controversy, includes four assertions. **First**, specific arts are composed of two elements: form and matter. Form, e.g., color in painting, words in poetry, and sound in music, is used to capture or represent a mood, feeling, or some sort of aspiration, be it moral, political, or some other goal. Matter is the specific landscape, poem, or song. **Second**, each art tries to "find guidance from the other arts." (*The Renaissance*, p. 60) For example, architecture aspires to embody the qualities of a picture, or sculpture, or the flow of poetry. **Third**, the ideal art is one in which the distinction between form and matter disappears. Pater speculates that "form and matter, in their union or identity, present one single effect to the 'imaginative reason,'...." **Fourth**, music best represents the union of matter and form in art. The art of music, according to Pater, "most completely realizes this artistic ideal, this perfect identification of form and matter...the end is not distinct from the means, the form from the matter, the subject from the expression; they inhere in and completely saturate each other;" (*The Renaissance*, p. 62) For Pater, music, by its abstract nature, conveys meaning and beauty without recourse to anything other than itself.

Aside from Proust's novels, there are few anecdotal stories of Proust's involvement with Wagner's music. George Painter's biography cites an incident in 1902 when Proust and his friends sang the Good Friday motif from *Parsifal*.[23] Jean-Jacques Nattiez argues that while Vinteuil's sonata and septet are not based on Wagner's music, Vinteuil, as a musician of revolutionary stature, is based on Wagner.[24] We find textual evidence of Nattiez's claim throughout *In Search of.* For example, in *The Captive*, p. 489, the Narrator is playing Vinteuil's music and says: "I could not help murmuring 'Tristan,' with the smile of an old friend of the family discovering a trace of the grandfather in an intonation, a gesture of the grandson who never set eyes on him." The Narrator is making a clear genealogical connection between Wagner and Vinteuil. Paul du Quenoy writes of Proust: "A devoted Wagnerian among other exploits Proust claimed that he had nearly memorized all of the composer's works . . . but his more mature and widely beloved *Remembrance of Things Past* stands as a Wagnerian epic par excellence." Du Quenoy continues, "No musician is mentioned more frequently in it [*In Search of*] than Wagner, whose person, works, and legacy, according to my latest reading merited no fewer than 62 references in the complete text."[25]

Wagner was a Romantic *par excellence*: ecstatic emotions, romantic heroes, redemption through love, and art as a transformative force in society. None of these qualities is expressed in the modernistic novels *Ulysses* or *In Search of.* *Ulysses* shows us a depressed and downtrodden Dublin in 1904 absent of any redemptive powers. *In Search of* shows us the Parisian aristocracy on its last gasps of air during the *fin de siècle*.

So how does Wagner fit into the literary art of the early twentieth century and specifically into these two early twentieth-century literary masterpieces? Answering this question is the focus of this work. First, I provide illustrations that Joyce and Proust consciously made Wagnerian references in *Ulysses* and *In Search of.* Second, I show how Joyce and Proust transformed Wagner's formal or technical musical innovations of *leitmotifs*, endless melody, and *Gesamtkunstwerk* into literary works. In chapters 3 and 4, I provide an abundant number of illustrations particularly of

---

[23] George D. Painter, *Marcel Proust: A Biography*, vol. 1, p. 303.

[24] Jean-Jacques Nattiez, *Proust as Musician*, p. 88.

[25] Paul du Quenoy, *Wagner and the French Muse: Music, Society, and Nation in Modern France*, p. 107. The number of Wagner references depends on how one counts a unique reference. See Tables 2 and 3 in chapter 4.

leitmotifs in these two works. The reason that I include so many illustrations is to demonstrate that *Ulysses* and *In Search of* are replete with these Wagnerian tools.

A brief review of the above Wagnerian operatic tools in *Ulysses* and *In Search of* are discussed in the next three sections.

a. Wagner's *Leitmotifs*: Brief Description

Listening to Wagner's music conjures up a range of associations: loud, emotional, women dying to redeem their men, long symphonic orchestration, and enriching aesthetic experiences. Wagner's operas are associated with intricate stories; his characters have complex, and often dark, psychological lives. Wagner expresses and develops these deep complexities through three fundamental devices: *leitmotifs*, endless melody, and *Gesamtkunstwerk*. Each of these terms is pivotal to Wagner's oeuvre in a different way. We first discuss *leitmotifs*.

At their most basic, *leitmotifs* are characterized as short pieces of music that have an audible identity and recur throughout the work. Wagnerian *leitmotifs* or motifs often are named by what is occurring on stage when the piece of music is first heard. In one way, this naming method makes good sense. For example, it is a lot easier to label the descending scale we hear when Wotan enters with his spear as Wotan's Spear *leitmotif* rather than displaying the descending scale every time we want to talk about Wotan's Spear motif.

Two popular and easily recognizable *leitmotifs* are the Jaws motif in the movie *Jaws* and the Darth Vader motif in *Star Wars*. When we hear the Jaws or Darth Vader music, we can be fairly certain who will soon appear on the screen.

Referring to Wagner's *leitmotifs*, Claude Debussy derogatorily labeled them as "calling cards."[26] However, Debussy's criticism does not do justice to Wagner musical innovation, although this "calling card" analysis has its origin in Bayreuth, particularly in the writings of Hans von Wolzogen.

Hans von Wolzogen (1848–1938) has a permanent place in the Wagner story. He attended the first Bayreuth festival, which featured *The Ring*, in 1876.

---

[26] Interview in *Le Figaro*, May 16, 1902. "Certainly, my compositional process, which consists above all of dispensing with compositional processes, owes nothing to Wagner. In his work, each character has, one might say, his 'calling card,' his photograph, his 'leitmotif' which always precedes him. I confess that I consider this method to be rather crude." See *Berlioz and Debussy: Sources, Contexts and Legacies: Essays in Honour of François Lesure*, edited by Barbara L. Kelly and Kerry Murphy, chapter seven: Michael Strasser, *Grieg, the Société nationale, and the Origins of Debussy's String Quartet*, p. 132.

In 1877, Wagner invited him to edit the Wagnerian journal, the *Bayreuther Blätter* He edited this in-house publication from 1878 to his death in 1938. Wolzogen was among "old friends such as Heinrich von Stein and Hermann Levi" who met Wagner's train from Venice/Vienna when Wagner's body was brought to Bayreuth in February 1883. "The burial took place late on the Sunday afternoon in the presence of only Wagner's immediate family and his most intimate friends, accompanied by Wagner's dogs, Adolf von Gross, Hermann Levi, Hans Richter, Hans von Wolzogen, and others."[27]

In 1879, three years after the first production of *The Ring*, Hans von Wolzogen published a commentary on *The Ring* identifying and giving names to many of its *leitmotifs*. For better or worse, many of those names are still with us. Deryck Cooke identifies four shortcomings of Wolzogen's analysis, which may have contributed, although unlikely since Debussy certainly knew better, to Debussy's superficial and probably insincere analysis of them in terms of calling cards.[28]

First, Cooke identifies Wolzogen's presentation of short musical examples as giving the impression that the score was a patchwork (calling cards) of musical ideas. Second, the name, *Leitmotiv*, meaning "leading motives," again gives the impression that each motif is complete in itself. Third, his list of *leitmotifs* is grossly incomplete. And fourth, and most important, Wolzogen ignored "the continual transformation of existing motives into new ones," their evolution, their plasticity,

---

[27] Oliver Hilmes, *Cosima Wagner: The Lady of Bayreuth*, p. 155–56. Wolzogen's devotion to Wagner and Wagnerism was remarkable. On his honeymoon in 1872, he visited the hole where the Bayreuth Festival house eventually would stand. Lest one be left with a positive impression of von Wolzogen, he, along with Wagner's wife Cosima, Chamberlain, and others, ignored Wagner's earlier left wing radical liberal political writings of the late 1840s. They appropriated Wagner's political writings to support the politically conservative members of the plutocracy and then later to support Hitler's National Socialism. The Bayreuth monthly newsletter, the *Bayreuther Blätter*, became a creed and vehicle for spouting anti-Semitism, xenophobic, German/Aryan anti-democratic nationalistic doctrine. To quote Johnathan Carr, *The Wagner Clan*, p. 97: "All in all he wrote more than four hundred usually muddled and bombastic articles himself, and edited some twenty thousand pages of text, in which ultra-conservatism and racism went hand in hand with the worship of German art—especially, of course, Wagner's." His legacy, however, is naming *leitmotifs* in several of Wagner's operas, including *The Ring* and *Parsifal*.

[28] Deryck Cooke, *I Saw the World End: A Study of Wagner's Ring*, p. 37f. Cooke attributes some of the confusion surrounding the nature of *leitmotifs* to Wagner. In fairness to Wagner, Wagner did not use the term *leitmotifs* ("leading motives") but called them *Haupmotiv*, or "principal motives." Cooke's book is a must-read for anyone interested in the mythological roots and analysis of *The Ring*. Unfortunately, Cooke was able to complete his analysis only of *Das Rheingold* and *Die Walküre* before being killed in a car accident in 1976.

their ability to change into very different yet related motifs. For example, on the surface, in *The Ring*, the Ring motif and Valhalla motif sound very different and evoke opposite emotional responses in the audience. One is sinister and reeks of evil whereas the other is majestic and pompous. Once demonstrated, one can see that getting from one motif to the other is through a step-by-step transformation.[29]

Wagner's innovative use of *leitmotifs* is their ability to morph into different keys, rhythms, and orchestration and combine with other motifs to reflect the dramatic situation on stage. Wagner transforms these basic motives or ground themes by altering their speed, their rhythm, their melody, changing from minor to major, inverting them, taking pieces of one motive, e.g., their first or middle notes, and developing new, but related motifs. One purpose of these transformations is to create associations between *leitmotifs*. Returning to the Ring and Valhalla motifs discussed above, while these motifs sound different from each other, one sinister and the other majestic, both represent the quest for power, even at the cost of forfeiting love.

Jeffrey Swann refers to Wagner's *leitmotifs* as "pregnant with meaning," i.e., they carry the past and, in embryonic form, they point to the future.[30,31] In other words, their psychological significance changes and develops with the passage of time. This is the function and beauty of *leitmotifs*; they move you through time creating an integrated whole; they call up forgotten memories and impressions and link these memories and impressions together to create a unified story. However, the passage of time requires memory, for without memory there would only be discrete isolated moments of time and the function of *leitmotifs* would be lost.

---

[29] For musical examples of *leitmotifs* and illustrations of their musical transformation in Wagner's *Ring*, see Deryck Cooke's two-CD collection *An Introduction to* Der Ring des Nibelungen, (Decca Record Company, 1968, set 443 581–82).

[30] For several of Jeffrey Swann's lectures on Wagner's music, see "Wagner Society of Washington DC," YouTube, https://www.youtube.com/user/WSWDC. There are dozens of books cataloging Wagner's *leitmotifs*. For example, see J. K. Holman, *Wagner's Ring: A Listener's Companion & Concordance*, chapter 3. Counting *leitmotifs* in Wagner's *Ring of the Nibelung* can be a full-time job. For example, Dr. Allen Dunning identifies 178, Wolzogen 90, Sabor's commentary 80, Stone's *Ring* Disc 124, and the list goes on.

[31] For a further explanation of Wagner's *leitmotifs* and an exploration of their use in Proust's *In Search of Lost Time*, see Jeffrey Swann, "Wagner and Proust," *The Wagner Journal* 12, no. 2: 34–55, especially pp. 45f. Swann quotes Thomas Mann: "I mean by the use of the leitmotiv, the magic formula that works both ways and links the past with the future, the future with the past. The leitmotiv is the technique employed to preserve the inward unity and abiding presentness of the whole at each moment" (pp. 45–46). In addition to taking the listener to the past and to the future, I would add that they also take one inward into the psychology of the occurring event.

Two illustrations will suffice: Wotan's Spear motif and Brünnhilde's Valkyrie motif. In its basic form, Wotan's Spear motif is a descending scale. However, it is no ordinary descending scale, one can feel the power in Wotan's descending scale in one's gut. The motif inspires authority and strength in the beholder or awe and fear in the recipient depending on Wotan's intent. However, in act 2 of *Die Walküre*, toward the end of Wotan's losing confrontation with his wife, Fricka, the muscular, commanding, solid, and unyielding descending scale spear motif grovels to a whimper and virtually disintegrates into pieces. We feel Wotan's humiliation and impotence. The audible impression remains that of the Spear motif, but the motif is now breaking apart, creating sound that foreshadows the spear's physical breaking in act 3 of *Siegfried*.

A similar change occurs to Brünnhilde's identity as a Valkyrie. When we first meet her in act 1 of *Die Walküre*, she is represented by the energetic and triumphant Ride of the Valkyrie motif. In acts 2 and 3 of *Die Walküre*, Brünnhilde's Valkyrie motif gradually fragments and disintegrates as Wotan, her father, tells her that she is not to protect Siegmund from Hunding's murderous intent. Toward the end of act 3 of *Die Walküre*, Brünnhilde learns her punishment for disobeying her father— she will lose her godhead, become a human, and become the wife of the first man who sees her. After some interesting pleading, Wotan relents and then assures her that she will be awakened only by a hero. Again, we hear fragments of the Ride of the Valkyries motif as Brünnhilde recalls her past. However, in this context, we experience not her humiliation and degradation, but rather her nascent growing happiness as she realizes the richness of her new life with Siegfried. The same basic sounds, but with a totally different significance.

Another way to understand how *leitmotifs* function, to borrow a metaphor from *In Search of*, is that they act as both a telescope and microscope.[32] Their telescopic functions enable the reader or listener to bring within reach events from the past and the future. Those familiar with Wagner's *Ring* will recognize Wotan's "Great Idea," i.e., the Sword motif, at the end of *Das Rheingold*. Our recognition of the Sword motif reminds us of the mess in which Wotan finds himself (he needs to get the ring from Fafner, but as the god of laws and contracts, he cannot get it himself). Simultaneously, this motif foreshadows the future story of the Sword: Siegmund will pull it out of Hunding's tree, Wotan will shatter it, Brünnhilde retrieves

---

[32] Marcel Proust, *In Search of*, PR, vol. 2, p. 1118.

it, Mime finds it, Siegfried re-forges it, kills Fafner with it, offers it as a token of friendship to Gunther, etc. These events are embedded in the Sword motif in its telescopic design.

The microscopic function of *leitmotifs* is to focus on the specificity of an event. This function provides a psychological insight, rather than a broad temporal and spatial view, into the situation. See the illustration below for a graphic representation of the telescopic and microscopic function of *leitmotifs*.

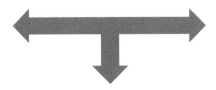

The horizontal arrows represent telescopic movement through objective space and time, and the vertical arrow represents microscopic travel through subjective or psychological time.

At the end of *Das Rheingold*, we hear Wotan's Great Idea, i.e., the Sword motif. In this context, the Sword motif gives us insight into Wotan's psychology; it tells us that Wotan's solution to his dilemma is through power and violence, i.e., getting someone to kill for him. For Wotan, the Sword is the instrument for this murderous task. Wotan persists in this same violent vein that is at the root of his current personality—to continue his rule of the world through his laws. He now needs someone to kill for him, and he is in the mental process of working out the details.

At the start of *Die Walküre* we discover the manifestation of Wotan's plan: to father two children (Sieglinde and Siegmund) who will perform the deed that he, as the keeper of contracts, cannot perform. The telescopic perspective on the Sword generally is unchanged. However, with each new context in which the Sword motif appears, the microscopic view reveals the personality of the character associated with this motif. For example, we see that Siegmund is not a power-hungry, violent person, but someone whose interests are to use the Sword in self-defense as he and Sieglinde flee from the morning's battle with Hunding. Siegmund is not like his father, Wotan. If he were like Wotan, he would have killed Hunding either while Hunding slept or as soon as he woke up. Instead, they flee. In *Siegfried*, when Siegfried forges the Sword, he thinks of the Sword as a tool to acquire knowledge of fear through his encounter with Fafner and to break the psychic hold that Mime has over him. In *Götterdämmerung*, the function of the Sword morphs into a gift of friendship from Siegfried to Gunther.

Another example of the microscopic, as well as the telescopic, function of *leitmotifs* is the "Prize Song" in *Die Meistersinger*. At the telescopic level, the "Prize Song" tells us about sixteenth-century Nuremberg and the process for admittance into the Meistersinger Guild. At the microscopic level, the "Prize Song" shows us the sexually romantic nature of Walter. The "Prize Song," to which Hans Sachs is the midwife, also describes Sachs's reminiscence of early love and reflections on the passing of generations. When we hear versions of the "Prize Song," our intellect and emotions should travel through both the outer world of space and time around sixteenth-century Nuremberg and to the psychologies of Walter and Sachs.

Matthew Bribitzer-Stull, in his book, *Understanding the Leitmotif, From Wagner to Hollywood Film Music*,[33] shows how music can have both an internal coherence and an association with things outside itself.[34] He argues that our initial association of a piece of music with extra-musical ideas primarily is cultural (cultural tropes) along with idiosyncratic personal or subjective elements.[35] He further argues that unlike reminiscence motives, *ideés fixes*, motto themes and other extra-musical associative techniques, Wagnerian leitmotifs have the following three properties:

1. *Leitmotifs* are bifurcated in nature, comprising both a musical physiognomy and an emotional association.
2. *Leitmotifs* are developmental in nature, evolving to reflect and create new musico-dramatic contexts.
3. *Leitmotifs* contribute to and function within a larger musical structure.[36]

---

[33] Matthew Bribitzer-Stull, *Understanding the Leitmotif, From Wagner to Hollywood Film Music*.

[34] Bribitzer-Stull, p. 82. He further argues on page 95 that *leitmotifs* sit at the "intersection of emotion, memory, and meaning."

[35] I am reminded of a play I recently saw in which the sound of raindrops (culturally associated with nature) was associated with gun shots (subjective experience of the narrator).

[36] Bribitzer-Stull, p. 10.

Bribitzer-Stull analyses Wagnerian *leitmotifs* using the vocabulary of musicology. These terms include consonant triads, diminished seventh chords, falling thirds, rising sixth, and tritones. He also discusses thematic truncation, thematic evolution, thematic fragmentation, and thematic irony. [37]

We have spent a long time on the function of Wagner's *leitmotifs*. While there are hundreds of examples, I must leave a more in-depth analysis to more competent hands and heads and ears. Our question is how Joyce and Proust use *leitmotifs* in literature. But first a brief analysis of two additional Wagnerian tools: the endless melody and the concept of *Gesamtkunstwerk*.

b. Wagner's Endless Melody: Brief Description

In Thomas Mann's 1947 novel *Doctor Faustus*, Mann (or, rather, the narrator) writes, "I can only repeat that the paragraphs and asterisks in this book are simply a concession to the reader's eyes, and that if it were up to me, I would write the whole thing in one fell swoop, in one breath, without any divisions, indeed without paragraphs and indentations. I merely lack the courage to present so inconsiderate a printed text to the eyes of the reading public." [38] Unlike Mann, Joyce and Proust had no problems with long sentences replete with endless subordinate clauses (*In Search of*) and fragmented sentences and thoughts and unpunctuated text (*Ulysses*). The source of this emerging literary style has its roots in Wagner's endless melody.

Wagner rejected the traditional operatic tools, such as arias, duets, ensembles, cabalettas, and cavatinas, as well as the general structure of numbered pieces. A string of numbered pieces, he believed, artificially disrupted the dramatic flow of the story, be it the spoken poetic word or musical development. Yet Wagner needed some structure and structural elements to hold the piece together. In place of numbered pieces and

---

[37] See Bribitzer-Stull, chapter 7 for additional examples.
[38] Thomas Mann, *Doctor Faustus*, p. 187.

traditional formal musical structures, Wagner composed endless melodies using *leitmotifs* as building blocks. [39] [40]

This endless melody is not endless, but it does go on much longer than a traditional melody and pushes the idea of melody to its limit. However, the passage of music creates one continuous, unified sound. [41] Since *leitmotifs* intrinsically are temporally (and emotionally) fluid, they recall the past and anticipate the future. For example, at the end of the prologue of *Götterdämmerung*, we hear Siegfried's eleven-minute "Journey down the Rhine." It includes the following *leitmotifs*: Laughing at Death, Siegfried's Horn Call, Loge Fire, Rhine, Lovelessness, Joy, Rhinemaidens, Gold Fanfare, Rhine Daughters' Lament, Ring, Woe, Tyranny, and Hagen's motif. [42] We hear one continuous melody, although admittedly, not a hummable melody.

Nearing the end of *Götterdämmerung* we hear Siegfried's eight-minute "Funeral March." While virtually nothing occurs on stage, the "Funeral March" is a retelling of Siegfried's lineage and story constructed from at least ten *leitmotifs*. In addition to providing a telescopic view of Siegfried's family and personal history, which is quite glorious, Siegfried's "Funeral March" delves microscopically into Siegfried's failure to fulfill his potential. At the microscopic or psychological level, we cannot help but hear Siegfried's funeral music

---

[39] Some argue that an endless melody is not a melody at all. See Jed Rasula, *History of a Shiver: The Sublime Impudence of Modernism*, chapter 7: "Endless Melody: A Theoretical Excursion." Nietzsche levies a battery of criticism of Wagner's operas in *The Case of Wagner*. See Walter Kaufmann, *Basic Writings of Nietzsche*, particularly sections 7 and 8 where he attacks Wagner as "our greatest miniaturist in music who crowds into the smallest space an infinity of sense and sweetness." (Nietzsche is being sarcastic.) His attack on *leitmotifs* continues: "The word becomes sovereign and leaps out of the sentence, the sentence reaches out and obscures the meaning of the page, the page gains life at the expense of the whole—the whole is no longer a whole. . . . To say it plainly: Wagner does not give us enough to chew on. His recitativo-little meat, rather more bone, and a lot of broth." Nietzsche has a love/hate relationship with Wagner's music. He loves it in how it can mesmerize and hypnotize one's self to the point of losing one's self. He also hates it for that very reason. He finds losing one's identity, even momentarily, as frightening.

[40] Cinema is the twentieth-century version of endless melody and *Gesamtkunstwerk*. Movie theaters currently are designing kinesthetic motion into seats to enhance the patron's visual and auditory experience.

[41] See Aaron Copland, *What to Listen for in Music*, pp. 39–48. "A beautiful melody, like a piece of music in its entirety, should be of satisfying proportion. It must give us a sense of completion and inevitability. . . . But, most important of all, its expressive quality must be such as will arouse an emotional response in the listener" p. 40.

[42] See Monty Stone, The Ring *Disc*. Although many shun labeling *leitmotifs*, labels assist the listener to identify them and recognize their transformations. Labeling or naming them also makes possible discussing them in books and talks.

as having an ironic flavor; glorious music for a person who is drawn in by the big city lights (Hall of the Gibichungs), betrays his lover (Brünnhilde), and is ignobly stabbed in his back (by Hagen) while bragging about his exploits, such as killing Fafner, walking through fire, and waking up Brünnhilde. Yes, Siegfried was great in potential, but a failure as a person. The same music can be heard and understood from two different perspectives: one historic and one psychological. Each perspective creates a different musical experience.

Before addressing how literature, particularly that of Joyce and Proust, employs endless melodies in *Ulysses* and *In Search of*, we first must address the concept of *Gesamtkunstwerk*.

c. Wagner's *Gesamtkunstwerk*: Brief Description

The term "*Gesamtkunstwerk*" is translated as a "total work of art," "ideal work of art," "synthesis of the arts," and "comprehensive artwork." While we associate this term with Wagner, the term originated in 1827 with the German writer and philosopher, K. F. E. Trahndorff, and was used by other artists including Lessing, Tieck, Novalis, and Weber.[43] The purpose of a "synthesis of the arts" was not to put together unrelated parts to create something big and grand (effects without cause). Rather, the purpose was to harmonize the parts to create a higher unity; the whole being greater than its parts. In the nineteenth century, opera seemed most suitable for this transformative goal of *Gesamtkunstwerk*. A successful opera must include an interesting libretto, excellent music, insightful conducting,[44] and outstanding singing. In addition, it must include convincingly conceptualized set design, props, blocking, costumes, and lighting. All of these components must work in unison.[45]

---

[43] See *Wikipedia, Gesamtkunstwerk*, last updated October 14, 2020, https://en.wikipedia.org/wiki/Gesamtkunstwerk. Virtually any book on Wagner mentions *leitmotifs*, endless melody, and *Gesamtkunstwerk*. As stated above, my purpose is not to provide a comprehensive analysis of these Wagnerian tools, but rather to show how Joyce and Proust applied them to their literary works. For an in-depth explanation of Gesamtkunstwerk, see Robert Laudon, *Sources of the Wagnerian Synthesis* (Munich: Katazbichler, 1979), referred to in Simon Williams, *Richard Wagner and Festival Theatre*, p. 60.

[44] Richard Wagner, *Essays on Conducting*, translated with critical commentary by Chris Walton (Rochester: Rochester University Press, 2021).

[45] Comfortable seats and air conditioning could help, but Bayreuth seems to have successfully skirted these requirements.

Wagner discussed the term *Gesamtkunstwerk* in two of his 1849 essays, *Art and Revolution* and *The Artwork of the Future,* and further analyzed the concept in his 1851 opus *Opera and Drama.*[46] Arguably, Wagner was a walking and talking human *Gesamtkunstwerk.*

Wagner created theoretical underpinnings for his operas (he called them dramas, we call them music dramas) in his theoretical works. He wrote his libretti to create an organic connection between the drama on stage and the music in the orchestra pit. He trained his singers to better enact the drama on stage. He designed the set and props. He directed many of his operas and wrote detailed directing notes for his productions. Moreover, his treatise *On Conducting* is, in part, a guide to how symphonies and his operas should be conducted. He advocated for the lowering of lights during performances and finally, built his own opera house to his specifications at Bayreuth, Germany.[47] In other words, Wagner synthesized different art forms to create an operatic experience in which multiple arts are coordinated to create the desired dramatic effect. Wagner wanted audiences' total absorption into his music dramas; he wanted to create an audio-visually absorbing experience that would literally transport the viewer to a different reality.

The latter part of the nineteenth century and the early twentieth century consciously sought to manifest the idea of a *Gesamtkunstwerk* within poetry, theater, visual arts, and film.[48] During this period, the goal of *Gesamtkunstwerk,* i.e., the mutuality or synthesis of the arts, was not to create complexity and confusion, but rather to facilitate entry into the infinite and the ineffable.

---

[46] See William Ashton Ellis for English translations of many of Wagner's theoretical writings. According to Wagner, the downfall of ancient Greek opera and theater happened when the individual arts split into separate disciplines. This occurred with the demise of Athenian fourth-century BCE playwrights. Much of Wagner's theoretical analyses should be viewed as a conceptual rather than as a historical analysis. Concepts, however, are important. For Wagner, *Gesamtkunstwerk* aimed to create a bond between art and society. For Wagner, art is public, art is political.

[47] See Simon Williams, *Richard Wagner and Festival Theatre,* and Frederic Spotts, *Bayreuth: A History of the Wagner Festival,* p. 55: "Production of the first *Ring* at Bayreuth in 1876: . . . the entire burden fell directly on Wagner's shoulders. Producer, stage manager, director, singing coach, orchestral advisor, final arbiter on sets and costumes-he was each of them."

[48] See Jed Rasula, *History of a Shiver,* for a detailed analysis of how artists worked in different mediums to synthesize different art forms. Central to Rasula's book is how Wagnerism, melomania (excessive passion for music), and synesthesia, i.e., the convertibility of one sense into another, i.e., hearing sounds in color or tasting words, permeated the artistic culture around the turn of the century.

The Russian composer Alexander Scriabin stated in 1914: "Through music and color, with the aid of perfume, the human mind or soul can be lifted outside or above merely physical sensations into the region of purely abstract ecstasy and purely intellectual speculation."[49] In less esoteric and more practical terms, in Figure 1, *Nude Descending a Staircase, No. 2* (1912), Marcel Duchamp captured the temporal flow of music by painting a figure "walking down a staircase" on a spatially two-dimensional canvas.

Figure 1: Marcel Duchamp,
Nude Descending a Staircase,
No. 2 (1912)[50]

The extent to which Wagner succeeded in creating an operatic *Gesamtkunstwerk* is debatable. Equally debatable are the merits of *Gesamtkunstwerk*. This debate centers on the question of whether this "maximal grandeur" diminishes each individual art form by inhibiting a more profound investigation into each independent art form.[51] Another way to phrase the question is whether the

---

[49] See Rasula, *History of a Shiver*, p. 26.

[50] Marcel Duchamp, *Nude Descending a Staircase, No. 2* (1912), oil on canvas, Philadelphia Museum of Art, accessed on September 10, 2020, *Wikipedia*,
https://en.wikipedia.org/wiki/File:DuchampNude_Descending_a_Staircase.jpg.

[51] Rasula, History of a Shiver, p. 219.

subordination and intermingling of individual art forms for a common purpose devalues the autonomy of each individual art form.

Regardless of the merits of this intellectual and aesthetic debate, multimedia art is here to stay. For two examples, see Suzanne Lacy's *The Crystal Quilt* at the Tate Modern (2018) or *Manifesto Art x Agency* at the Hirshhorn in Washington, DC (2019). The former performance art event is composed of a video, documentary, quilt, photographs, sound, and performance. The latter is composed of multiple parts, one of which is thirteen video projections playing simultaneously.

Before returning to the question of how Joyce and Proust used the concept of *Gesamtkunstwerk* in *Ulysses* and *In Search of*, we must get from Wagner's Romanticism to Joyce's and Proust's modernism. To get there, we must pass through the artistic period referred to as symbolism.

d. Brief Detour to Symbolism

A prominent position during the Romantic period was music's ability to transport an individual to a non-cognitive subjective, yet universal realm of feeling, to the ineffable, to the essence of reality.[52, 53] During the second half of the nineteenth

---

[52] A problem with making anything ineffable, in this context, an aesthetic experience of music, is that, by being ineffable, we cannot talk about it, even to ourselves, since knowledge is a cognitive activity and the aesthetic experience is non-cognitive. This paradoxical position of talking about that which cannot be talked about also haunts religious mysticism. In the mid-to-late nineteenth century, music, which aspired to replace religion, found itself in the same position: How do we talk about that which we cannot talk about? In the *Tractatus*, the early Wittgenstein recognized this dilemma in his concluding proposition 7: "What we cannot speak about we must pass over in silence." Most writers have a difficult time passing over in silence.

[53] The theoretical foundation for the metaphysical status of music was provided in Arthur Schopenhauer's *The World as Will and Representation*. Schopenhauer's metaphysics is difficult to understand without a background in Plato (Platonic Forms), and particularly in Kant's phenomenon/noumena distinction. That said, see Schopenhauer's *The World as Will and Representation*, vol. 1, chapter 52, and vol. 2, chapters XXXIV ff, and chapter XXXIX: "On the Metaphysics of Music." Schopenhauer's metaphysics provides the foundation for aesthetic experiences. On the aesthetic experience in general, Schopenhauer writes, "an aesthetic experience, in which, e.g., we see different beautiful sculptures, we are experiencing the universal or Form Beauty." He continues, "Music does not express this or that particular and definite pleasure, this or that affliction, pain, sorrow, horror, gaiety, merriment, or peace of mind, but joy, pain, horror, gaiety, merriment, peace of mind themselves" (vol. 1, p. 261). Schopenhauer goes on at great length discussing the significance of harmony, melody, rhythm, base notes, fourth and fifth intervals, in terms of his theory of the Will objectifying itself (vol. 1, p. 258; vol. 2, p. 447). For Schopenhauer, the Will's objectification explains music's independence of what we ordinarily call experience of the objective world.

century, the Wagnerian-inspired symbolist movement focused on the inexpressible, incomprehensible, esoteric, and ethereal properties of music, specifically Wagner's music—"the dream of deepest sleep, entirely remote from the waking cerebral consciousness. . . ."[54]

The symbolists had two contrasting intellectual and aesthetic explanations for this extraordinary property of music. The first was in Schopenhauer's metaphysics and the other was in non-cognitive subjective experience. Wagner, who was all things to all people, provided inspiration for both camps.

Wagner's *Beethoven* essay (1870) is anchored in the metaphysics of Arthur Schopenhauer. In this essay, Wagner writes: "We have called Music the revelation of the inner vision of the Essence of the world. . . ." (*Beethoven*, op. cit., p. 108) In Wagner's essay we hear echoes from Schopenhauer: ". . . for it [music] never expresses the phenomenon, but only the inner nature, the in-itself, of every phenomenon, the will itself." (*World as Will and Representation*, vol. 1, p. 261) Schopenhauer continues, "Music, if regarded as an expression of the world, is in the highest degree a universal language. . . . The inexpressible depth of all music, by virtue of which it floats past us as a paradise quite familiar and yet eternally remote, and is so easy to understand and yet so inexplicable, is due to the fact that it reproduces all the emotions of our innermost being, but entirely without reality. . . ." (Schopenhauer, vol. 1, pp. 262, 264) This metaphysical position argues that music can show what language is unable to say. In even more esoteric language, music brings the infinite into the finite.

---

[54] Wagner supports this ethereal nature of music in his 1870 essay *Beethoven*. (See Ellis) In *Beethoven*, Wagner deviates from his earlier theoretical works on the special status, à la Schopenhauer, given to music. "But it was Schopenhauer who first defined the position of Music among the fine arts with philosophic clearness, ascribing to it a **totally different nature** from that of either plastic or poetic art" (p. 65, emphasis added). And in what does this totally different nature consist? Music transcends individual consciousness and points us to the "oneness of all human beings" p. 71, "to the universal Will," p. 72; it displays essences without having to "pass through the medium of the understanding," i.e., concepts, p. 72; ". . . speechless Feeling . . . she [Music] transports us to the highest ecstasy of consciousness of our infinitude," p. 77. Music, rather than speech, drives the drama: "Who can ever hear that thrilling tone-piece [here Wagner is speaking of Beethoven's overture to Leonora] without being filled with the conviction that Music includes within itself the most consummate Drama?" p. 106.

Another intellectual and aesthetic underpinning for the symbolists was Walter Pater's (1839–1894) maxim that "All art constantly aspires towards the condition of music." In his essay, "The School of Giorgione," Pater writes:

> **All art constantly aspires towards the condition of music.** For while in all other kinds of art it is possible to distinguish the matter from the form, and the understanding can always make this distinction, yet it is the constant effort of art to obliterate it. That the mere matter of a poem, for instance, its subject, namely, its given incidents or situation – that the mere matter of a picture, the actual circumstances of an event, the actual topography of a landscape – should be nothing without the form, the spirit, of the handling, that this form, this mode of handling, should become an end in itself, should penetrate every part of the matter: this is what all art constantly strives after, and achieves in different degrees. (*The Renaissance* , p. 60, emphasis added)

This non-metaphysical maxim means that all art should strive to embody emotions, feelings, and non-linguistic/non-conceptual experience.

Beginning with Baudelaire's review of Wagner's *Tannhäuser*, artists began turning away from the external and objective world to focus on exploring the inner subjective world of "the subject." They maintained that the subjective, private experience was not less real than objective reality. They asserted that the subjective was as real as objective reality.

Both the metaphysical and non-metaphysical approaches gave primary importance to the subjective inner realm of experience. The difference between these two viewpoints is in what they theorized was being disclosed during, for example, dreams, clairvoyance, or any emotional experience, such as desire, or an aesthetic experience. When the metaphysical symbolists went inward, they discovered the essence of reality: Plato's Forms, Kant's Noumena, and Schopenhauer's Will. When the non-metaphysical symbolists went inward, they discovered psychological complexity and an abundance of human emotions. Both maintained that art should make the invisible, subjective inner world visible. The difference between them is in what they believed was being made visible.

Regardless of their theoretical underpinnings, both approaches gave birth to melomania, the love of music. Both approaches also had the ambition to make music the root of all art and took Wagner's music as their guiding force. This aspiration spawned Wagnermania[55] and soon became manifest in the non-musical arts as well.[56]

Stéphane Mallarmé (1842–1898), a symbolist poet, championed the relationship between poetry and music. He argued that the theme within a poem should be "orchestrated" by the manipulation of harmonies, tones, and colors inherent in carefully chosen words. Figure 2 is an example of a poem designed to look like a musical score. To quote Alex Ross's discussion of Figure 2, "The layout has the look of musical notation, with voices rising and falling amid expectant silences." Mallarmé invokes Wagner in his introductory note: "A sort of general leitmotiv that unfolds itself constitutes the unity of the poem: accessory motifs have gathered around it."[57]

---

[55] Wagnerism and Wagnermania were not restricted to Europe, but also inundated the musical taste and behavior in the United States. See Joseph Horowitz, *Wagner Nights: An American History*. For a narrative short story describing the effect of Wagner's music, see Willa Cather, *A Wagner Matinée*.

[56] See Alex Ross, *Wagnerism: Art and Politics in the Shadow of Music*, p. 11: "The truly extraordinary thing is that after his death the shadow [of Wagner's impact] grew still larger. The chaotic posthumous cult that came to be known as Wagnerism was by no means a purely or even primarily musical event. It traversed the entire sphere of art—poetry, the novel, painting, theater, dance, architecture, film." Modern political rallies, with music blaring and video screens, adopted *Gesamtkunstwerk* techniques. Wagnerism also permeated restaurants with Siegfried Schnitzels, Wotan Ham à la Wallhall, and Nibelung Dumplings. See Ross, p. 203. I started keeping track of the individual artists classified as Wagnerites in Ross's and Rasula's (*History of a Shiver*) books. The list of Wagnerites quickly became unmanageable.

[57] Ross, *Wagnerism*, p. 107. The general sentiment among many artists was that music, as represented by Wagner's music, had moved ahead of other art forms. See p. 104.

Figure 2: Stéphane Mallarmé, excerpt from *"Un coup de dés jamais n'abolira le hazard"* (A throw of the dice will never abolish chance) (1897)[58]

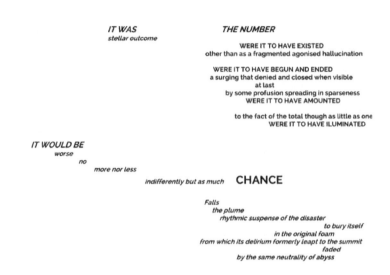

Occultist Édouard Schuré thought Wagner was "perhaps the most perfect and amazing artist that ever lived" for having made a "bold incursion into the three worlds-the material, the astral, and the divine."[59] Whether these "three worlds" pointed toward the metaphysical or toward the psychological, artists of the late nineteenth century aimed to depict nonobjective images. These images were not extensions of ordinary experience, but as something entirely different, as something surreal or even as something ultra-real. For example, Figures 3-5, based on scenes from Wagnerian operas, are not representations of reality, but representations of what Wagner's music evokes in the listener.

---

[58] Figure 5: Stéphane Mallarmé, excerpt from *"Un coup de dés jamais n'abolira le hazard"* (A throw of the dice will never abolish chance) (1897), poem, accessed on September 9, 2020, https://www.poetryintranslation.com/PITBR/French/MallarmeUnCoupdeDes.php.

[59] Rasula, *A History of a Shiver*, p. 79.

Figure 3: Henri Fantin-Latour, *Tannhäuser* (1886)[60]

Figure 4: Charles Temple Dix, *The Flying Dutchman* (1860s)[61]

---

[60] Henri Fantin-Latour, *Tannhäuser* (1886), oil on canvas, Cleveland Museum of Art, accessed on September 10, 2020, https://www.clevelandart.org/art/1916.1038. Fantin-Latour was one of the first avowed French Wagnerian painters. He spent decades trying to capture on canvas in oils and on paper in pastels scenes from Wagner's music dramas. See Ross, op. cit., p. 94.

[61] Charles Temple Dix, *The Flying Dutchman* (1860s), oil on canvas, accessed on September 9, 2020, Wikimedia Commons, https://commons.wikimedia.org/wiki/File:The_Flying_Dutchman_by_Charles_Temple_Dix.jpg.

Figure 5: Koloman Moser, *Brünnhilde and Wotan* (circa 1916)[62]

In theater, Maurice Maeterlinck's *Pelléas et Mélisande* (1892) takes place in a mysterious and dreamlike setting with an eerie cast of characters. Maeterlinck's play provided the basis for Debussy's 1902 opera by the same name. During the *fin de siècle*, artists strove to capture our interior and subjective life. However, this subjective view morphed into something no longer beautiful and esoteric but rather into the base, into our Freudian id, and into what will be depicted in the Modern era.

e. From Symbolism to Modernism

As we enter the twentieth century, particularly the time period around World War I, Western European aesthetics morphed from the Romantic period to the Modern

---

[62] Koloman Moser, *Brünnhilde and Wotan* (circa 1916), oil on canvas, Leopold Museum, accessed on September 10, 2020, Wikimedia Commons, https://commons.wikimedia.org/wiki/File:Koloman_Moser-Wotan and_Br%C3%BCnhilde-Google_Art_Project.jpg.

period.[63] The idyllic countryside mutates into a polluted and poverty-ridden city. The hero becomes the anti-hero and humor becomes ironic. No longer do lovers leap into the ocean (Senta, from Wagner's *Flying Dutchman*) or into flames (Brünnhilde, from Wagner's *Ring*), and the erotic sentiment mutates into the pornographic and the violent.

In Figure 6, *The Hay Wain* (1821), John Constable paints a romanticized idyllic landscape with a family living in harmony with nature. One hundred years later, the worldview has drastically changed. In Figure 7a, *After the Push* (1917), Christopher Nevinson depicts a desolate landscape. In Figure 7b, *La Patrie* (1916), Nevinson shows wounded soldiers waiting to die in a crowded room filled with strangers. In Figures 8a and 8b, *War Cripples* (1920) and *Skat Players* (1920), Otto Dix shows us the condition of those who survived World War I, an entirely different landscape than Constable's idyllic space. Where does that leave humanity? Marcel Duchamp reduced the landscape to a urinal. (Figure 9: Marcel Duchamp, *Fountain* [1917]). How did that transformation happen?

---

[63] Charles A. O'Connor III, *The Great War and The Death of God*. O'Connor discusses the impact of World War I on Western society and culture including on theology, philosophy, literature, and art. One cannot speak of the Modern period without speaking of the Postmodern period, which by some accounts began in 1945 with the dropping of the atomic bombs on Hiroshima and Nagasaki. The Modern period retained an implicit belief in historical progress and an element of hope for personal and social growth and development. These aspirations are captured in Ezra Pound's imperative: "Make It New." We see hope expressed toward the end of *Ulysses* in Bloom and Molly's desire to try again to bond as a married couple and in the last book of *In Search of* with the Narrator's determination to become a writer. Contrast those endings with Richard Powers's 2018 Pulitzer Prize–winning novel *The Overstory: A Novel*. In the Romantic era, *The Overstory* would have had a happy, uplifting ending with the trees saved. In the Modern era, those particular trees would be killed but there would be hope for future trees. In this postmodern book, the trees are killed, there's little hope for future trees, and the characters end in death, betrayal, abject failure, and loneliness. Those entering the Postmodern period are to abandon all hope.

Figure 6: John Constable, *The Hay Wain* (1821)[64]

Figure 7a: Christopher R. W. Nevinson, *After the Push* (1917)[65]

---

[64] John Constable, *The Hay Wain*, (1821), oil on canvas, The National Gallery, Room 34, accessed on September 10, 2020, Wikimedia Commons, https://commons.wikimedia.org/wiki/File:John_Constable_The_Hay_Wain.jpg.

[65] Christopher R. W. Nevinson, After the Push: *After the Push* (1917), painting, Imperial War Museum, accessed on September 10, 2020, Wikimedia Commons, https://commons.wikimedia.org/wiki/File:After_The_Push_by_CRW_Nevinson_1917.JPG.

Figure 7b: Christopher R. W. Nevinson, *La Patrie* (1916)[66]

Figure 8a: Otto Dix, *War Cripples* (1920)[67]

---

[66] Christopher R. W. Nevinson, *La Patrie* (1916), oil on canvas, Birmingham Museums Trust, accessed on September 10, 2020, Wikimedia Commons, https://commons.wikimedia.org/wiki/File:La_patrie_Christopher_Richard_Wynne_Nevinson_(1889%E2%80%931946)_Birmingham_Museums_Trust.jpg.

[67] Otto Dix, *War Cripples* (1920), reproduction taken from a period photo of original painting exhibited at the First International Dada Fair and believed to have been destroyed in World War II, accessed on September 9, 2020, https://www.ottodix.org/catalog-item/129.006.

Figure 8b: Otto Dix, *Skat Players* (1920)[68]

Figure 9: Marcel Duchamp, *Fountain* (1917)[69]

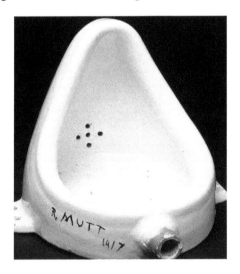

---

[68] Otto Dix, *Skat Players* (1920), oil on canvas, Alte Nationalgalerie, accessed on September 10, 2020, https://www.wikiart.org/en/otto-dix/the-skat-players-1920.

[69] Marcel Duchamp, *Fountain* (1917), ready-made installation, Tate Modern, accessed on September 10, 2020, WikiArt, https://www.wikiart.org/en/marcel-duchamp/fountain-1917.

Many factors explain the transition from Romanticism to modernism. Darwinism and the rise of scientific materialism replaced the assumed transcendent purpose of human life and reduced ontological and metaphysical explanations to scientific and empirical explanations. Rapid industrialization and urbanization created a culture in which people became alienated from nature and from each other. The Belle Époque was supported by an expanding urban working class living in poverty with the associated maladies that arise from poverty.

World War I, with its massive and senseless destruction of life, property, and the prior world order, had an immense impact on the demise of the Romantic worldview. The result was a distrust of government and church, the traditional institutions of order and fundamental explanation of the world.[70] Within this growing pessimism, artists began to illustrate a different worldview. Like Freia's apples in Wagner's *Ring of the Nibelung*, speculative metaphysics and religious belief withered. A radical break with the past became an artistic mandate.[71]

In response to a sense of alienation from society and a loss of spiritual meaning at the root of existence, writers turned inward to their subjective experiences. Writers began discarding the traditional structure of a novel: plot,

---

[70] The impact of World War I was different in the United States than in Europe. Europe was devastated economically, psychologically, and politically. Economically, in the United States, World War I proved to be a financial stimulus for farmers, ship builders, steel manufactures, and other industries that produced products that were needed by war torn Europe. Psychologically, the American population viewed themselves as saviors of the Allies without whom the Allies would have lost the war to a totalitarian regime. Politically, the United States' rationale to enter the war was, to use President Wilson's words, "to make the world safe for democracy." This aspiration reinforced the United States' self-identity as both superior to other nations and having the mission to constructively transform the world. This self-identity often is referred to as "American exceptionalism." Although the United States soon returned to an isolationist policy, this self-identity of American exceptionalism remains the foundation of the United States' foreign policy to this day. See David M Kennedy, *Over Here: The First World War and American Society*, (Oxford: Oxford University Press, 1980, 2004).

[71] Christopher Butler describes this break with the past as a "transvaluation of all values," as the opening up of an "extraordinary avant-garde market-place of competing styles," as an "unprecedented freedom and confidence in stylistic experiment by what they saw as radically new ideas, current in that period, concerning consciousness, time, and the nature of knowledge, which were to be found in the work of Nietzsche, Bergson, Freud, Einstein, Croce, Weber, and others. And these ideas contested in a dramatic manner the beliefs of the older generation." Christopher Butler, "Joyce the modernist," in *The Cambridge Companion to James Joyce*, ed. Derek Attridge (Cambridge: Cambridge University Press, 1970), p. 67.

setting, characters, and linear flow of narrative. They probed interior experiences in place of narrative. This inward movement included an exploration of language itself. Language *qua* language becomes the subject of artistic literary exploration and expression.[72]

Subjective exploration no longer was an avenue to the universal and cosmic. It was no longer Tristan and Isolde expiring "in sweet perfume, in the surging swell, in the ringing sound, in the vast wave of the world's breath. . . ."[73] This "sweet perfume" morphed into the interior dank odor of unmet instincts. Freud's depiction of this inner self was not of fundamental religious or cosmic goodness. It was of antisocial drives and base instincts. Darkness, not light, was at the end of the tunnel.

Despite this shift in sentiment from Romanticism to modernism, Wagner remained hugely popular and culturally influential. What did Wagner offer to those early Moderns if the Romantic sentiment and social revolutionary spirit of the nineteenth century were replaced by social alienation and individual isolation? Wagner's legacy to the Moderns, particularly to writers, was not his romantic sentiment and a man's apotheosis through a woman's love. Rather, it was Wagner's formal or technical elements: the use of *leitmotifs*, endless melody, and the concept of *Gesamtkunstwerk*.

---

[72] The artistic exploration of language *qua* language may have reached its zenith with Joyce's 1939 *Finnegans Wake*. *Finnegans Wake* makes language, almost more than the story, the novel's subject.
[73] Wagner's *Tristan and Isolde*, closing lines of the Liebestod. Wagner's program notes referred to Isolde's closing piece as her *Verklarung* (Transformation). Wagner labeled the overture as the Liebestod. Franz Liszt flipped the labels and Wagnerians accepted Liszt's designations over Wagner's!

CHAPTER 2

Summary of James Joyce's *Ulysses*[74]
and Marcel Proust's *In Search of Lost Time*

In order to appreciate how Joyce and Proust creatively employed *leitmotifs*, endless melody, and *Gesamtkunstwerk* in their works, a brief overview of *Ulysses* and *In Search of* is helpful.

a. Joyce's *Ulysses*[75]

Ulysses is a modern-day retelling of Homer's *Odyssey*. Unlike Homer's epic, which takes place over ten years and is replete with heroic adventures that over time become legends, Joyce's *Ulysses* is encapsulated in one ordinary day in Dublin: June 16, 1904. Many of the sixty plus characters are lower middle class or poor, heavy drinkers, and lacking in anything even remotely close to the heroic. Leopold Bloom (hereinafter referred to simply as "Bloom") is our modern-day Ulysses. He is thirty-eight years old, works as an advertising canvasser for a local paper, and wanders around Dublin from one pseudo-Homeric adventure to another.

Homer's Odysseus was doing his best to get home to his son, Telemachus, and faithful wife Penelope. Due to powers beyond his control, i.e., the gods, Odysseus was fated to wander around the Mediterranean Sea before being allowed to return home. Upon arriving home, in heroic fashion, Odysseus slays the suiters who had occupied his home. In contrast, Bloom's

---

[74] See Appendix C for the structure of *Ulysses*.

[75] James Joyce, *Ulysses*. All references are to the episode number, name, and location, i.e., episode 4, Calypso: 4.25–27 refers to episode 4, lines 25–27.

son, Rudy, died in infancy eleven years ago, and his wife, Molly, is at home waiting for her 4:00 p.m. tryst with Blaze Boylan. Bloom, who knows of the tryst, does not want a confrontation and therefore avoids going home until the early hours of the following day.

Stephen Dedalus, the Telemachus of our modern Homeric tale, is a substitute grammar school teacher, who hates his job, despises his boss, and thinks himself superior to everyone in Dublin. He suffers from the sin of pride, and his financial irresponsibility would make Polonius moan in despair. Stephen's mother is dead, and he is estranged from his father. That morning, after relinquishing his apartment key to his housemate, he chooses to become homeless. The subtext of *Ulysses* is Stephen's longing for a surrogate father figure and Bloom's psychologically seeking a surrogate son.

In Joyce's earlier novel, *A Portrait of the Artist as a Young Man* (1916), Stephen Dedalus tells us that his aim is to become a writer who will "forge in the smithy of my soul the uncreated conscience of my race."[76] His writing thus far has produced only private verbal word play (also known as pseudo-profound nonsense) such as "His [Stephen's] mouth moulded issuing breath, unspeeched: ooeeehah: roar of catecractic planets, globed, blazing, roaring, wayawayawayawayaway. . . . Listen: a fourworded wavespeech: seesoo, hrss, rsseeiss, ooos. Vehement breath of water amid seasnakes, rearing horses, rocks. In cups of rocks it slops: flop, slop, slip: bounded in barrels." (episode

---

[76] The full passage from Stephen's diary reads: "Welcome, O life! I go to encounter for the millionth time the reality of experience and to **forge** in the **smithy of my soul** the **uncreated** consciousness of my **race**." (emphasis added) Why did Joyce have Stephen write this cryptic mini-manifesto? According to Pericles Lewis in *Modernism, Nationalism, and the Novel*, Joyce is putting forward the framework of his aesthetic theory. Lewis argues that the artist forges, i.e., reshapes, rather than invents reality. In Wagner's opera *Siegfried*, Siegfried rearranged the broken pieces of the sword; Siegfried did not make the material that constituted the sword. The smithy represents the artist's creative spirit. This spirit is circumscribed by the culture into which the artist is born. The artist inherits language, history, and foundational beliefs, i.e., a culture. The artist cannot create his inherited legacy which constitutes his individual consciousness and national identity. The artist can, however, give new shape to his individual consciousness and to his culture. This concept of race, culture, *Volk*, or nation defines groups of people who are connected by a shared history, language, and beliefs. In the years around the 1900s, the concept of race or culture became identified with a political entity called the state which is constituted by citizens. The conflict between the concepts of nation and state raises practical and theoretical questions. A practical question is defining the state's obligations to non-citizens. A theoretical question is whether the individual (liberal theory) or the group/community (twentieth century fascism) is the basic unit of society. See Lewis, *Modernism*, particularly chapter 1.

3, Proteus: 3.402–4 and 3.456–59) Homer's Odysseus would not mistake Stephen for his son, Telemachus.

The distinctive feature of both Stephen and Bloom, but more so of Bloom, is their semi-conscious subjective life.[77] Stephen's thoughts tend toward the abstract and esoteric. Bloom's thoughts trend toward the more mundane. Bloom's mental life, however, is rich with thoughts about history, current events, musical tunes, scientific queries, regrets, sexual fantasies, kind acts, future aspirations, and his daughter and wife, Milly and Molly. By using recurrent thoughts and experiences, a.k.a. *leitmotifs,* Joyce unifies the story and gives us insight into the characters' psychology. Several of these *leitmotifs* are discussed in chapter 3.

b. Proust's *In Search of Lost Time*[78]

In Search of is a seven-book work that spans the time period from about fifteen years before the Narrator's birth to several years after World War I. The year of the Narrator's birth is widely considered to be the same year as Proust's birth in 1871. Since the Narrator, the novel's protagonist, is writing his story toward the end of his life, that would make the Narrator around fifty years

---

[77] Molly Bloom's subjective life is a *tour de force* of meandering thoughts or, in its literary name, stream of consciousness. Her 22,000-word stream of conscious soliloquy (or shall we say 22,000-word endless melody) in the final chapter is bookended with the life-affirming word "yes." However, most of her mental twists and turns have to do with her past and current sexual activities.

[78] Moncrieff translated the French title *À la recherche du temps perdu* as *Remembrance of Things Past.* This was not a literal translation but taken from the first two lines of Shakespeare's Sonnet (30.1–2): "When to the sessions of sweet silent thought I summon up remembrance of things past." I chose to use the title *In Search of Lost Time* and abbreviate it as *In Search of. In Search of* is a more accurate translation and better captures Proust's project than *Remembrance of Things Past* for several reasons. First, much of what the Narrator describes as having objectively happened, i.e., his remembering, may not have happened as he describes it. See the passage in Book 7, (PR), vol. 2, pp. 881–90, where, after reading an account by the Goncourt brothers of an evening at the Verdurins', the Narrator tells us that his account is not of what really happened but rather psychological generalizations: "The result was that, when I came to put together all the notes I had been able to make on the guests at a dinner, the pattern of the lines I drew represented a collection of psychological generalizations in which the special interests of the guests' remarks occupied hardly any place." (PR, vol. 7, p. 888) Second, the French words *"du temps"* in the title translate as "time." And third, the word "time" appears as the first and last words of the novel: *"Longtemps, je me suis couché de bonne heure,"* signifying the importance of "time." To make matters more complicated is the tense of the first sentence—the present prefect tense. The present perfect tense describes an action that started in the past and continues in the present. See Roger Shattuck, *Proust's Way: A Field Guide to* In Search of Lost Time, pp. 265–68.

old. [79] About two thirds into the novel, we learn that the Narrator's name is Marcel (C, vol. 2, p. 429), but I will continue to refer to him as "the Narrator."

The Narrator is wealthy, hyper-intelligent, and a candid observer of society, particularly that of Parisian Society. He seldom drives the action but rather comments on and analyzes it, even his own actions. [80] The Narrator is not a nice or kind person. [81] He is self-centered, a social climber, arguably emotionally stunted, and shows very little loyalty or love to anyone save his grandmother and his mother. [82] We very seldom hear him converse but he must have been a wonderful conversationalist since everyone wants his company, and, therefore, he is able to move seamlessly in and out of various strata of the French aristocracy and upper bourgeoisie.

The Narrator's aspirations are three-fold. First, he wants to "make it into Society." [83] About one third into the novel, he is invited to the drawing room and

---

[79] Per George Painter's *Marcel Proust: A Biography*: "[*À la recherche*] is not, properly speaking a fiction, but a creative autobiography." (xvii) Since the Narrator describes events after World War I and Proust was born in 1871 and died in 1922, it is reasonable to place the Narrator around fifty years of age.

[80] Howard Moss, *The Magic Lantern of Marcel Proust*, p. 11: "He [Proust] is only too happy to stop and analyze every possible nuance of whatever it is, whether that means thirty-one pages on the reasons why Princesses de Parma is nice to the narrator at the Duchesse de Guermantes' dinner party (ten pages for the first reason, twenty-one on the second) or close to a thousand on the workings of jealousy."

[81] Proust, by all accounts had many idiosyncrasies, but he was not nasty or a user of people solely for his own financial and psychological benefit. Proust was financially independent and had several close friends. Joyce, however, followed in Wagner's footsteps as being someone who showed no appreciation for others' personal and financial support. Wagner had Otto Wesendonck, King Ludwig II of Bavaria (Crazy Ludwig), and Hans von Bülow as supporters. Joyce had Sylvia Beach, Harriet Shaw Weaver, and his brother John Stanislaus as his supporters. Wagner had Cosima and Joyce had Nora to look after their needs.

[82] The Narrator's conception of love is that of a solipsistic experience: "I knew that I was in love with Albertine; but alas! I had no thought of letting her know it. . . . For one thing, the avowal, the declaration of my passion to her whom I loved no longer seemed to me one of the vital and necessary incidents of love, nor love itself an external reality, but simply a subjective pleasure. And as for this pleasure, I felt that Albertine would do everything necessary to furnish it, all the more since she would not know that I was enjoying it." (*WBG*, vol. 1, p. 693)

[83] As an adolescent, when leaving Swann's home with the writer Bergotte: "'This is all between ourselves,' said Bergotte as he left me outside my own door. A few years later I should have answered: 'I never repeat things.' That is the ritual phrase of society. . . . It is what I should have said then and there to Bergotte, for one does not invent all one's speeches, especially when one is acting merely as a card in the social pack. But I did not yet know the formula. What my great aunt . . . would have said on a similar occasion was: 'If you don't wish it to be repeated, why do you say it?' That is the answer of the unsociable, of the quarrelsome. I was nothing of that sort: I bowed my head in silence." (*WBG*, vol. 1, pp. 435–36)

dinner table of a member of the Parisian aristocracy, i.e., into Parisian Society. As his number of invitations to the most exclusive drawing rooms and dinner tables increases, his infatuation with Society decreases and changes to disgust as he observes the hypocrisy and shallowness of Society and all those aspiring to enter it. The Narrator takes special delight in exposing this hypocrisy to the reader. On that level, *In Search of* is a gigantic social satire, and, once that is recognized, *In Search of* is a hilarious read.[84]

Second, the Narrator wants to experience love. This desire for love leads to several unhealthy love relationships. These relationships are grounded on the Narrator's need to possess and control an object, rather than a mutually nurturing love relationship between two people. The reader witnesses several perplexing sexual scenes between the Narrator and his mistress, Albertine, during which he thinks of his mother. During these psycho/sexual stunted scenes we cannot help but recall when, early in the novel, the Narrator, as a child, manipulated his mother into giving him a goodnight kiss. Following that kiss, his mother spends the night with him on an adjacent cot in his bedroom.

The Narrator's third goal is a composite of aspirations. He wants to penetrate the essence of an aesthetic experience, capture that essence as a writer, and understand how that essence creates the experience of joy.

Physical decay and death permeate *In Search of*. The Narrator seeks to defeat the decaying power of time. He comes to realize that art, if it lasts beyond that artist's death, might be the closest we can come to defeating or at least taming the all-powerful smothering grip of time.[85] The Narrator discovers another way to defeat time. He realizes this through a serious of epiphanies, the madeleine cake experience being the first of such epiphanies. (*SW*, vol. 1, p. 34) This discovery unfolds through involuntary memory. This type of memory has the power to conjure up the past with such vividness and veracity that the memory is experienced as in the present. Both methods give the Narrator the experience of joy. But what does this concept of involuntary memory mean?

---

[84] For a six-minute summary, "Summarize Proust Challenge," YouTube, 5:59, 8/23/2009, https://www.youtube.com/watch?v=CdIZUomR21M. This is a reading taken from Patrick Alexander, *Marcel Proust's Search for Lost Time: A Reader's Guide to* The Remembrance of Things Past, pp. 13–14.

[85] Joyce asserts a comparable idea. In response to Benoist-Méchin's request to see the scheme of the Penelope episode in *Ulysses*, Joyce responded, "If I gave it all up immediately, I'd lose my immortality. I've put in so many enigmas and puzzles that it will keep the professors busy for centuries arguing over what I meant, and that's the only way to insuring one's immorality." Ellman, *James Joyce*, p. 521.

What we call "ordinary" memory occurs when someone asks you to recall an event, i.e., the name of the street you crossed (street X) to get to the beach. This type of memory is intentional and directed. Another type of ordinary memory is when the memory just pops into our consciousness. This experience also happens often, although we might not be aware of it. A common example is the free association that occurs when daydreaming.

Involuntary memory, as used by Proust, is when the memory of crossing street X is enriched with all the sensations, emotions, thoughts, etc., that were present when we originally crossed street X. Admittedly rare, in Proust's lexicon, it is an experience outside the normal flow of time; it is an aesthetic experience as the past becomes present. The memory of the event comes alive; it is in our present consciousness with the immediacy of our prior experience and becomes a new experience. This new experience is more vivid, more significant since it now is accompanied with a rich history of experience. Proust describes this type of involuntary memory as defeating time. Similarly, the emotional content of a *leitmotif* contains a vivid history enriched by prior memories. While objective or scientific time is linear and forever moving forward, *leitmotifs* move bi-directionally through time. This trans-temporal feature of *leitmotifs*, to use Proustian concepts, simultaneously joins several moments of experience and in this sense defeats our normal or linear experience of time.

c. A Tenuous Connection between Joyce and Proust

Proust (1871–1922) was French and Joyce (1882–1941) was Irish. They met once on May 18, 1922, in Paris at a party for Igor Stravinsky and Sergei Diaghilev. There are several slightly divergent accounts of their conversation, but they all point to the total absence of a meaningful encounter.[86] Both appeared in character: Joyce had been drinking heavily and Proust was covered in furs. They discussed their respective illnesses. Proust reportedly said that "I regret that I don't know Mr. Joyce's work." Joyce counted with "I have never read

---

[86] Richard Ellman, pp. 508–9. Interestingly Joyce attended Proust's funeral. And perhaps equally as interesting, Paul de Kock (the author of the semi-porn book that Molly enjoys reading) is mentioned both in *Ulysses* and *In Search of*. The Narrator compares Paul de Kock with Gogol (*C*, vol. 2, p. 645). There was an actual Paul de Kock (1793–1871) who was a popular French writer of Parisian life to whom both Proust and Joyce seem to be referring. Joyce seems to enjoy the last name and perhaps Proust is being ironic in his comparison to Gogol.

Mr. Proust." Apparently neither cared for the writing of the other. There is no reason to believe that there was any influence of one on the other.

In fairness to Proust, he was very sick and would be dead in six months. Proust died on November 18, 1922. In fairness to Joyce, Joyce included several cryptic references to Proust in *Finnegans Wake* (*FW*): "Prost bitte!" (*FW*, 424:9); "the prouts will invent a writing" (*FW* 482:31); "swansway" (*FW* 450:5, 465:35); "two legglegels in blooms" (*FW* 587:26); and "pities on the plain" (*FW* 564:28).[87] However, in addition to their connection to their respective physical maladies was their profound intellectual and cultural link to Wagner and Wagnerism.

One could wonder whether Joyce had Proust in mind when he wrote in *Ulysses* in the style of John Cardinal Newman:

> There are sins or (let us call them as the world calls them) evil memories which are hidden away by man in the darkest places of the heart but they abide there and wait. He may suffer their memory to grow dim, let them be as though they had not been and all but persuade himself that they were not or at least were otherwise. Yet a **chance word will call them forth** suddenly and they will rise up to confront him in the most various circumstances, a vision or a dream, or while timbrel and harp soothe his senses or amid the cool silver tranquility of the evening or at the feast, at midnight, when he is now filled with wine. (episode 14, Oxen of the Sun: 14.1345– 53, emphasis added.)[88]

"Yet a chance word will call them forth. . . ." One must agree this sounds very Proustian.

With this chapter as background, we now move to the heart of our discussion: the impact of Wagner on Joyce and Proust's literary masterpieces.

---

[87] See Painter, *Marcel Proust: A Biography*, vol. 2, p. 342, n1. Painter's five references have an air of plausibility except "two Legglegels in blooms". I do not see a Proust reference. William York Tindell, *A Reader's Guide to Finnegans Wake*, (Syracuse University Press, 1969), p. 118 cites additional references to Proust in *FW*, 49:23-4, "…(who the lost time we had the pleasure we have had our little *recherché* brush with, what, Schott?)…" and on page 158, *FW*, 224:22–23, "The youngly delightsome filles-in-pleyurs are now showen drawen, if but one…" as possibly a reference to book 2 of *In Search of: Jeunes Filles en Fleurs. Jeunes Filles en Fleurs* is translated into English as *In the Shadow of Young Girls in Flower* or *Within a Budding Grove*.

[88] In terms of the number of words in each work, *Ulysses* has more than 265,000 and *In Search of* has about 1.5 million, 5.6 times more words than *Ulysses*.

CHAPTER 3
Wagnerism in James Joyce's *Ulysses*

T his chapter includes the heart of my analysis of Wagner's impact on Joyce's novel *Ulysses*. The chapter is divided into five sections. Section a shows the biographical connection between Wagner and Joyce. Section b presents selected Wagnerian references within the text of *Ulysses*. Sections c, d, and e provide examples of *leitmotifs*, endless melody, and *Gesamtkunstwerk* within *Ulysses*.

a. Background on the Wagner-Joyce Connection [89]

Joyce had detailed knowledge of Wagner's works. Over time, his relationship to Wagner changed from one of admiration to hostility to reconciliation. As the saying goes, it's complicated.

According to Stoddard Martin, George Moore (1852-1933) was the most influential Irish novelist before Joyce and had a major influence on Joyce. [90] [91] Moore also was a devoted Wagnerian. The link between Wagner, Moore, and Joyce is more direct than just one of influence. Scholars, including Stoddard Martin, Richard Blissett, and Cóilín Owens, suggest that Joyce heavily borrowed from Moore. Per Martin: "it should not come as any surprise that Joyce imitated Moore, parodistically at times, even stole motifs outright from

---

[89] Major sources for this section are Ellmann, *James Joyce*; T. Martin, *Joyce and Wagner*; and Stoddard Martin, *Wagner to the Waste Land: A Study of the Relationship of Wagner to English Literature*.

[90] S. Martin, *Wagner to the Waste Land*, chapter 6. Martin devotes individual chapters to discussing Wagner's influence on Swinburne, Wilde, Symons, Shaw, Moore, Yeats, Joyce, Lawrence, and Eliot.

[91] Ellmann tells us that as early as 1899, when Joyce was seventeen, Joyce "was already beginning to feel he might outdo George Moore, Hardy, and Turgenev, if not Tolstoy". Ellmann, *James Joyce*, p. 83.

him."[92] In discussing Joyce's *The Dubliners*, Owens comments: "It is clear, in any event, that before he [Joyce] wrote "After the Race" (September 1904), Joyce had read *Evelyn Innes*, since "Eveline," written the previous July, exhibits a number of details with analogues in Moore's novel."[93] Moore incorporated the narrative equivalent of Wagner's *leitmotifs* and unending melodies as unending narratives in many of his novels, as well as creating prose representations of Wagnerian operas.

In *Ulysses*, episode 9, Scylla and Charybdis, Joyce makes several references to George Moore. For example, at 9.305–310 Stephen observes, and mentally comments on, three men talking in the library reading room: "I hope you'll be able to come tonight. Malachi Mulligan is coming too. Moore asked him to bring Haines. Did you hear Miss Mitchell's joke about Moore and Martyn? That Moore is Martyn's wild oats? Awfully clever, isn't it? They remind me of Don Quixote and Sancho Panza. Our national epic has yet to be written, Dr Sigerson says. Moore is the man for it. A knight of the rueful countenance here in Dublin."

At the outbreak of World War I, Joyce was teaching English in Italy. He exclaimed to one of his English language students, Oscar Schwarz, "Wagner *puzza di sesso* (stinks of sex)."[94] Richard Ellmann, the writer of the definitive biography of Joyce, notes ironically that this is a strange comment coming from someone who was starting on a book that was going to be banned as pornographic. While *puzza di sesso* is meant as an insult and gives the appearance of someone not wanting anything to do with *puzza*, Joyce always had a place for Wagner in his major literary works.

Joyce concludes *A Portrait of an Artist as a Young Man* (1916) with the famous reference to Wagner's character Siegfried from *The Ring*: "Welcome, O life! I go to encounter for the millionth time the reality of experience and to *forge in the smithy* of my soul the uncreated consciousness of my race" (emphasis added). In "James Joyce in the Smithy of His Soul," William Blissett argues for "the depth and centrality of the identification of Stephen and Siegfried in *A Portrait* and *Ulysses*."[95] Stephen Dedalus as a twentieth-century Siegfried is

---

[92] S. Martin, *Wagner to the Waste Land*, p. 117.
[93] Cóilín Owens, *Before Daybreak "After the Race" and The Origins of Joyce's Art*, p. 87.
[94] Ellman, *James Joyce*, p. 382.
[95] Blissett, "James Joyce in the Smithy of His Soul."

about as heroic as a wet tissue. Nonetheless, Joyce links Stephen to Siegfried and thereby to Wagner.

As Joyce finished writing the Sirens episode (June 1919) in *Ulysses*, his friend, George Borach, reports Joyce telling him:

> I finished the Sirens chapter during the last few days. A big job. I wrote this chapter with the technical resources of music. It is a fugue with all musical notions: piano, forte, rallentando, and so on. A quintet occurs in it, too, as in *Die Meistersinger*, my favorite Wagnerian opera.[96]

In 1919, five years after Joyce's "Wagner *puzza di sesso*" outburst, Joyce was with a friend, Ottocaro Weiss, at a performance of *Die Walküre*. Joyce asks, "Don't you find the musical effects of my Sirens better than Wagner's?" When Weiss replied in the negative, Joyce "turned on his heel and did not show up for the rest of the opera, as if he could not bear not being preferred."[97]

Finnegans Wake, which is replete with references to Wagner, begins the first full sentence (it starts in mid-sentence) with a reference to Wagner's *Tristan and Isolde*:

> riverrun, past Eve and Adams, from swerve of shore to bend of bay, brings us by a commodius vicus of recirculation back to Howth, Castle and Environs. Sir Tristan, violer d'amores, fr'over the short sea, has passencore rearrived from North Armorica on this side of scraggy isthmus of Europe Minor to wielderfight his penisolate war...

Critics have argued that *Finnegans Wake* (FW) uses the themes of Wagner's *Tristan and Isolde* and the structure of *The Ring* tetralogy. Tristan and Isolde's relationship unfolds in the realm of night, somewhat similar to the realm of dreams in which FW takes place. Structurally, Joyce's FW is a tetralogy, like *The Ring* tetralogy. FW shows human development through four distinct states: Book One/*Das Rheingold*—theocracy or the age of the gods; Book Two/*Die*

---

[96] Ellmann, *James Joyce*, p. 459.
[97] Ellmann, *James Joyce*, p. 460.

Walküre—aristocracy or the age of heroes; Book Three/*Siegfried*—age of people; Book Four/*Götterdämmerung*—chaos.[98]

Again, to quote Stoddard Martin:

> From the time of the triumph of *Ulysses*, Joyce's disparaging remarks about Wagner began to disappear; and during the latter 1920s and 1930s, while he was at work on a book which was in some sense the apotheosis of the musical ideal of the 1890s, he let his lifelong interest in Wagner and Wagnerian method flow as a subterranean current recognizable to all who might care to count the ways in which he could say "gutterdoomering" or "Welhell" or to "exagiminate" the *Ring*-like texture and scope of his most sublime yet pranksterish literary experiment.[99]

So why this somewhat schizophrenic relationship to Wagner? Stoddard Martin argues that Joyce's psychological attitude toward Wagner changed from early adoration, to middle-aged coolness and denunciation, to later reconciliation. The relationship, as Martin states, was "first reverence, then imitation, then competition, then repudiation, finally peaceful coexistence."[100] This reflects the psychology of a child breaking free of his or her parent and then later coming to appreciate the parent's impact on his or her life. Is Martin's analysis psychological babble or psychological insight? That question takes us outside the domain of this discussion, but what remains uncontroversial is that Joyce had intimate knowledge of Wagner's works.

b. Textual Reference to Wagner in *Ulysses*[101]

It is difficult to obtain a consistent count of Wagnerian references in *Ulysses*. In *Joyce and Wagner: A Study of Influence*, Timothy Martin cites about forty

---

[98] S. Martin, *Wagner to the Waste Land*, p. 153. Also see Blissett, "James Joyce in the Smithy of His Soul," p. 131. This is only one of many interpretations of *FW*.

[99] S. Martin, *Wagner to the Waste Land*, p. 139.

[100] S. Martin, *Wagner to the Waste Land*, p. 137.

[101] Textual references to *Ulysses* are to the Hans Walter Gabler edition. References to Wagner are bolded.

references within *Ulysses* to Wagner and Wagnerian operas.[102] However, some of these references might be a stretch, and some are repeated under different operas as a "proximate reference." For example, in episode 13, Nausicaa, 1076–78, Bloom ponders: "A star I see, Venus? Can't tell yet. Two. When three it's night. Were those nightclouds there all the time? Looks like a phantom ship." Martin attributes this reference both to *Tannhäuser* and as a proximate reference to *The Flying Dutchman*.

Don Gifford's Ulysses *Annotated: Notes for James Joyce's* Ulysses corroborates some of Martin's cites but excludes others. (See Table 1 in Appendix A.) For example, in episode 3, Proteus: 3.397–98: "He comes, pale vampire, through storm his eyes, his bat sails, bloodying the sea, mouth to her mouth's kiss," Martin cites this as a reference to *The Flying Dutchman* whereas Gifford cites a poem translated from the Irish by Douglas Hyde (1860–1949). I suspect the discrepancy arises from one's musical knowledge. Perhaps Martin studied Wagner's operas and therefore was more sensitive to spotting Wagner references whereas Gifford's musical interests were elsewhere.

While the exact number of Wagner references in *Ulysses* is undetermined, within *Ulysses* there are many uncontested Wagnerian references. Several Wagner references are in the Circe episode. This episode is written in the style of a theatrical play.

After Stephen's long day of heavy drinking, including consuming the hallucinogen-laden absinthe, the time is midnight and Stephen and Bloom find themselves in a brothel. Stephen is hallucinating images of his mother and her condemnation of his lifestyle. The "dialogue" continues:

THE MOTHER
> (wrings her hands slowly, moaning desperately) O Sacred Heart of Jesus, have mercy on him! Save him from hell, O Divine Sacred Heart!

STEPHEN
> No! No! No! Break my spirit, all of you, if you can! I'll bring you all to heel!

---

[102] T. Martin, *Joyce and Wagner*, pp. 185–221.

THE MOTHER

(in the agony of her death rattle) Have mercy on Stephen, Lord, for my sake! Inexpressible was my anguish when expiring with love, grief and agony on Mount Calvary.

STEPHEN

Nothung! (He lifts his **ashplant** high with both hands and smashes the chandelier. Time's livid final flame leaps and, in the following darkness, ruin of all space, shattered glass and toppling masonry.) (episode 15, Circe: 15.4232–42, emphasis added)

Again, in the Circe episode, Bloom, hallucinating that he is mayor of Dublin, refers to Wagner's theoretical writings and to *The Flying Dutchman*:

BLOOM

. . . I say, from the cattlemarket to the river. That's **the music of the future.** That's my programme. *Cui bono?*[103] But our buccaneering **Vanderdeckens** in their **phantom ship** of finance. . . . (episode 15, Circe: 15.1367–69, emphasis added)

A few lines later we hear Bloom again:

(impassionedly) "These **flying Dutchmen** or lying Dutchmen as they recline in their upholstered poop, casting dice, what reck they? . . ." (episode 15, Circe: 15.1390–91, emphasis added)

A few lines later, various individuals and groups are in a marching procession that is a clear reference to act 3 of *Die Meistersinger*:

Prolonged applause. Venetian masts,[104] maypoles and festal arches spring up. . . . (episode 15, Circe: 15.1398–99)

---

[103] "*Cui bono?*" Latin: "Who benefits by it?" Or, in popular idiom, "Of what use is it?" See Don Gifford and Robert Seidman, Ulysses *Annotated: Notes for James Joyce's* Ulysses, p. 470. Gifford's book is indispensable for starting to make sense of the many references in *Ulysses*.

[104] Venetian masts are tall poles spiral-wound with multicolored ribbons and used to decorate streets on festive occasions.

In episode 16, the time is now past 1:00 a.m., and Bloom and Stephen are walking down a street trying to determine where to go. The text continues:

> So they turned on to chatting about music, a form of art for which Bloom, as a pure amateur, possessed the greatest love, as they made tracks arm in arm across Beresford place. **Wagnerian music**, though confessedly grand in its way, was a bit too heavy for Bloom and hard to follow at the first go-off but the music of Mercadante's *Huguenots*, Meyerbeer's *Seven Last Words on the Cross* and Mozart's *Twelfth Mass* he simply revelled in. . . . (episode 16, Eumaeus: 16.1732–38) (emphasis added) [105]

Ulysses includes multiple references to Stephen referring to his **ashplant** (walking stick) as his sword (an allusion to Siegfried's sword):

> "My **ash sword** hangs at my side." (episode 3, Proteus: 3.16)

> He took the hilt of his **ashplant**, lunging with it softly, dallying still. (episode 3, Proteus: 3.489)

> Stephen looked down . . . on his **ashplanthandle** over his knee. "My casque, **my sword**." (episode 9, Scylla and Charybdis: 9.295–96)

In the Sirens episode there is reference to Alberich's cave in *Das Rheingold*, act 3:

> But wait. But hear. Chords dark. Lugugugubrious. Low. In a cave of the dark middle earth. Embedded ore. The voice of dark age, of unlove, earth's fatigue made grave approach and painful, come from afar, from hoary mountains, called on good me and true. (episode 11, Sirens: 11.1005–8)

---

[105] This is typical Joycean humor. Bloom misidentifies all the references. Only a music scholar, or someone with Gifford's *Ulysses Annotated*, would get the humor.

Timothy Martin attributes many of the hallucinogenic dance scenes by the prostitutes in the Circe episode (#15) as references to Klingsor's magic garden and the Flower Maidens in *Parsifal*:

> The kisses, winging from their bowers fly about him, twittering, warbling, cooing. . . . They rustle, flutter upon his garments, alight, bright, giddy flecks, silvery sequins. (episode 15, Circe: 15.1268–70)

> The Yews: (rustling) She is right, our sister. Whisper. (Whispered kisses are heard in all the wood. Faces of hamadryads[106] peep out from the boles and among the leaves and break, blossoming into bloom.) (episode 15, Circe: 15.3340–42)

In Circe, 15.3649–60), we hear references to three individual operas within Wagner's *Ring* cycle: *Götterdämmerung*, act 1, scene ii; *Walküre*, act 1, scene ii; and *Siegfried*, act 1, scene i.

STEPHEN
> (*extends his hand to her smiling and chants to the air of the bloodoath in* The Dusk of the Gods)

> *Hangender Hunger,*
> *Fragende Frau,*
> *Mach tuns alle kaputt.*[107]

LYNCH
> Sheet lightening courage. The youth who could not shiver and shake. (To Zoe) Who taught you palmistry? (Circe: 15.3649–60)

---

[106] Hamadryads are nymphs who live in trees.

[107] *Hangender Hunger* = intense desire; *Fragende Frau* = questioning woman; *Macht uns alle kaput* = destroys us all.

The above two sections provide ample evidence that Joyce was well-acquainted with Wagner's operas and directly referred to Wagner and Wagnerian characters in the text of *Ulysses*.[108] Now let us see how Joyce used Wagner's formal techniques of *leitmotif*, endless melody, and *Gesamtkunstwerk*.

c. Leitmotifs

Joyce's *Ulysses* is replete with literary *leitmotifs*.[109] These literary *leitmotifs* function in a similar manner to Wagner's musical *leitmotifs*. Wagnerian *leitmotifs*, as discussed in chapter 1a, remind the listener of the history embedded in the current situation and foreshadow the future; they link the present to the past and future. *Leitmotifs* have both a telescopic and microscopic function; they have both an outward and inward vector. They bring distant objects of the past and future closer to view and simultaneously focus into the psychology of the character.

Literary *leitmotifs* function in a similar way. In *Ulysses*, when we read the word "jingle" in episode 11, for example, our memory travels to earlier uses of that word in the novel. Moreover, the jingle *leitmotif* provides insight into the character or situation by showing us how the character, e.g., Bloom, reacts to the jingle sound as he hears it throughout the day.

Ulysses includes many types of *leitmotifs*, such as recurring persons, real or imagined, and objects. Examples that appear throughout the novel include Simon Dedalus, Stephen's ashplant, the bar of soap and potato in Bloom's pocket, the envelope containing Martha's letter, Buck Mulligan, Hamlet, and political revolutionaries including Robert Emmet, Charles Parnell, and Arthur Griffith.

There also are recurring images, memories, and places such as clouds, Stephen's dead mother, Bloom's dead father and dead son, bee sting, Sandymount shore, sex and sexual fantasy, and color *leitmotifs* such as those of

---

[108] For a list of Wagner references in *Ulysses*, see Appendix A.

[109] Beginning with Hans von Wolzogen, it became a popular sport to identify and label Wagner's musical *leitmotifs*. Joyce scholarship participates in a similar sport. Blissett, in "James Joyce in the Smithy of His Soul," states: "There are more than 150 motifs in the book [*Ulysses*]." (p. 115) Blissett makes a stronger claim for the use of *leitmotifs* in *Finnegans Wake*: "As for Wagnerism, the *Wake* is not like music, it is music; it does not use *leitmotifs* occasionally or habitually, it is comprised of *leitmotifs*; Wagnerian references do not adorn, they nourish." (p. 130)

Stephen and Bloom's pants. Moreover, references often are indirect, such as when Molly Bloom refers to Arthur Griffith as "that little man he [Bloom] showed me without the neck." (episode 18, Penelope: 18.385)

We find recurring sounds and words such as "jingle" and "Tap Tap", and many songs from Molly's upcoming concert tour: *La ci darem la mano*" from *Don Giovanni* and "Love's Old Sweet Song," Irish protest songs such as "The Croppy Boy," the Saint George's church bells, and words such as "one and eightpence too much," and "odour/breath of whetted ashes", rocks, and "Agenbite of inwit." We also find recurring concepts such as Irish patriotism, the Gaelic League, English domination, anti-Semitism, death and birth, poverty, metempsychosis (met her pike hoses), scientific terms such as parallax and refraction, paternity and anti-Semitism, and love,[110] to name just a few.

Wagner uses a host of musical tools to expand a *leitmotif's* dramatic significance. These tools include changing a *leitmotif's* speed and rhythm, altering its key from major to minor, inverting it, using different orchestration, and taking pieces of the *leitmotif*, e.g., its first or middle note and developing it into new but related *leitmotifs*.[111] There are various literary tools that serve the same function as musical *leitmotifs*. These tools include repetition, ambiguity, synonyms, misinterpretation, mishearing, irony, sarcasm, declaring, ordering, accentuating words, lying, and inserting another language.

There are several ways in which Joyce uses ordinary language to create literary *leitmotifs*. The below illustrations move from the simple to the more complex.

One technique is to use the same word in different contexts. Four examples are discussed below: Buck Mulligan, Stephen's ashplant, Bloom's potato, and black pants.

---

[110] "Love" is an ideal shared by Bloom and Stephen. Perhaps love falls within the family of paternity *leitmotifs*. In the Cyclops episode, Bloom affirms the centrality of love in our life: "'But it's no use,' says he. 'Force, hatred, history, all that. That's not life for men and women, insult and hatred. And everybody knows that it's the very opposite of that that is really life.' 'What?' says Alf. 'Love,' says Bloom. 'I mean the opposite of hatred.'" (episode 12, Cyclops: 12.1481–85) Stephen struggles with whether he can love or be loved and speaks of a mother's love. In episode 15, Circe, when confronted with violence, Stephen asserts: "Struggle for life is the law of existence, but human philirenists. . . ." (episode 15, Circe: 15.4434–35) "Philirenist" means a lover of peace.

[111] See Cooke's two-CD set *An Introduction to* Der Ring des Nibelungen. For example, Bryan Magee points out the similarity in chord sequence between Alberich's ring and Valhalla's *leitmotifs* signifying their association with the quest for power. *The Tristan Chord: Wagner and Philosophy*, p. 115.

Buck Mulligan. *Ulysses* opens with the following words: "Stately, plump Buck Mulligan came from the stairhead. . . ." And within those first few words we find our first *leitmotif* in the form of a person, Buck Mulligan. We learn very quickly through descriptions ("stately, plump") and innuendos (he is at the top of the stairs looking down upon everyone) that Buck Mulligan is a very intelligent, loud-mouth, arrogant jokester who takes nothing seriously. He is Stephen's foil. Mulligan appears in only a handful of episodes: episode 1, Telemachus (the place where he, Stephen, and Haines live); episode 9, Scylla and Charybdis (the National Library); episode 10, Wandering Rocks (the streets of Dublin); and episode 14, Oxen of the Sun (a birthing hospital). Yet his personality is so dominant that when mentioned we cannot help but remember his other appearances and what was occurring during those moments. Where Mulligan goes, our memory follows.

Stephen's ashplant. In episode 15, Circe: 15.4242,[112] Stephen shouts "Nothung!" The word "Nothung" refers to Siegmund/Siegfried's sword in *The Ring*. Siegmund sings: "Highest need of holiest love, consuming need of yearning desire burns brightly within my breast, urging me on to deed and death! Nothung! Nothung! So I name you, sword! Fearsome steel!" as he withdraws the sword from Hunding's ash tree, freeing Sieglinde from a loveless marriage. (*Die Walküre*, act 1) And Stephen? He is in a brothel hallucinating from drinking absinthe, "the greeneyed monster." It is now past midnight, and the craziness of the past hour is reaching a crescendo:

STEPHEN
Nothung!
(He lifts his ashplant high with both hands and smashes the chandelier. Time's livid final flame leaps and, in the following darkness, ruin of all space, shattered glass and toppling masonry.)

THE GASIET
Pwfungg!

---

[112] The Circe episode is written as a theatrical play, hence the unusual formatting for a novel. The reader also will notice that Joyce does not conform to normal punctuation, e.g., quote marks.

BLOOM
   Stop!

LYNCH
   (rushes forward and seizes Stephen's hand) Here! Hold on! Don't
   run amok!

BELLA
   Police!

(Stephen, abandoning his ashplant, his head and arms thrown back
stark, beats the ground and flies from the room, past the whores at the
door.)

BELLA
   (screams) After him!

(The two whores rush to the halldoors. Lynch and Kitty and Zoe
stampede from the room. They talk excitedly. Bloom follows, returns.)

THE WHORES
   (Jammed in the doorway, pointing) Down there.

ZOE
   (pointing) There. There's something up.

BELLA
   Who pays for the lamp? (She seizes Bloom's coattail). Here, you
   were with him. The lamp's broken. (episode 15, Circe: 15.4242–69)

Here we see our modern hero in action. Drunk, he breaks a lamp, abandons
his weapon, and runs. Like a good father, Bloom pays for the damage and retrieves
Stephen's ashplant.

We first learn of the sword as Wotan's "great idea" at the end of *Das Rheingold* as the gods enter their new home, Valhalla. We first learn of Stephen's ashplant[113] as Stephen, Mulligan, and Haines are leaving their home to go for a swim:

> Stephen, taking his ashplant from its leaningplace, followed them out and, as they went down the ladder, pulled to the slow iron door and locked it. He put the huge key in his inner pocket. (episode 1, Telemachus, 1.528–30)

And a few lines later:

> He walked on waiting to be spoken to, trailing his ashplant by his side.... (episode 1, Telemachus: 1.627)

Stephen's ashplant accompanies him throughout the day but not as a symbol of power or of the dawn of a new age, but as a coat rack for his cap: "Stephen looked down on a wide headless caubeen, hung on his ashplanthandle over his knee. 'My casque and sword.'" (episode 9, Scylla and Charybdis: 9.295–96) And "Stephen looked on his hat, his stick, his boots. 'Stephanos, my crown, My sword, His boots are spoiling the shape of my feet. Buy a pair. Holes in my socks. Handkerchief too.'" (episode 9, Scylla and Charybdis: 9.946–48)[114]

In the Circe episode discussed above, Stephen brandishes his ashplant/sword several times in the brothel, culminating with him majestically breaking the lamp. This sword-bearer from *A Portrait of the Artist as a Young Man*, like Siegfried, was going to "forge in the smithy of my soul the uncreated conscious of my race." Stephen is falling a bit short of his aspiration, but as a *leitmotif* it is quite successful.

First, Stephen's ashplant fulfills a *leitmotif*'s telescopic function. Stephen's ashplant brings into focus, via memory, different parts of Stephen and Bloom's day. This "Nothung" scene occurs around 1:00 a.m., yet it prompts us to remember that at 8:00 a.m. the preceding morning, Stephen, Mulligan, and

---

[113] See Gifford, Ulysses *Annotated*, p. 22. An ashplant is an inexpensive walking stick made from the un-barked sapling of an ash tree. In the Celtic tradition, the ash tree was associated with king-making and its wood made up the handles of spears. The association with Wotan's spear is not accidental. Wotan's spear was made from a limb of the World Ash Tree.

[114] We learn in episode 1 that Stephen is wearing Buck Mulligan's hand-me-down pants.

Haines were in their residence at Martello Tower on Sandycove. Sandycove also is the same place where Bloom and Gerty MacDowell had an unusual sexual encounter earlier that evening. In this same vein, the "Nothung" scene refers to Joyce's earlier novel, *A Portrait of the Artist as a Young Man*, and to an opera from the prior century, *Siegfried*. Second, it also fulfills a *leitmotif*'s microscopic function. We see into Stephen's psychology as he handles his ashplant/sword. He is not heroic in any sense of the word, but borders on being an impotent fool.

Bloom's potato. Several objects accompany Bloom as he meanders around Dublin on June 16, 1904. These objects take on a *leitmotific* function as they acquire layers of psychological significance and meaning throughout the day. Examples include a potato (a link to his Jewish past), a bar of soap and the book *Sweets of Sin* (reminders of Molly), a "white slip of paper" (his clandestine pen pal romance with Martha), and the ache from a bee sting he received three weeks earlier. For illustrative purposes, we will focus on the potato.

We first hear of the potato early in Bloom's day and again and again throughout the day. Shortly after Bloom dressed to begin his day, he decides to buy a pork kidney for breakfast: "On the doorstep he felt in his hip pocket for the latchkey. Not there. In the trousers I left off. Must get it. Potato I have. Creaky wardrobe no use disturbing her." (episode 4, Calypso: 4. 72–74) In episode 8, Lestrygonians, we find Bloom in a mental frenzy trying to avoid Boylan both physically, by ducking behind a gate, and psychologically, by directing his consciousness to items in his pocket:

> I am looking for that. Yes, that. Try all pockets. Handker. Freeman. Where did I? Ah, yes. Trousers. Potato. Purse. Where? Hurry. Walk quickly. Moment more. My heart. His hand looking for the where did I put found in his hip pocket soap lotion have to call tepid paper stuck. Ah soap there I yes. Gate. Safe! (episode 8, Lestrygonians: 8.1188–93)

In the episode 15, Circe, Bloom loses the potato to Zoe, a prostitute in Bella's brothel:

ZOE

I feel it.

(Her hand slides into his left trouser pocket and brings out a hard black shrivelled potato. She regards it and Bloom with dumb moist lip.)

BLOOM

A talisman. Heirloom.

ZOE

For Zoe. For keeps? For being so nice, eh?

(She puts the potato greedily into a pocket then links his arm, cuddling him with supple warmth. He smiles uneasily. Slowly, note by note, oriental music is played. He gazes in the tawny crystal of her eyes, ringed with kohol. His smile softens.) (episode 15, Circe: 15.1309–19)

Bloom expresses his regret at 15.2795: "I should not have parted with my talisman." Fortunately, Bloom gets it back and in so doing we learn the significance of the "potato":

BLOOM

(With feeling) "It is nothing, but still, a relic of poor mamma.

ZOE

Give a thing and take it back
God'll ask you where is that
You'll say you don't know
God'll send you down below.

BLOOM

There is a memory attached to it. I should like to have it." (episode 15, Circe: 15.3508, 3520)[115]

---

[115] There are early associations made between the potato and Bloom's mother in the Circe episode, e.g., at 15.202, 15.208, and 15.289, but, as readers, we make the emotional association between the potato and Bloom when Bloom attached it to the memory of his mother.

We sense the growing significance of the potato throughout the day. However, this *leitmotif* is fully developed only very late in the day when we learn its meaning for Bloom. Our understanding of earlier encounters with the word "potato" becomes, in retrospect, enriched. Our memory literally has changed. Our memory has become enhanced with this new information. This layering of meaning with the passage of time is one way in which *leitmotifs* function. In this case, a very humble object, the potato, becomes a *leitmotif*.

Black pants and a bit of science. The time is shortly after 8:00 a.m., and Bloom is walking to the grocer to buy a pork kidney for his breakfast. He is contemplating the black pants he is wearing for Dignam's 11:00 a.m. funeral:

> He crossed to the bright side, avoiding the loose cellarflap of number seventyfive. The sun was nearing the steeple of George's church. Be a warm day I fancy. Specially in these black clothes feel it more. Black conducts, reflects, (refracts it is?), the heat. But I couldn't go in that light suit. (episode 4, Calypso: 4.77–80)

Bloom's science is incorrect; black absorbs heat. As a *leitmotif*, this question of the nature of the color black fleetingly enters Bloom's mind several times during the day. In episode 11, Sirens, inside the Ormond tavern Bloom is considering what to drink. His mind momentarily returns to his earlier puzzle about the properties of the color black:

> Bald Pat, bothered waiter, waited for drink orders. Power for Richie. And Bloom? Let me see. Not make him walk twice. His corns. Four now. How warm this black is. Course nerves a bit. Refracts (is it?) Heat. Let me see. Cider. Yes, bottle of cider. (episode 11, Sirens: 11.444–48)

In episode 15, Circe, Bloom reflects: "Seasonable weather we are having this time of year. Black refracts heat. Short cut home here. Interesting quarter..." (episode 15, Circe: 15.400–1) Each time we read about black and its heat-related properties, erroneously analyzed by Bloom, we are reminded of the hours and events that preceded its mention: Bloom getting breakfast, Molly in bed, Dignam's funeral, and the five shillings Bloom donates to Dignam's wife.

Stephen also wears black pants. (episode 1, Telemachus: 1.120; episode 6, Hades: 6.38–40) Stephen wears black in mourning for his mother's death and because Hamlet wore black. From a *leitmotific* perspective, both Bloom and Stephen wear black. This creates a visual link between them. This link represents a father-son relationship that will be discussed below under the "paternity" *leitmotif.*

Using the same word, but with different meanings, is another technique to create a *leitmotif.* The following humorous yet frightening illustration begins around 11:00 a.m.

Newspapers and horses: Throwaway. The setting: Bloom exits a pharmacy with a bar of special soap for his wife Molly and with a newspaper in his hand. He encounters a fellow Dubliner, Bantam Lyons. Lyons plans to bet on that day's Gold Cup horse race. Lyons is holding the race sheets. Bloom never gambles:

> He [Bloom] strolled out of the shop, the newspaper baton[116] under his armpit, the coolwrapped soap in his left hand.
>
> At his armpit Bantam Lyons' voice and hand said:
> - Hello, Bloom. What's the best news? Is that today's? Show us a minute.
>
> Shaved off his moustache again, by Jove! Long cold upper lip. To look younger. He does look balmy. Younger than I am.
>
> Bantam Lyon's yellow blacknailed fingers unrolled the baton. Wants a wash too. Take off the rough dirt. Good morning, have you used pears' soap? Dandruff on his shoulders. Scalp wants oiling.
> - I want to see about that French horse that's running today, Bantam Lyons said. Where the bugger is it?
> He rustled the pleated pages, jerking his chin on his high collar. Barber's itch. Tight collar he'll lose his hair. Better leave him the paper and get shut of him.

---

[116] Is "newspaper baton" an allusion to Wotan's spear? Maybe, maybe not. With little effort, one can find a *leitmotif* under every rock.

- You can keep it, Mr. Bloom said.

- Ascot. Gold cup. Wait, Bantam Lyons muttered. "Half a mo.
Maximum the second.

- I was just going to **throw it away**, Mr. Bloom said. Bantam Lyons
raised his eyes suddenly and leered weakly.

- What's that? His sharp voice said.

- I say you can keep it, Mr. Bloom answered. I was going to **throw it
away** that moment.

Bantam Lyons doubted an instant, leering: then thrust the outspread
sheets back on Mr. Bloom's arm.

- I'll risk it, he said. Here, thanks. (episode 5, Lotus Eaters: 5.516–
41, emphasis added)

Bantam Lyons mistook Bloom throwing away the paper as an insider tip
on the horse, Throwaway. This horse, Throwaway, has 20:1 odds in that
afternoon's Gold Cup horse race. Here the words "throw away" have two
different meanings: an activity (throwing away the paper) and a name (the horse
"Throwaway"). The words "throw away" also serve as a placeholder for several
Dubliners' anti-Semitic attitude toward Bloom.

Lyons changed his mind and did not bet on Throwaway. However,
throughout the day Bloom's alleged "tip" spread throughout Dublin's horse-
betting community.[117] In a local pub, we hear people talking about Bloom: "He
has some bloody horse up his sleeve for the Gold cup. A dead snip."[118] (episode
8, Lestrygonians: 8.1008) Unbeknownst to Bloom, Throwaway wins the race.

Later that afternoon, Bloom is in a courthouse seeing about a pension fund
for Mrs. Dignam, the widow whose husband had been buried that morning. In
a bar across the street the patrons are discussing the huge amount of money
Bloom "won" and his stinginess for not using some of his winnings for a round
of drinks:

---

[117] The betting community is very wide in Dublin. The Gold Cup race of that day, was discussed at
Bello's house of prostitution where the medical students, Stephen, and Bloom visited during the late
hours of June 16. In characteristic fashion, Bloom was referred to as "that Goddamned outsider."
(episode 15, Circe: 15.2936)
[118] "Snip" means racing tip.

Courthouse my eye and your pockets hanging down with gold and silver. Mean bloody scur. Stand us a drink itself . . . Cute as a shithouse rat. Hundred to five. (episode 12, Cyclops: 12.1759-61)

Upon returning to the pub, Bloom is verbally attacked for reasons unknown to him. After a barrage of anti-Semitic insults and an all-around ugly scene, Bloom leaves the bar. As Bloom is riding away in a carriage, the drunken bigot, the Citizen, throws a tinbox at Bloom:

"Begob he [the Citizen] drew his hand and made a swipe and let fly. Mercy of God the sun was in his eyes or he'd have left him for dead. Gob, he near sent it into the county Longford. The bloody nag took fright and the old mongrel after the car like bloody hell and all the populace shouting and laughing and the old tinbox clattering along the street." (episode 12, Cyclops: 12.1853–57) [119]

In a display of Joycean humor, Joyce connects "Throwaway" to its original two elements: the newspaper and the horse race. It is after 1:00 a.m. and Bloom and Stephen are in a cabman's shelter, a place where drivers of horse-drawn vehicles come to chat, have a cup of coffee, or work off their hangover:

While the other was reading it on page two Bloom (to give him for the nonce his new misnomer) whiled away a few odd leisure moments in fits and starts with the account of the third event at Ascot on page three, his side. Value 1000 sovs with 3000 sovs in specie added. For the entire colts and fillies. Mr F. Alexander's *Throwaway*, b.h.by *Rightaway-Thrale*, 5 yrs, 9 st 4 lbs (W. Lane) 1, lord Howard de Walden's *Zinfandel* (M. Cannon) 2, Mr W. Bass's *Sceptre* 3. Betting 5 to 4 on *Zinfandel*, **20 to 1 *Throwaway*** (off). *Sceptre* a shade heavier. . . . (episode 16, Eumaeus: 16.1274–81, emphasis added)

Continuing to develop the Throwaway *leitmotif*, Joyce gives a few torn pieces of paper (that should have been thrown away) additional meanings. It is now after

---

[119] This is one of many references to Homer's *Odyssey*. The Citizen is a modern-day Polyphemus, the cyclops who threw boulders at Odysseus as Odysseus sailed away from the cyclops' cursed island.

2:00 a.m. Bloom is at home and looking at his dresser. He sees "four polygonal fragments of two lacerated scarlet betting tickets numbered 8 87, 88 6." (episode 17, Ithaca: 17.320) We know from an earlier scene that Boylan, Molly's current lover, placed two bets on Sceptre, one for himself and one for Molly. (episode 11, Sirens: 11.375; episode 12, Cyclops: 12.1222) These torn pieces of horse racing tickets remind us of two facets of Bloom's alienation and dejection: the unjustified condemnation of Bloom for not buying a round of drinks with his non-winnings and Boylan's affair with his wife, Molly.

Just as Wagner's musical *leitmotifs* mutate, transform, and take on multiple layers of meaning during his operas, Joyce's linguistic *leitmotifs* mutate and transform and take on multiple layers of meaning during the course of his novel. The words "throw away" refer to a newspaper, the name of a horse, a focus of conversation among Dubliners, the motivation for anti-Semitic splatter, torn-up betting tickets, and proof that Boylan was in his and Molly's home that afternoon having sex. To use a musical analogy, that *leitmotif* modulates from one key to many different keys.

Sound *leitmotifs* permeate *Ulysses*, whether in chants, songs, boots crushing on sand and shells as Stephen contemplates the "ineluctable modality of the visible" (episode 3, Proteus: 3.1), cat meowing, and church bells. The Sirens episode (#11) inundates us with sounds, particularly those of singing at the piano in the Ormond bar.[120] Several of these sounds function as *leitmotifs*. When we hear/read them, we are reminded of their past occurrences, and they acquire greater significance with each encounter. Below is an analysis of two sound *leitmotifs*: "Tap Tap" and "jingle."

Tap Tap. The sound "Tap Tap" is closer to a noise than music but it serves at least two *leitmotific* functions: first, to remind us of Bloom's intrinsic kindness, and second, even the simplest of sounds, here a single note or pitch, can be perceived as music. Music, Bloom tells himself, can be heard everywhere if we allow our ears to hear it. These two properties of the Tap Tap *leitmotif* become layered during the Sirens episode (#11).

---

[120] The Sirens episode explicitly is written with music in mind. On June 18, 1919, as Joyce and Georges Borach walk around Lake Zurich, Joyce says: "I finished the Sirens chapter during the last few days. A big job. I wrote this chapter with the technical resources of music. It is a fugue with all musical notations: piano, forte, rallentando, and so on. A quintet occurs in it, too, as in *Die Meistersinger*, my favorite Wagnerian opera. . . . Since exploring the resources and artifices of music and employing them in this chapter, I haven't cared for music any more. I, the great friend of music, can no longer listen to it. I see through all the trick and can't employ it any more." See Ellmann, *James Joyce*, p. 459.

Bloom's kindness is exhibited earlier in the day in the below scene. Here Bloom comes to the aid of the blind stripling "with his slender cane," the tool that makes the "Tap Tap" sound:

A blind stripling stood tapping the curbstone with his slender cane. No tram in sight. Wants to cross.

- Do you want to cross? Mr Bloom asked.

The blind stripling did not answer. His wallface frowned weakly. He moved his head uncertainly.

- You're in Dawson street, Mr Bloom said. Molesworth street is opposite. Do you want to cross? There's nothing in the way.

The cane moved out trembling to the left. Mr Bloom's eye followed its line and saw again the dyeworks' van drawn up before Drago's. Where I saw his brillantined hair just when I was. Horse drooping. Driver in John Long's. Slaking his drouth.

- There's a van there, Mr Bloom said, but it's not moving. I'll see you across. Do you want to go to Molesworth street?

- Yes, the stripling answered. South Frederick street.

- Come, Mr Bloom said.

He touched the thin elbow gently: then took the limp seeing hand to guide it forward. (episode 8, Lestrygonians: 8.1075–89)

Three hours later, in the musical Sirens episode, we learn that the blind stripling is a piano tuner.(episode 11, Sirens: 11.280, 11.312–13) This new information creates a musical connection between the "Tap Tap" sound of his cane and his occupation as a piano tuner.

In the Sirens episode, line 64, we hear a small orchestra outside the bar:

Bronze by gold, miss Douce's head by miss Kennedy's head, over the crossblind of the Ormond bar heard the viceregal hoofs go by, ringing steel. (episode 11, Sirens: 11.64–65)

Soon we hear from Simon Dedalus:

He [Simon Dedalus] looked towards the saloon door.

- I see you have moved the piano.

- The tuner was in today, miss Douce replied, tuning it for the smoking concert and I never heard such an exquisite player. (episode 11, Sirens: 11.275–79)

One could argue that the Tap Tap *leitmotif* could fall under a broader "music" *leitmotif*. True enough, but the Tap Tap *leitmotif* can stand on its own. It soon begins to acquire significance as one of many unique musical sounds, like its own musical instrument, that permeates the Sirens episode. One of the barmaids is holding a seashell to a patron's ear:

Ah, now he heard, she holding it to his ear. Hear! He heard. Wonderful. She held it to her own. And through the sifted light pale gold in contrast glided. To hear.
Tap.
Bloom through the bardoor saw a shell held at their ear. He heard more faintly that that they heard, each for herself alone, then each for other, hearing the plash of waves, loudly, a silent roar (episode 11, Sirens; 11.930-936)

- What are the wild waves saying? He asked her, smiled.
Charming, seasmiling and unanswering Lydia on Lidwell smiled
Tap.
By Larry O'Rourke's, by Larry, bold Larry O', Boylan swayed and Boylan turned. (episode 11, Sirens: 11.949–53)

We read and Bloom hears the sound Tap Tap throughout the singing of *The Croppy Boy*:

- *Bless me, father,* Dolland the croppy cried. *Bless me and let me go.*
Tap.
Bloom looked unblessed to go. Got up to kill: on eighteen bob a week. Fellows shell out the dibs. Want to keep your weathereye open. Those girls, those lovely. By the sad sea waves. Chorusgirl's romance. Letters read out for breach of promise. From

Chickabiddy's owny Mumpsypum. Laughter in court. Henry. I never signed it. The lovely name you.

Low sank the music, air and words. Then hastened. The false priest rustling soldier from his cassock. A yeoman captain. They knew it all by heart. The thrill they itch for. Yeoman cap.

Tap. Tap.

Thrilled she listened, bending in sympathy to hear. (episode 11, Sirens: 11.1074–85)

A few lines later:

With hoarse rude fury the yeoman cursed, swelling in apoplectic bitch's bastard. A good thought, boy, to come. One hour's your time to live, your last.

Tap. Tap.

Thrill now. Pity they feel. To wipe away a tear for martyrs that want to, dying to, die. For all things dying, for all things born. Poor Mrs Purefoy. Hope she's over. Because their wombs. (episode 11, Sirens: 11.1097–1102)

The meaning of Tap Tap becomes clearer as the episode proceeds. Near the end of the episode we learn Bloom's rather humorous theory of music and appreciate its significance:

Numbers it is. All music when you come to think. Two multiplied by two divided by half is twice one. Vibrations: chords those are. One plus two plus six is seven. Do anything you like with figures juggling. Always find out this equal to that. Symmetry under a cemetery wall. He doesn't see my mourning. Callous: all for his own gut. Musemathematics. And you think you're listening to the etherial. But suppose you said it like: Martha, seven times nine minus x is thirtyfive thousand. Fall quite flat. It's on amount of the sounds it is. (episode 11, Sirens: 11. 830–37)

Later Bloom considers: "Sea, wind, leaves, thunder, waters, cows lowing, the cattlemarket, cocks, hens don't crow, snakes hissss. There's music everywhere" (11.962–63). Bloom then contemplates, with playing and singing in the background, the variety of instruments:

> A blade of grass, shell of her hands, then blow. Even comb and tissuepaper you can knock a tune out of it. . . . Hunter with a horn. Haw. Have you the? *Cloche. Sonez la.* Shepherd his pipe. Policeman a whistle. Locks and keys! Sweep! Four o'clock all's well! Sleep! All is lost now. Drum? Pompedy. Wait. I know. Towncrier, bumbailff. Long John. Waken the dead. Pom. Dignam. Poor little *nominedomine.* Pom. It is music. I mean of course it's all pom pom pom very much what they call *da capo.* Still you can hear. As we march, we march along march along. Pom. (episode 11, Sirens: 11.1237–47)

Bloom finds music and aesthetic pleasure in the simple sound of a blind person's stick hitting the ground, a police whistle, the clicking of glasses, and those able to hear the sound from the text, *Pprrpffrrppfff.* (episode 11, Sirens: 11.1286–94) But we must not ignore the terrifying sound in Bloom's ear of "jingle." The jingle *leitmotif* begins innocently but gains greater and greater significance the more we hear it.

Jingle. Jingle is a pleasing sound, but it morphs into a sound of misery. As an audible sound it remains unchanged, but our understanding of that sound changes as the novel progresses. The sound begins innocuously enough. Shortly after 8:00 a.m. from the hallway of their home, Bloom asks Molly:

> - You don't want anything for breakfast?
>> A sleepy soft grunt answered:
> - Mn.
>> No. She didn't want anything. He heard then a warm heavy sigh, softer, as she turned over and the loose brass quoits of the bedstead **jingled.** (episode 4, Calypso: 4.55, my emphasis)

At 8:00 a.m. the word "jingle" means nothing more to us than the rattling of Molly's bed springs as she rolls over in bed. About fifteen minutes later, upon returning home from the butcher, Bloom finds the mail on the hall floor:

Two letters and a card lay on the hallfloor. He stooped and gathered them. Mrs Marion Bloom. His quickened heart slowed at once. Bold hand. Mrs Marion.
- Poldy!
Entering the bedroom he halfclosed his eyes and walked through warm yellow twilight towards her tousled head.
- Who are the letters for?
He looked at them. Mullingar. Milly.
- A letter for me from Milly, he said carefully, and a card to you. And a letter for you.
He laid her card and letter on the twill bedspread near the curve of her knees.
- Do you want the blind up?
Letting the blind up he gently tugs halfway his backward eye[121] saw her glance at the letter and tuck it under her pillow. (episode 4, Cyclops: 4.243–57)

We soon learn that the letter is from Blazes Boylan, Molly's music manager who, as Bloom knows and the reader soon discovers, will be "visiting" Molly at 4:00 p.m.

The jingle *leitmotif* gradually acquires two meanings. First, that of the person Blazes Boylan, the suiter who penetrates our modern-day Penelope. And second, where the adultery will occur, i.e., in Bloom and Molly's bed. Each time we read "jingle" we know that a stake is driven further into Bloom's heart.

We read, and Bloom hears, "jingle" throughout the day, particularly in the 4:00 p.m. Sirens episode. Once the *leitmotif* is in our ear, it can appear in other contexts and have the same intellectual and emotional effect. In episode 7 (Aeolus) in the *Freeman's Journal* newspaper office, the editor, Myles Crawford,

---

[121] "Backward eye" refers to a cuckolded husband. Also, since Molly is married, the custom was for the envelope to have been addressed to "Mrs. Leopold Bloom" and not "Mrs. Marion Bloom." See Gifford, p. 76.

is looking for his keys: "He worked jerkily into the office behind, parting the vent of his jacket, jingling his keys in his back pocket. They jingled then in the air and against the wood as he locked his desk drawer." (episode 7, Aeolus: 7.458–60) Since Bloom is not present, the "jingling" sound is not a reminder for him, but it is for us. Once the *leitmotif* is in our ear, the *leitmotif* comes alive and there is no avoiding its meaning(s).

I close this section with examples of two complex *leitmotifs*: paternity and metempsychosis. These *leitmotifs* are conceptual rather than physical objects or sounds. They are a composite family of *leitmotifs*.

Paternity *leitmotifs*. In Homer's *Odyssey*, Odysseus spends ten years travelling home from Troy to Ithaca to reunite with his son, Telemachus, and wife, Penelope. Telemachus longs for his father. Penelope, despite a house full of suitors, remains faithful to her husband. In Joyce's *Ulysses*, our modern-day Odysseus, Bloom, has a fifteen-year-old daughter, Milly, who is living away from home. Their son, Rudy, died eleven years ago at the age of eleven days,[122] and Molly is a far cry from being faithful to her husband.

Bloom and Stephen are acquainted with each other, but only remotely. To mirror the Homeric father-son relationship, Joyce must create some sort of paternity relationship between Bloom and Stephen. Joyce creates this paternity *leitmotif* through a series of related *leitmotifs* showing Bloom and Stephen's connection. Appropriately, that connection comes to fruition when they finally meet in a maternity hospital in episode 14: Oxen of the Sun.

Below we will examine four *leitmotifs* that I classify within the paternity family of *leitmotifs*: rain, house key, near encounter, and Sandymount shore.[123] While these names are arbitrary, their *leitmotific* function is not. When these terms or events occur in the text, we are reminded of the developing connection between Stephen and Bloom. On subsequent readings we cannot encounter these words or events without a telescopic view of their entire day and a microscopic view into their individual personalities.

---

[122] Shakespeare's son Hamnet died when he was eleven years old. Stephen is obsessed with Shakespeare's *Hamlet*, a play centering on a father-son relationship.

[123] I previously discussed in "Black pants and a bit of science" the visual link of black pants that both Stephen and Bloom wear.

For example, in the morning Stephen walks around Sandymount shore in contemplation, like a student in Aristotle's Peripatetic school. During Stephen's stroll we learn a great deal about him, but since we have not encountered Bloom, we make no connection to Bloom. In the early evening Bloom takes a rest on Sandymount shore probably stepping in Stephen's washed-away footprints. Here we learn a great deal about Bloom and his proclivity for self-pleasure. More important, the name "Sandymount shore" is now rich and pregnant with meaning. As a *leitmotif*, Sandymount shore is a place where Stephen and Bloom meet in space but not in time. That will come later.

Earlier that morning (8:00 a.m.), we learned of the traumatic effect that Stephen's mother's death had on Stephen. (episode 1, Telemachus: 1.100ff) During the course of the novel, we learn that while Stephen and his father, Simon, both live in Dublin, they basically have no relationship. As a result, Stephen figuratively is fatherless. Around the same time (8:00 a.m.), we also learned that Bloom's only son, Rudy, died shortly after childbirth. Bloom now is contemplating how Mrs. Thornton, the midwife, helped with Molly's delivery:

> Lots of babies she must have helped into the world. She knew from the first poor little Rudy wouldn't live. Well God is good, sir. She knew at once. He would be eleven now if he had lived. (episode 4, Calypso: 4.418–20)

And three hours later, en route to Dignam's funeral:

> If little Rudy had lived. See him grow up. Hear his voice in the house. Walking beside Molly in an Eton suit. My son. Me in his eyes. Strange feeling it would be. From me. Just a chance. (episode 6, Hades: 6.75–78)

At the same time as Bloom is thinking about his son Rudy, we learn that Stephen associates himself with Hamlet by wearing only black pants (episode 1, Telemachus: 1.120) and is obsessed with Hamlet's paternity: [124]

---

[124] Stephen also wonders about Eve's maternity (episode 3, Proteus: 3.41–42). In the cabalistic tradition, Eve was not born of a woman and therefore did not have a navel.

- What is your idea of Hamlet? Haines asked Stephen
- No, no, Buck Mulligan shouted in pain. I'm not equal to Thomas Aquinas and the fiftyfive reasons he has made out to prop it up. Wait till I have a few pints in me first.

He turned to Stephen, saying, as he pulled down neatly the peaks of his primrose waistcoat:

- You couldn't manage it under three points, Kinch, could you
- It has waited so long, Stephen said listlessly, it can wait longer.
- You pique my curiosity, Haines said amiably. Is it some paradox? . . .
- It's quite simple. He proves by algebra that Hamlet's grandson is Shakespeare's grandfather and that he himself is the ghost of his own father.

- What? Haines said, beginning to point at Stephen. He himself?

Buck Mulligan slung his towel stolewise round his neck and, bending in loose laughter, said to Stephen's ear:

- O, shade of Kinch the elder! Japhet in search of a father! (episode 1, Telemachus: 1.545–61)[125]

We will have to wait until episode 9, Scylla and Charybdis, to hear the details of Stephen's Hamlet paternity theory.[126] However, we find early hints of Bloom and Stephen's paternity relationship as they unconsciously seek out each other.[127] To use Wittgenstein's term from the *Philosophical Investigations*, Stephen and Bloom share a strong "family resemblance."[128]

---

[125] We find other references to Hamlet by Stephen during these early hours of the day. See episode 2, Nestor: 2.152, and several references to Elsinore, e.g., episode 3, Proteus: 3.281.

[126] *Ulysses* is replete with references to *Hamlet* and without Gifford's Ulysses *Annotated*, they would be impossible to detect. For example, in episode 3, Proteus: 3.55: "Airs romped round him, nipping and eager airs" refers to Horatio and Hamlet watching on the battlement for the appearance of the Ghost (I.iv.2). Or, when Bloom is leaving a Catholic Mass and is thinking about the buttons on a woman's skirt, "Glimpses of the moon" (episode 5: Lotus Eaters: 5.455) refers to when Hamlet is speaking to the Ghost (Hamlet, 1.iv.51–56). Pretty obscure references, but that's Joyce's plan, to "keep professors busy for centuries arguing over what I meant. . . ."

[127] An early clue of Stephen and Bloom's connection is Haines's dream of a black panther that wakes Stephen. Panthers are in the same species as leopards, as in Leopold Bloom. Joyce is playing on the similarity of words between leopard and Leopold and gives Leopold Bloom certain leopard-like traits such as swift and independent movement.

[128] Ludwig Wittgenstein, *Philosophical Investigations*.

Stephen and Bloom share a sense of social alienation. Stephen tells us during these morning hours that he is enslaved by the imperial British state and the Roman Catholic Church (episode 1, Telemachus: 1. 640–64); his guilt from not praying with his mother on her death bed (episode 1, Telemachus: 1.87ff); his living quarters, "I will not sleep here tonight. Home also I cannot go." (episode 1, Telemachus: 1.739–40); "He has the key. I will not sleep there when this night comes" (episode 3, Proteus: 3.276); and history, "History, Stephen said, is a nightmare from which I am trying to awake" (episode 3, Proteus: 3.377). Bloom is a Jew, although a three-time converted Catholic, living in a very Catholic society. Anti-Semitism permeates Dublin from the ignorant school master Mr. Deasy in episode 3, Proteus to the grotesque Citizen in episode 12, Cyclops. Bloom has no friends, is the subject of mockery almost everywhere he goes, and has a strained relationship with his wife Molly. He also carries the guilt of not having been a good son. (See, for example, episode 15, Circe: 15.2300ff)

Joyce uses several atmospheric events, phrases, and descriptions to suggest the paternal bond between Stephen and Bloom. At 8:00 a.m., as the story begins to unfold, Stephen and his housemates are starting their day. Stephen observes a cloud beginning to cover the sun. (episode 1, Telemachus: 1.248) Three episodes later, also at 8:00 a.m., Bloom is starting his day and observes the same cloud slowly covering the sun. (episode 4, Calypso: 4.218) This "first thing in the morning" shared celestial experience begins to link the two characters and thus becomes a *leitmotif*.

This cloud *leitmotif* continues developing. Three hours later (11:00 a.m.), Bloom hears a donkey braying. This generates the following thoughts:

> Rain. No such ass. Never see a dead one, they say. Shame of death. They hide. Also poor papa went away. (episode 6, Hades: 6.837)

Joyce gives us a double meaning to the donkey braying. First, an Irish superstition is that a donkey braying midday forecasts rain. (Recall the clouds both Stephen and Bloom independently noticed.) And second, an ancient Roman belief was that a donkey was a beast of ill omen. This donkey association triggers in Bloom memories of his dead father. Analogous to Bloom's dead father, Stephen's father is figuratively dead to Stephen. Thus, both Bloom and

Stephen feel fatherless. Continuing the "cloud" *leitmotif*, at 10:00 p.m., with both Bloom and Stephen at the Maternity Hospital, there is a deluge.

> A black crack of noise in the street here, alack, bawled back. Loud on left Thor thunder: in anger awful the hammerhurler. (episode 14, Oxen on the Sun: 14.407)

Finally, it is now past midnight, and Stephen and Bloom are walking to Bloom's house:

> As neither of them were particularly pressed for time, as it happened, and the temperature refreshing since it cleared up after the recent visitation of Jupiter Pluvius,[129] they dandered along past by where the empty vehicle was waiting without a fare or a jarvey. (episode 16, Eumaeus: 16.39f)

Since it is helpful to name *leitmotifs*, what shall we name the above series of connected words: Clouds? Rain? The sky? Companionship? Father-son relationship? The point is that Joyce has associated several different words and names: clouds, donkey braying, rain, Thor, and Jupiter Pluvius to identify Stephen and Bloom's shared weather experiences. Their "first thing in the morning" shared celestial experience occurred in separate locations; now, close to the end of their day, we find them literally arm in arm. (episode 16, Eumaeus: 16.1720f) The cloud *leitmotif* has become part of the mosaic of *leitmotifs* that make up the paternity *leitmotif*.

Their loss of their respective house keys also occurs early in their day. "Give us that key, Kinch," Buck Mulligan said. . . . (episode 1, Telemachus: 1.720, 1.322) Mirroring Stephen's loss of his latchkey is Bloom's less dramatic but equally troublesome experience: "On the doorstep he felt in his hip pocket for the latchkey. Not there. In the trousers I left off. Must get it." (episode 4,

---

[129] *Jupiter Pluvius* is Latin for "Jupiter the Rainmaker." Gifford, Ulysses *Annotated*, p. 535.

Calypso: 4.72) Stephen is forced to relinquish his house key and Bloom forgets to retrieve his house key, signifying their respective homeless conditions.[130]

Further developing the paternity *leitmotif*, Bloom and Stephen cross paths, but at a distance, several times during the day, the first time on the way to Dignam's funeral. In the below passage, Bloom and Stephen's father, Simon Dedalus, share a carriage:

> All watched awhile through their windows cap and hats lifted by passers. Respect. The carriage swerved from the tramtrack to the smoother road past Watery lane. Mr Bloom at gaze saw a lithe young man, clad in mourning, a wide hat.
> - There's a friend of yours gone by, Dedalus, he said.
> - Who is that?
> - Your son and heir.
> - Where is he? Mr Dedalus said, stretching over across.
>
> The carriage, passing the open drains and mounds of rippedup roadway before the tenement houses, lurched round the corner and swerving back to the tramtrack, rolled on noisily with chattering wheels. Mr Dedalus fell back saying:
> - Was that Mulligan cad with him? His *fidus Achates*!
> - No, Mr Bloom said. He was alone. (episode 6, Hades: 6.37-50)

Their paths almost cross in the newspaper offices of the *Freeman's Journal* and *Evening Telegraph*. As Stephen and the office staff are leaving for drinks (around 12:45 p.m.), Bloom is returning from the office and sees them walking to the bar: "Wonder is that young Dedalus the moving spirit. Has a good pair of boots on him today. Last time I saw him he had his heels on view. Been walking in muck somewhere. Careless chap. What was he doing in Irishtown?" (episode 7, Aeolus: 7.984–86)

In episode 9, Scylla and Charybdis, in the National Library they again come into close contact. Stephen and others are in the library discussing Shakespeare,

---

[130] Bloom is not technically homeless, but he does have to break into his house. (episode 17, Ithaca: 17.70–90) Bloom is "homeless" in a more devastating manner since that day another man occupied his home and bed.

specifically *Hamlet*, and Bloom is researching material for an advertisement. Here they are brought in close contact twice.

The first is when Bloom is requesting material from a library: "'There's a gentleman here, sir,' the attendant said, coming forward and offering a card. 'From the *Freeman*. He wants to see the files of the *Kilkenny People* for last year.'" (Scylla and Charybdis: 9.586) A few lines later Mulligan says to Stephen, "'He knows you. He knows your old fellow too'" (Scylla and Charybdis: 9.615), i.e., Stephen's father. It is interesting that when Stephen is regurgitating the conversation a few lines later, he mistakenly recollects: "Says he's your father." (Scylla and Charybdis: 9.820) At the end of the episode their paths cross a second time (9.1203–11) as they pass by each other at the Library's exit door. They still have not met!

It is now dusk, 8:00 p.m., and Bloom sits resting on Sandymount shore watching three young women in their early twenties babysitting three young children:

> The summer evening had begun to fold the world in its mysterious embrace. Far away in the west the sun was setting and the last glow of all too fleeting day lingered lovingly on sea and strand, on the proud promontory of dear old Howth guarding as ever the water of the bay, on the weedgrown rocks along Sandymount shore.... (episode 13, Nausicaa: 13.1–5)

In episode 13, Nausicaa, Bloom is sitting in the same place where Stephen meandered in contemplation in episode 3, Proteus.[131] Stephen and Bloom are getting very close. What started out as the two noticing the same cloud formation has now come down to earth, where the two are touching each other in space but not yet in time. That comes, not surprisingly, in a maternity hospital where "father and son" finally meet.

---

[131] Stephen and Bloom have very different personalities. Stephen contemplated Aristotle, whereas Bloom contemplates Gerty's petticoat. We are reminded that personality differences exist between father and son.

The description of their encounter is written in the style[132] of the fifteenth-century prose of Sir Thomas Malory. Stephen and Bloom share a bench in the maternity hospital:

> Now let us speak of that fellowship that was there to the intent to be drunken an they might. There was a sort of scholars along either side of the board . . . young Stephen, he was the most drunken that demanded still of more mead and beside the meek sir Leopold. (episode 14, Oxen of the Sun: 14.187–95)

> But sir Leopold was passing grave maugre his word by cause he still had pity of the terrorcausing shrieking of shrill women in their labour and as he was minded of his good lady Marion that had borne him an only manchild which on his eleventh day on live had died and no man of art could save so dark is destiny...and now sir Leopold that had of his body no manchild for an heir looked upon him his friend's son and was shut up in sorrow for his forepassed happiness and as sad as he was that him failed a son of such gentle courage (for all accounted him of real parts) so grieved he also in no less measure for young Stephen for that he lived riotously with those wastrels and murdered his goods with whores. (episode 14, Oxen of the Sun: 14.264–76)

Finally, at the close of episode 15, Circe: 15.4923–67, after Stephen is beaten unconscious by a drunk British soldier (which itself is a highly ironic action) and everyone has left the scene, Bloom retrieves Stephen's ashplant. Bloom looks toward Stephen, who is lying in the street in the position of a newborn baby. Bloom hallucinates his dead son Rudy:

> (Silent, thoughtful, alert he stands on guard, his fingers at his lips in the attitude of secret master. Against the dark wall a figure appears slowly, a fairy boy of eleven, a changeling, kidnapped,

---

[132] Episode 14: Oxen of the Sun is written in the style that mirrors the development of the English language and therefore can be very cumbersome for the reader. The style quoted above imitates the fifteenth-century prose style of Sir Thomas Malory. See Gifford, Ulysses *Annotated*, pp. 408–49, and Stuart Gilbert, *James Joyce's* Ulysses, chapter 14.

dressed in an Eton suit with glass shoes and a little bronze helmet, holding a book in his hands. He reads from right to left inaudibly, smiling, kissing the page.) (Circe, 15: 4955–60)

From this point forward we watch the father-son relationship unfold. Bloom begins by taking care of Stephen as would any father: he looks after Stephen, brings Stephen back to his house, and offers him a place to stay that night. Stephen acts first like a bratty teenager:

- What belongs, queried Mr Bloom bending, fancying he was perhaps under some misapprehension. Excuse me. Unfortunately, I didn't catch the latter portion. What was it you. . . ?
   Stephen, patently crosstempered, repeated and shoved aside his mug of coffee or whatever you like to call it none too politely, adding:
   - We can't change the country. Let us change the subject. (episode 16, Eumaeus: 16.1165–70)

Exhausted, Stephen temporarily accepts Bloom as a surrogate father:

The night air was certainly now a treat to breathe though Stephen was a bit weak on his pins.
   - It will (the air) do you good, Bloom said, meaning also the walk, in a moment. The only thing is to walk then you'll feel a different man. Come. It's not far. Lean on me.
   Accordingly, he passed his left arm in Stephen's right and led him on accordingly. (episode 16, Eumaeus: 16. 1716–22)

Finally, they arrive at Bloom's house where they spend a long time conversing. Their conversation ends when they urinate together in Bloom's yard. (episode 17, Ithaca: 17.1186–98) A few moments later (episode 17; Ithaca: 17. 1220–25), they depart. Stephen to who knows where and Bloom into his house:

How did they take leave, one of the other, in separation?

Standing perpendicular at the same door and on different sides of the base, the lines of their valedictory arms, meeting at any point and forming any angle less than the sum of two right angles.

What sound accompanied the union of their tangent, the disunion of their (respectively) centrifugal and centripetal hands?

The sound of the peal of the hour of the night by the chime of the bells in the church of Saint George.

What echoes of that sound were by both and each heard?

By Stephen:
Liliate rutilantium. Turma circumdet.
Iubilantium te virginum. Chorus excipiat.

By Bloom:
Heigho, heigho,
Heigho, heigho.

This ends their relationship, at least for that day. The reader can only speculate whether that end will be forever or just for that evening. However, what is of note is that Stephen "hears" Latin, the prayer for the dying, i.e., his mother, the sound of his past. Bloom hears the lyrical sound of bells in the here and now. Stephen is esoteric; Bloom is practical. Stephen is morose; Bloom is optimistic. The chimes, however, connect them. We have heard those chimes before during Bloom's early hours (episode 4; Calypso: 4:546–48) and in the Sirens episode (episode 11, Sirens: 11.858), a reminder, if nothing else, that it has been a very long day. Stephen's day continues because, by choice, he has nowhere to go. Bloom's day is nearing an end. He will crawl into bed with Molly, his Penelope, soon to begin a new day.

Metempsychosis or Met Him Pike Hoses. The concepts metempsychosis, metamorphosis, transubstantiation—and its related concepts, consubstantiation and reincarnation—all refer to the concept of one thing changing into another. On the metatextual level, Bloom is the metamorphosis of Odysseus, Stephen of Telemachus, Molly of Penelope, Boylan of Antinous, the Citizen of Polyphemus. The Homeric link also can be made with many other characters in Joyce's *Ulysses*.

We first are introduced to the concept of metempsychosis in a humorous exchange in episode 4, Calypso, between Molly and Bloom. We have to wait for Bloom's reminiscence of the below event to learn of Molly's mispronunciation of "Metempsychosis" as "Met Him Pike Hoses." (episode 8, Lestrygonians: 8.1148) It is shortly after 8:00 a.m. at Bloom and Molly's home at 7 Eccles Street. Molly asks about a word in a book that she does not recognize or know how to pronounce:

> - Show here, she said. I put a mark in it. There's a word I wanted
>   to ask you.
> She swallowed a drought of tea from her cup held by nothandle
>   and, having wiped her fingertips smartly on the blanket, began
>   to search the text with the hairpin till she reached the word.
> - Met him what? He asked
> - Here, she said. What does that mean?
> He leaned downward and read near her polished thumbnail.
> - Metempsychosis?
> - Yes. Who's he when he's at home?
> - Metempsychosis, he said, frowning. It's Greek: from the Greek.
>   That means the transmigration of souls. (episode 4. Calypso:
>   4.331–42)

Nearly at the same time, at Martello Tower, on Dublin Bay about seven miles from 7 Eccles Street, Buck Mulligan is mimicking the Catholic mass. Buck Mulligan's performance is ripe with parody and blasphemy[133] and is directed at Stephen. This parody gains significance if we recall from Joyce's earlier novel, *A Portrait of the Artist as a Young Man*, that Stephen desperately is trying to free himself from his Catholic Jesuit upbringing. Buck Mulligan is

---

[133] See Gifford's Ulysses *Annotated*, pp. 12–13.

coming down the stairs, hence elevated, carrying his shaving tools: "a bowl of lather on which a mirror and a razor lay crossed."[134] The text continues:

> He [Buck Mulligan] added in a preacher's tone:
> - For this, O dearly beloved is the genuine Christine: body and soul and blood and ouns. Slow music, please. Shut your eyes, gents. One moment. A little trouble about those white corpuscles. Silence, all.
> He peered sideways up and gave a long slow whistle of call, then paused awhile in rapt attention, his even white teeth glistening here and there with gold points. Chrysostomos. Two strong shrill whistles answered through the calm.
> - Thanks, old chap, he cried briskly. That will do nicely. Switch off the current, will you? (episode 1, Telemachus: 1.21–29)

"A little trouble about those white corpuscles" refers to the transubstantiation or the changing of the bread and wine into the body and blood of Christ, i.e., one object changing into another. "Switch off the current" refers to the Holy Ghost during the process of transubstantiation.

We encounter this Metempsychosis *leitmotif*, i.e., one thing changing into another, at the beginning of each of Stephen's and Bloom's day.[135] This *leitmotif* is instantiated multiple times throughout the novel. For example, we soon learn of Stephen's fixation with Aristotle's theory of potentiality and actuality, i.e., an object changing into another. In addition, we learn of Stephen's somewhat puzzling theory "that Hamlet's grandson is Shakespeare's grandfather and that he himself is the

---

[134] Episode 1, Telemachus, 1.2. *Ulysses* opens with the following sentence: "Stately, plump Buck Mulligan came from the stairhead, bearing a bowl of lather on which a mirror and a razor lay crossed." These few words "bowl of lather on which a mirror and a razor lay crossed" contain a plethora of references. Buck Mulligan is standing on a staircase, i.e., elevated like a member of the clergy. Among the many references, the "bowl" refers to a shaving bowl, a chalice, the bay of Ireland (which looks like a bowl), and the bowl in which Stephen's mother would vomit during her last days. "Mirror" refers to a shaving mirror, Wilde's *The Picture of Dorian Gray*, and Hamlet's claim that a play should reflect reality. The "razor" is a reference to clergy as butchers and "lay crossed" references the Vatican. Credit to Christopher Griffin, who teaches *Ulysses* and other topics at Politics and Prose bookstore in Washington, DC, for discussing these references.

[135] *Ulysses* begins with a metempsychosis of a day that has two beginnings: once with Stephen in episode 1 at 8:00 a.m. and then again with Bloom in episode 4 at 8:00 a.m.

ghost of his own father." (episode 1, Telemachus: 1.555–57) Aristotle's theory and Stephen's Hamlet theory both are related to metempsychosis.[136]

Major changes or metamorphoses occur in nearly every episode. Episode 6, Hades, involves the transformation of life into death with the burial of Paddy Dignam. Throughout the novel, but particularly in the Hades episode, Bloom's thoughts return to his and Molly's son, Rudy, who died as a newborn. Episode 14, Oxen of the Sun, revolves around the birth of Mrs. Purefoy's (ninth) child. In the same episode, Bloom ponders how the present crude and insensitive drunk medical students will transform into eminent members of society merely by the acquisition of an academic title:

> Singular, communed the guest with himself, the wonderfully unequal faculty of metempsychosis possessed by them, that the puerperal dormitory and the dissecting theater should be the seminaries of such frivolity, that the mere acquisition of academic titles should suffice to transform in a pinch of time these votaries of levity into exemplary practitioners of an art which most men anywise eminent have esteemed the noblest. (episode 14, Oxen of the Sun: 14.897–902)

In episode 9, Scylla and Charybdis, Stephen ponders that his physical body has a complete makeover every five months: "Wait. Five months. Molecules all change. I am other I now." (episode 9, Scylla and Charybdis: 9.205) Episode 15, Circe, is replete with hallucinatory-induced transformations. In episode 17, Ithaca, Bloom marvels at the metamorphic property of water: "as vapor, mist, cloud, rain, sleet, snow, hail. . . ." (episode 17, Ithaca: 17.216–17)

There are other cases of metamorphosis such as Bloom's recognition that his daughter Milly is growing into a woman and soon will be sexually active. Will Molly and Bloom rekindle their relationship and try to have another child? If yes, that would be a major change in their relationship. Bloom acquired a

---

[136] Stephen argues that the characters in Shakespeare's plays mirror people in Shakespeare's life, or generalizing, that all literature is autobiographical, which Stephen may or may not actually believe. Stephen also is discussing the implications of Aristotle's theory that actuality contains its possibilities within it, and vice versa. (Think of the acorn and oak tree example.) This actuality/potentiality relationship exists in relation to paternity: we are the result of our past generation(s) and will be the source of the next generation(s). This notion of paternity can be applied to literature and the arts in general. Homer's tale gave birth to countless epics, including Joyce's *Ulysses*.

momentary son in Stephen and Stephen a fleeting father in Bloom. During the course of their day, did we witness a metamorphosis in Bloom and Stephen? Fifty years earlier, during the Romantic period, the answer would have been a resounding "yes." As Moderns, the answer would be "probably not." I suspect their tomorrows will be similar to their todays. Joyce, however, leaves that question open for each reader to answer, and perhaps the same reader gives a different answer with each rereading.

d. Endless Melody

Wagner created the technique of endless melody in part to break free of traditional operatic structures, such as arias, duets, choruses, and intermittent recitative.[137] Author Édouard Dujardin consciously took this innovative musical idea from Wagner and applied it to his novel *Les Lauriers sont coupés* ("*The laurels are cut*"). Joyce consciously took this literary idea from Dujardin and applied it to his literary works, including *Ulysses*.[138] Joyce knew Dujardin had acquired the idea of an interior monologue and its associated stream of consciousness[139] from Wagner, and so, with no stretch, we can attribute Joyce's use of these styles in *Ulysses* to Wagner. To show the link, I quote from Dujardin's book on *Le Monologue intérieur*, where Dujardin discusses the technique of *Les Lauriers sont coupés*:

---

[137] See Chapter 1b for a discussion of Wagner's endless melody.

[138] "But he [Joyce] bought *Les Lauriers sont coupés* at a railway kiosk in 1903, and after *Ulysses* had made the 'interior monologue' famous, he was always careful to credit Dujardin's book as its inspiration. Dujardin, it turns out, got the idea from Wagner's 'infinite melody.'" T. Martin, p. 8, n36. Martin's source is Blissett, pp. 113–15.

[139] The terms "interior monologue" and "stream of consciousness" have different meanings and different histories. Interior monologue was first used by Édouard Dujardin in his 1887 novel *Les Lauriers sont coupés* ("*The laurels are cut*"). Stream of consciousness was used by William James in 1890 in *The Principles of Psychology*. The two terms often are used interchangeably, but they indicate different structures of conscious reflection. In both interior monologue and stream of consciousness the reader witnesses the character's mental life, i.e., their thoughts, memories, wishes, fears, etc. However, in interior monologue the narrative is structured along accepted grammatical conventions. In stream of consciousness the narrative is characterized by leaps of thought and freely violates grammatical conventions. Visually, stream of consciousness often lacks punctuation.

I am going to reveal a secret: *Les Lauriers sont coupés* was undertaken with the crazy ambition to transpose into the literary domain Wagnerian methods that I defined to myself as follows: the life of the soul represented by the ceaseless urging of musical motifs that express, one after another, indefinitely and successively, "states" of thought, sentiments, or sensations; which [i.e., the ambition] realizes itself, or attempted to realize itself, in the indefinite succession of short phrases, each rendering one of these states of thought, without logical order, in the manner of surges rising from the depths of self—one would say nowadays from the unconscious or subconscious. [140]

Richard Ellmann, in his definitive Joycean biography, also notes the impact of Dujardin on Joyce:

The most famous of the devices of *Ulysses*, the internal monologue, was also the result of early experiments. Joyce had been moving rapidly towards a conception of personality new to the novel. . . . He (Joyce) had observed approaches to the interior monologue in Dujardin, George Moore, Tolstoy, even in his brother's journal. He had toyed with Freud's theories of verbal association. . . Having gone so far, Joyce in *Ulysses*. . . let thoughts hop, step, jump, and glide. [141]

The important point is the direct link between Joyce and Wagner through Dujardin. To quote Timothy Martin:

He (Joyce) was certainly aware of attempts by Moore and D'Annunzio to borrow Wagnerian orchestral techniques; but another track of influence, albeit unconscious, may have been of greater importance. Joyce's account of the origin of the interior monologue in *Ulysses* winds its way back to Wagner and his *leitmotifs*. Joyce always maintained that Dujardin's *Les Lauriers sont coupés*

---

[140] Dujardin, *Les Lauriers sont coupés*, p. 258; translated by T. Martin, p. 150, n31.
[141] Ellmann, *James Joyce*, p. 358.

which he had read during his first stay in Paris in 1902 and 1903. . .
inspired this technique. . . the internal monologue was inspired by
Wagner.

In *Ulysses*, we witness Bloom's thoughts, half thoughts, and quarter
thoughts. They meander like a breeze through a forest, a leaf on a stream
floating by flora and fauna, and civilization in all its discontent. Bloom's
thoughts flow continuously and endlessly. There are no natural breaks.
Sometimes the connection between his thoughts is obvious, but often they jump
from one topic to the next.[142] Like musical *leitmotifs*, Blooms thoughts reappear,
in whole or in fragments, throughout the novel. These fragments serve both to
unify the story and to heighten our understanding of Bloom.

In episode 8, Lestrygonians, we return to the blind stripling we discussed
when analyzing the Tap Tap *leitmotif*. Bloom is walking down the street having
just helped the blind stripling cross the street. He is trying to remember
someone he met years earlier:

> Penrose! That was that chap's name.[143]
>
> Look at all the things they can learn to do. Read with their
> fingers. Tune Pianos. Or we are surprised they have any brains. Why
> we think a deformed person or a hunchback clever if he says
> something we might say. Of course the other senses are more.
> Embroider. Plait baskets. People out to help. Workbasket. I could
> buy for Molly's birthday. Hates sewing. Might take an objection.
> Dark men they call them. (episode 8, Lestrygonians: 8.1114–20)

First, Bloom remembers the name of someone, Penrose, but not while
trying to remember it, the name simply pops into his head. Then he
contemplates people's shortsightedness in thinking that a person with a physical

---

[142] Observing your own thoughts as you fall asleep is one way to capture the "stream of consciousness" experience.

[143] The name "Penrose" pops into Blooms head. This refers to Bloom's earlier thinking about someone he knew but could not remember his name: "Stream of life. What was the name of the priestylooking chap was always squinting in when he passed? Weak eyes, woman. Stopped in Citron's saint. Kevin's parade Pen something. Pendennie? My memory is getting. Pen. . . ? Of course it's years ago. Noise of the trams probably. . . ." (episode 8, Lestrygonians: 8.176–79)

handicap is mentally handicapped. Next, he thinks of jobs that a blind person could do, for example, make baskets. That leads him to thoughts of his wife, Molly, and perhaps he could buy her a workbasket to make baskets. He drops that idea quickly on grounds that she might take offense. Then he returns to a slang term for persons who are blind.

In this passage of six lines, we witnessed an endless melody in literature. In actuality, Bloom's musings continue for over a dozen more lines, hence endless. It is a melody of sorts because it is constructed from bits of memory with which we are acquainted: the blind piano tuner, Bloom's kind heart, his scientifically inclined mind, his practicality, and his wife Molly.

Ulysses includes many examples of long stretches of text that appear disjointed but are constructed from familiar elements. At the end of episode 14: Oxen of the Sun, 1440–1590, we find an excellent example of an endless melody taking on an orchestral sound. In this scene, a band of drunken revelers spill onto the street. For 150 lines we witness language disintegrating into a multitude of intermingling disjointed sentences and phrases. It's an auditory mishmash but quite coherent given the context. [144]

Nothing, however, surpasses Molly's soliloquy in the last episode, (episode 18, Penelope). [145] Molly's thoughts are composed of much of what we learned during the day. As a literary endless melody, her 4,000+ word sentence is strung together by *leitmotifs*, i.e., words, phrases, events, and memories that we learned from Bloom and others during the course of Bloom's day.

Molly begins her long stream-of-consciousness sentence in response to Bloom's final words as he drifts into sleep. The setting takes place around 3:00 a.m. and Bloom has just climbed into bed. He mutters the following as he falls into a deep sleep:

---

[144] This use of verbal endless melody is similar to the riot scene at the end of act 2 of Wagner's *Die Meistersinger*.

[145] Some commentaries assert that Molly's monologue is comprised of eight sentences that are identified by spaces rather than by a period. Visually the 22,000 words do not appear to have any grammatical or semantic breaks. See Gifford, p. 610. If there are eight sentences, then Molly's 4,391-word sentence was the longest English sentence until Johnathan Coe's *The Rotters' Club* from 2001, which has 13,955 words.

> Going to dark bed there was a square round Sinbad the Sailor roc's auk's[146] egg in the night of the bed of all the auks of the rocs of Darkenbad the Brightdayler. (episode 17, Ithaca: 17. 2328–30)

The text continues with Molly's two-hour-and-fifteen-minute midnight ramble:[147]

> Yes, because he never did a thing like that before as ask to get him breakfast in bed with a couple of eggs since the City Arms hotel when he used to be pretending to be laid up with a sick voice doing his highness to make himself interesting for that old faggot Mrs Riordan that he thought he had a great leg of and she never left us a farthing all for masses for herself and her soul greatest miser ever was actually afraid to lay out 4d for her methylated spirit telling me all her ailments she had too much old chat in her about politics and earthquakes and the end of the world let us have a bit of fun first God help the world if all the women were her sort down on bathingsuits and lownecks of course nobody wanted her to wear them I suppose she was pious because no man would look at her twice I hope Ill never be like her a wonder she didn't want us to. . . . (episode 18, Penelope: 11.1–13)[148]

And on and on we go into Molly's conscious and unconscious life. There is no natural place to stop, it just keeps flowing and flowing, much like Wagner's operas. Nor do we want Molly's soliloquy or Wagner's operas to stop.

---

[146] Rocs are mythical Arabian giant birds and auks are subarctic flightless birds. See Gifford, p. 606. Bloom's closing sentence is comprised of elements previously discussed in the novel. Bloom contemplates several times the problem of squaring the circle and the Arabian Nights. "Auk" is mentioned by Stephen in episode 9: Scylla and Charybdis, 446, providing yet another connection between Stephen and Bloom.

[147] The 135-minute estimate is from the *Ulysses* audiobook: James Joyce, *Ulysses* (Internet Archive, Oct 2, 2010), https://archive.org/details/Ulysses-Audiobook.

[148] Molly's soliloquy is replete with poor grammar and misspelled words. For example, instead of "I'll" Joyce wrote "Ill." Per Christopher Griffin, Joyce was parodying his wife Nora and her spelling in letters she wrote to him.

e. *Gesamtkunstwerk*

Unlike a staged or three-dimensional creation, e.g., opera or sculpture or architecture, literature is confined to words on a page. Yet, literature can be a "complete work of art" in the sense of *Gesamtkunstwerk*, by containing multiple references and allusions. Joyce tells us that this was his intent during an interview regarding *Ulysses*. He said: "I've put in so many enigmas and puzzles that it will keep professors busy for centuries arguing over what I mean and that's the only way of insuring one's immortality."[149]

Joyce's development of *Gesamtkunstwerk* begins with the title. The title *Ulysses* has an obvious historic reference to Homer's *Odyssey*. In addition, the novel, *Ulysses*, mirrors the Homeric tale, *The Odyssey*, with Bloom, Stephen, and Molly standing in for Odysseus, Odysseus's son Telemachus, and Penelope. Odysseus's dog, Argos, also is replaced by an unsentimental cat.[150] Many of the characters Bloom encounters have their counterpart in *The Odyssey*. For example, the drunk bigot, the Citizen, mirrors the cyclops Polyphemus, and the two barmaids in the Sirens episode, Lydia Douce and Mina Kennedy, mirror Homer's two seductive sirens.

We have geographic references. In Homer's *Odyssey*, we follow Odysseus's ten-year journey around the Mediterranean on his travels home to his faithful wife. In Joyce's *Ulysses*, we follow Bloom's one-day journey around Dublin, finally arriving back home to his not-so-faithful wife.[151]

Joyce's language reflects different writing styles, both contemporary and historic. For example, episode 13, Nausicaa, reads like a cheap romance novel; episode 15, Circe, is a theatrical play; episode 14, Oxen of the Sun, mirrors

---

[149] Ellmann, *James Joyce*, p. 521. Ellmann quotes from an interview with Jacques Benoist-Méchin. See Ellmann, p. 791, n104. By coincidence, Joyce's epigram reads like something Proust would have written. Proust considers works of art as one avenue to conquer time.

[150] There is not a dry eye to be found when Homer's Odysseus meets his dog Argos after a twenty-year absence, who wags his tail in recognition and dies. Bloom's cat? Bloom finally is home, some eighteen hours after leaving in the morning. We learn all there is to know about this cat and it carries nothing sentimental with it: "For what creature was the door of egress a door of ingress? For the cat." (episode 17, Ithaca: 1034–35)

[151] See Jack McCarthy and Danis Rose, *Joyce's Dublin: A Walking Guide to* Ulysses. Joyce declared that if Dublin "one day suddenly disappeared from the Earth it could be reconstructed out of my book [*Ulysses*]."

English writing styles from the sixth century through the nineteenth century; and episode 11, Sirens, is an homage to music.

Joyce's words mirror the mood of the moment. In the Hades episode (episode 6), when Bloom is going to a funeral, the words are slow, quiet, and halting. When Bloom and Gerty orgasm in episode 13, Nausicaa, the language quickens to a climax. After his orgasm as Bloom falls asleep, the language slows to a halt capturing the lethargy that is sweeping over his body and mind. In episode 12, Cyclops, bigots are getting drunk and the language is offensive, vulgar, boorish, and hurtful. In contrast, in episode 15, Circe, the characters are hallucinating, and the words are fast and bizarre. And, in episode 3, Proteus, Stephen is deep in thought contemplating Aristotle and Aquinas, and the language is almost incomprehensible:

> Ineluctable modality of the visible: at least that if no more, thought through my eyes. Signatures of all things I am here to read, seapawn and seawrack, the nearing tide, that rusty boot. Snotgreen, bluesilver, rust: coloured signs. Limits of the diaphane. But he adds: in bodies. Then he was aware of them bodies before of them coloured. How? . . . (Proteus: 3.1–6)

Moreover, Joyce weaves his novel into a vast spatial and temporal tapestry, including threads from Dante[152] and Shakespeare to writers of soft porn and Dublin slang. He includes Irish myths, Irish history, and many references to the Irish-English conflict. He fondly mocks Yeats and Wilde and refers to dozens of singers and songs. *Ulysses* is an encyclopedia of human history seen through the eyes of an early twentieth-century Dubliner. Comprehending *Ulysses* requires understanding the world. *Ulysses* is a literary *Gesamtkunstwerk*.

---

[152]Joyce's identification with Dante is biographical, autobiographical, and textual. Biographically, while not exactly parallel, Dante's political exile from Florence mirrors Joyce's self-imposed exile from Dublin. Autobiographically, Joyce asserted that Dante's *Divine Comedy* was Europe's epic. Oliver Gogarty, Joyce's one-time good friend and the model for Buck Mulligan in *Ulysses*, dubbed Joyce "Dante of Dublin." (See Ellmann, pp. 4, 75) Textually, both *Divine Comedy* and *Ulysses* are multi-layered works containing several internal and external references with multiple meanings imbedded in almost every line. Joyce refers to the *Divine Comedy* in *Ulysses*. Typical of Joyce, most of the references are arcane. For example, at 1.631, Stephen says "Now I can eat salt bread." This phrase refers to Dante's *Paradiso*, 1757-78: "You are to know the bitter taste of others' bread, how salt it is...." For a sample of other references, see Stephen Tardif, "Joyce's Dantean Piety, or The Survival of Acceptable Ideas," https://scholar.harvard.edu/files/tardif/files/tardif-joyce-dante.pdf.

CHAPTER 4
Wagnerism in Marcel Proust's
In Search of Lost Time

This chapter includes the heart of my analysis of Wagner's impact on Proust's novel *In Search of Lost Time*. The chapter is divided into five sections. Section a gives the biographical connection between Wagner and Proust. Section b delineates Wagnerian references within the text. Sections c, d, and e illustrate with textual examples Proust's use of *leitmotifs*, endless melody, and *Gesamtkunstwerk*.

a. Background on the Wagner-Proust Connection

While Joyce tried to minimize and even deny his Wagnerian roots, Proust made no attempt to hide his homage to Wagner. In discussing Proust's high esteem of Wagner, Paul du Quenoy quotes from Proust's *Correspondence*:[153]

> Writing a confidante in 1895, the novelist [Proust] waxed that "the essence of music is to awaken in us a mysterious depth of soul. . . a depth which begins where finite things and all the arts that have finite things as their object, end, and where science ends-and which may thereby be called religious." Mallarmé could scarcely have said it better. A devoted Wagnerian, among other exploits Proust claimed that he had nearly memorized all of the composer's works and wrote in a 1904 article that only Wagner's *Parsifal* approached the aesthetic beauty of a Catholic service in a Gothic cathedral. His earlier and less well known epic *Jean Santeuil* included plenty of Wagnerian references, but

---

[153] Paul du Quenoy, *Wagner and the French Muse*, p. 107.

his more mature and widely beloved *Remembrance of Things Past* stands as a Wagnerian epic par excellence.

By his early twenties, Proust had become a Wagnerite. In late 1892 or early 1893, he wrote that, "His preferred musicians were a trio of Germans: Schumann, Beethoven, and Wagner, the last whose music had become the rage among many in French society, creating a division between those who, like Proust, considered themselves Wagnerites and those who vehemently denounced this new foreign music. Marcel and his friends had discovered Wagner at the Sunday concerts they attended."[154]

Proust refers to Wagner in his 1904 article "La Mort des cathédrales" in which he argues for maintaining cathedrals as functioning religious centers rather than as secular museums. Proust argued that the liturgical ceremonies were of "such historical, social, artistic, and musical interest" that "only Wagner had approached its beauty, by imitating it in *Parsifal*."[155]

In 1910, Proust sent Reynaldo Hahn a humorous drawing of a stained glass depicting scenes from Hahn's daily life. The second panel shows Hahn playing the overture to Wagner's *Die Meistersinger*.[156] In 1911, after installing a theatrophone (an early acoustical device connected through telephone lines to eight Parisian theaters), Proust asserted that "if the opera was one of Wagner's that he practically knew by heart, he could supply the missing words as he listened."[157]

Another example of Proust referring to Wagner outside of his novel, occurred during the early months of World War I, when anti-German and anti-Wagner propaganda was beginning to fill the pages of the French press, Proust wrote to his friend: "As I wrote to Léon the other day, I remain as Beethovenian and Wagnerian as ever and I find the articles of Masson and Saint-Saëns idiotic."[158]

---

[154] Carter, pp. 140–1. In late June of 1893, Proust compared Montesquiou's poems to the creations of Wagner and de Vinci. (Carter, p. 150) In 1894, in a letter to his close friend, Reynaldo Hahn, Proust wrote: "You are hard on *Lohengrin*, I think. The herald and the king throughout, Elsa's dream, the arrival of the swan, the chorus of judgment, the scene between the two women, the refaldo, the Grail, the leave-taking, the gift of the horn, the sword and the lamb, the prelude – isn't all that beautiful?" Carter, p. 172.

[155] Carter, p. 375.

[156] Carter, p. 492.

[157] Carter, p. 497.

[158] Carter, p. 581.

Scholars who have studied drafts of *À la recherche du temps perdu* (*In Search of Lost Time*) make a case that Wagner, and in particular Wagner's opera *Parsifal*, provides the clue to the meaning of Proust's novel. For example, in his notes of 1913–1916, Proust writes: "I shall present the discovery of Time regained in the sensation induced by the spoon, the tea, etc., as illumination 'à la *Parsifal*.'" Nattiez explains Proust's comment as "The psychological progression embodied in *À la recherche* parallels that of *Parsifal*."[159]

Here Proust sounds more like an offspring of the surrealists insofar as "memory" is mysterious and provides access to an esoteric and ineffable essence of Being. My own opinion is that Proust is not referring to some ineffable realm available to a select few. Rather, these heightened experiences are present at the surface of conscious experience if we were only to pay attention and enjoy them.

Regardless of how we interpret Proust's message, Proust absorbed the cultural milieu of his day, and in the center of this musical and artistic environment was Wagner. We know from George Painter's biography of Proust that by the age of twenty (1890) Proust was "an ardent Wagnerian, devoted to Faure and intrigued by Debussy. . . ."[160] But perhaps the clearest evidence of Wagner's impact on Proust is the number of times Wagner or Wagnerian operatic characters are mentioned in *In Search of*.

b. Textual Reference to Wagner in *In Search of Lost Time*

Identifying Wagnerian textual references in *In Search of* presents at least two types of problems. The first is determining what constitutes a single reference. The second is classifying each reference into a heuristically and manageable

---

[159] Jean-Jacques Nattiez, *Proust as Musician*, p. 31. Nattiez discusses at length potential sources for Vinteuil's "little phrase." His conclusion is that "the game quickly becomes fruitless" in part because Proust provides so few technical descriptions thus "leaving the field open to the most diverse interpretations." George Painter's *Marcel Proust: A Biography* is more definitive. Painter recognizes that Vinteuil's sonata, as with many of Proust's fictional characters, has many models. However, just as some characters and places have a strong identity with a single object, e.g., Swann with Charles Haas and Balbec with Cabourg, Vinteuil's sonata has close ties to Saint-Saëns' *Sonata in D Minor* and César Frank's *Sonata in A Major*: "But to each of these confidants he also revealed the profounder models, for the 'little phrase' in Saint-Saëns's Sonata in D Minor, and for the sonata as a whole in César Franck's *Sonata in A Major*." Painter, *Marcel Proust*, vol. 2, p. 245.
[160] Painter, *Marcel Proust*, vol. 1, p. 172. Also see Ross, *Wagnerism*, pp. 391–99.

number of categories. Both du Quenoy and Jean-Jacques Nattiez have made valuable contributions to the understanding of Wagner's impact on Joyce and Proust in terms of the number of Wagnerian references and the significance of these references. Each, however, addresses only one of the two above-mentioned problems.

"No musician," says du Quenoy,[161] "is mentioned more frequently in it [*In Search of*] than Wagner, whose person, works, and legacy, according to my latest reading, merited no fewer than 62 references in the complete text." With the proviso "no fewer than," du Quenoy gives himself some wiggle room. A methodological problem arises in determining what objects are being "counted." What constitutes a reference? For example, in the illustration below, are there one, four, or five references to Wagner? du Quenoy does not tell us but, by inference, it appears he counts it as one reference.

> M. de Guermantes begins. "As for **Wagner**, he sends me to sleep at once." "You are wrong there," said Mme. de Guermantes, "in spite of his insufferable long-windedness, **Wagner** was a genius. **Lohengrin** is a masterpiece. Even in **Tristan** there are some amusing passages scattered about. As the Chorus of Spinners in **The Flying Dutchman** is a perfect marvel." (*GW*, vol. 1, p. 1067, emphasis added)

Paul du Quenoy offers a count of sixty-two Wagnerian references.[162] However, he does not identify those references, nor does he tell us the significance of those references. Jean-Jacques Nattiez argues that embedded in the novel is a classification system "outlining a typology of the musical (and artistic)" appreciation by the public. To capture this typology, Nattiez suggests the following three-tier classification system into which all Wagnerian references can be assigned: ". . . the snobs who do not understand but behave as if they do; the cultivated amateur who makes an effort to penetrate the work but

---

[161] Paul du Quenoy, *Wagner and the French Muse*, p. 107.

[162] I identified sixty-three references, although one reference could be a stretch. In *Swann's Way*, vol. 1, p. 324, the Narrator, speaking as an older person, reflects on the changes he observes in society. He comments: ". . . as if it was in that belief and not in ourselves that the divine spark resided, and as if our present incredulity had a contingent cause – the death of the gods." "Death of the gods" is close to "Twilight of the gods" which could refer to the fourth opera in *The Ring*: *Götterdämmerung*.

remains, like the critic and the musicologist at the mere stage of rational enquiry; and the man of the elite who will enter upon the scene only later and achieve authentic understanding."[163] Nattiez does not provide illustrations of his classification system. Using the above illustration and Nattiez's classification system, I would assign M. de Guermantes into the snob category and his wife, Mme. de Guermantes, into the cultivated amateur category.

In reading *In Search of*, with an eye toward applying Nattiez's classification system, I developed an additional category that I believe is helpful to better understand Wagnerian references. Expanding on Nattiez's three-tier system, I added a fourth category and labeled it "literary." There are many references in the novel that do not fit into any of Nattiez's three-tier system; for example, when Odette wants Swann to pay for a trip to Bayreuth sans Swann,[164] or when Saint-Loup's vitality is compared to Siegfried, or when German bombs are said to sound like the Valkyrie. These Wagnerian references function more as literary references than snob (name dropping), cultivated amateur (an analysis of Wagner's music), or elite (authentic understanding). By my count, the majority of Wagnerian references best fit within this literary category.

I created a table (Table A below) that uses a four-tier classification system that combines Nattiez's three categories: snob, cultivated amateur, and elite references, with my fourth category, literary reference. Table A includes three column headings: Page, Description, and Category, arranged by volume and book title. The Description column includes a summary of the reference, and the Category column includes the assignment of the reference within my four-tier classification system. For example, in *Swann's Way*, vol. 1, pp. 136–37, we find the first Wagnerian reference in the following sentence:

> Her eyes waxed blue as a periwinkle flower, wholly beyond my reach, yet dictated by her to me; and the sun, bursting out again from behind a threatening cloud and darting the full force of its rays on to the square and into the sacristy, shed a geranium glow over the red

---

[163] Nattiez, *Proust as Musician*, p. 45. Nattiez does, however, cite the Verdurins as falling into the snob category.

[164] Jeffrey Swann, "Wagner and Proust," p. 41, writes "This trip to Bayreuth, by the way, is a very rare example of an anachronism in Proust, who is usually painstakingly careful about dates: this episode takes place just before the Narrator's birth, presumably, like Proust's, in 1871. There was no Bayreuth Festival until 1876. . . ."

carpet laid down for the wedding, along which Mme. de Guermantes smilingly advanced, and covered its woolen texture with a nap of rosy velvet, a bloom of light, giving it the sort of tenderness, of solemn sweetness in the palm of a joyful celebration, which characterizes certain pages of **Lohengrin,** certain paintings by Carpaccio, and makes us understand how Baudelaire was able to apply to the sound of the trumpet the epithet "delicious." (emphasis added)

In Table A, this reference to *Lohengrin* is summarized under the Description column as *Lohengrin*. Mme. de Guermantes coming to Combray for a wedding— inside the wedding chapel. The *Lohengrin* reference in the above passage is classified as "literary." Proust assumes that the reader knows the reference is to Wagner's opera *Lohengrin*, which includes a wedding scene in act 3.

Table A: Wagnerian References in *In Search of Lost Time*

Page	Description	Category
Volume 1: *Swann's Way*		
p. 137	*Lohengrin.* Mme.de Guermantes coming to Combray for a wedding - inside the wedding chapel	Literary reference
p. 144	Two references: Ride of Valkyries and *Tristan* Prelude—at the Verdurins'	Snobbery
p. 158	*Meistersinger*—at the Verdurins'	Snobbery
pp. 231–33	Three; mentions of Bayreuth and Wagner. Odette wants to treat the Verdurins to Bayreuth, sans Swann	Literary reference
p. 255	Reference to Wagner at Mme. de Saint-Euverte's home	Literary reference/Snobbery
p. 268	Reference to *Tristan* when discussing Vinteuil	Elite
p. 324	Reference to *Götterdämmerung:* "the death of the Gods." The narrator reflecting in old age on changes in society	Literary reference
Volume 1: *Within a Budding Grove*		
p. 333	Nietzsche and Wagner—The narrator speaking of subjects of intelligent conversation	Literary reference
p. 402	Klingsor's laboratory. Marcel is describing how he feels waiting for Mme. Swann in her waiting room	Literary reference
p. 422	*Meistersinger.* The narrator is comparing emotional expression in speech and literature	Elite
p. 439	Mention of Wagner as Marcel is being introduced to a house of ill repute	Cultivated amateur

Page	Description	Category
p. 460	*Lohengrin.* At Odette's home used to illustrate someone's ignorance	Snobbery
p. 464	*Tristan and Isolde.* Their continued love long after their having drunk the love potent. (Indirect ref. on p. 265?)	Literary reference
p. 482	*Parsifal.* As Holy Week approaches and spring approaches, reference to Good Friday music in *Parsifal*	Literary reference
pp. 529–30	Two; reference to Prelude to *Lohengrin* and Overture to *Tannhäuser.* Concert at Balbec	Cultivated amateur
pp. 555–56	Two; reference to Wagner and *The Ring*	Cultivated amateur
p. 627	King Mark. The Narrator imagining that he was someplace other than passing along poorly constructed buildings. This reference is questionable	Literary reference
Volume 1: *The Guermantes Way*		
p. 721	Wagnerian harmony as an example of richness of experience. Also reference back to wedding on pp. 133–37	Literary reference
p. 776	Siegfried. Describing the strength needed to wake oneself	Literary reference
p. 791	Siegfried. Describing the vitality of Saint-Loup	Literary reference
p. 834	Passing reference to Wagner by Rachel pretending to be a cultured person	Snobbery
p. 878	*Walküre.* Mme. de Guermantes illustration of love	Literary reference
p. 883	Reference to *Lohengrin* to signify no position in the Dreyfus affair: "like	Literary reference

Page	Description	Category
	Lohengrin landing from a skiff drawn by a swan"	
p. 998	Reference to the pilgrims' chants in *Tannhäuser* to describe the sounds of a draft on the staircase	Literary reference
p. 1000	Example of Wagner and Nietzsche on friendship	Literary reference
p. 1013	*Götterdämmerung.* Description of what a war would be like between France and Germany	Literary reference
p. 1020	Flower Maidens in *Parsifal*—how he felt the women were looking at him as he entered the Guermantes' dining room	Literary reference
p. 1024	Flower Maidens in *Parsifal.* (Reference to p. 1020) to describe the people in the room	Literary reference
p. 1054	Wagner's music: "... or that there was a great deal of Italian music in Wagner...."	Literary reference
p. 1054	*Tristan.* Discussing the ignorance of this society	Literary reference
p. 1067	Five references: Wagner, *Lohengrin, Tristan and Isolde, The Flying Dutchman.* "As for Wagner, he sends me to sleep at once." "You are wrong there," said Mme. de Guermantes	Cultivated amateur
p. 1099	Reference to the Wagner festival at Bayreuth	Snobbery (geographic ref.)
p. 1104	Two references to Flower Maidens in *Parsifal.* See reference on p. 1020 and 1024	Literary reference

Page	Description	Category
p. 1108	Wagner. Reference to his early music versus later music	Cultivated amateur
p. 1111	Wagner. "What would be said of a young Berliner who had never heard of the Walküre?"	Literary reference
p. 1119	Two references to Wagner. "Princess Metternich . . . believed she had started Wagner because Victor Maurel."	Snobbery
Volume 2: *Cities of the Plain*		
p. 38	*Tannhäuser*—". . . been picturing to himself the reception that occurs in *Tannhäuser* and himself as a Margrave, . . ."	Literary reference
p. 65	Reference to Beethoven, Wagner, Franck, Debussy as bores	Snobbery
p. 95	Reference to *Tristan*. Albertine's phone call described like the shepherd's pipe in *Tristan*	Literary reference
p. 107	"Wagnerian." Odette professing herself a Wagnerian	Snobbery
p. 108	Odette having been to Bayreuth	Snobbery
p. 152	Wagner. ". . . who would have been incapable of distinguishing between Mozart and Wagner, said. . . ."	Literary reference/Snobbery
p. 153	*Parsifal*. "I think it [*Pelléas*] is even finer than *Parsifal*. . . ."	Snobbery/Cultivated amateur
pp. 154–55	Five references to Wagner, Bayreuth, *The Ring*. The Narrator soliloquizing whether there is progress in music	Snobbery/Cultivated amateur
p. 203	Two references to *The Ring* and *Meistersinger*	Snobbery

Page	Description	Category
p. 218	Reference to the effect on Mme. Verdurin of listening to the music of Bach, Wagner, Vinteuil, and Debussy	Snobbery/Literary reference
p. 234	Mme. Verdurin: "I can see the day coming when they will have no more use for Wagner or Indy."	Snobbery
Volume 2: *The Captive*		
p. 478	Indirect reference to *Tristan?* Could be a stretch except in a few pages, he has a long discussion of Wagner	Literary reference
pp. 489–91	Seventeen references. Analysis of Wagner's creativity and the creative process; *Tristan*, Bayreuth. . . . Marcel playing on the piano and thinking about Wagner. Comparison between Vinteuil and Wagner	Elite
p. 496	Two references to a Wagner concert "Wagner," shepherd's pipe in *Tristan*	Literary reference
p. 553	Two references to Wagner and the Norn in *The Ring*	Literary reference
p. 563	Five references: Elizabeth's Prayer, *Tristan, Das Rheingold, Meistersinger.* These references come toward the end of the Narrator's profound analysis beginning on page 553 of Vinteuil's septet, which was a gateway to the Narrator's analysis of art, the aesthetic experience, and the defeat of time through art	Elite
p. 564	Reference to Ibsen, D'Annunzio, Tolstoy, Wagner, Strauss, as passing material for journalists	Snobbery/Literary reference
p. 570	Reference to Wagner by way of complementing someone else	Literary reference
p. 572	Reference to Beckmesser	Literary reference

Page	Description	Category
Volume 2: *The Sweet Cheat Gone*		
p. 693	"the multiplicity of the troubles that assail us, intertwined like Wagnerian leitmotiv. . . ."	Literary reference
p. 694	"But this leitmotiv. . . ." Reference to p. 693 above	Literary reference
p. 723	". . . surrendering myself without the restriction of a single care to Wagner's music, than await the..."	Literary reference
p. 860	Three reference to Wagner: "than a man who knew nothing of Wagner save the duet in *Lohengrin* would be able to foresee the prelude of *Tristan*"	Literary reference/Elite
Volume 2: *The Past Recaptured*		
p. 912	". . . in the sublime *Siegfried*. . . ."Letter to Marcel from Saint-Loup from the Front	Literary reference
pp. 914–15	Four references: *Ride of the Valkyrie.* Saint-Loup talking w/Marcel about the German planes	Literary reference
p. 928	During World War I, the French putdown of Germany: "the *predatory empire*, of Wagner"	Literary reference
p. 929	*Ride of the Valkyrie.* During World War I: the sirens would rend the air like the shrieking call of a Valkyrie	Literary reference

I created Table B as an abstract of Table A. Table B includes three columns: Book Title, Number of Wagner References, and Number of Wagnerian Illustrations. The difference between Reference and Illustration is that a sentence, paragraph, or page may include more than one illustration within that single reference. For example, on page 144 of *Swann's Way* we read: "If the pianist suggested playing the **Ride of the Valkyries**, or the Prelude to **Tristan**, Mme. Verdurin. . . ." (emphasis added). I counted this as one reference with two illustrations.

Table B: Count of References to
Wagner by Book in *In Search of Lost Time*

Book Title	Number of Wagner References	Number of Wagnerian Illustrations
Swann's Way	7	10
Within a Budding Grove	10	12
The Guermantes Way	19	25
Cities of the Plain	11	16
The Captive	8	30
The Sweet Cheat Gone	4	6
The Past Recaptured	4	7
TOTAL	63	106

Having identified and classified the Wagnerian references in *In Search of*, we can now turn to the issue of Proust's frequent incorporation of these references. The major artists in *In Search of* prima facie are fictitious: Elstir for painting, Bergotte for writing, Vinteuil for music, and Berma for drama. Proust's many textual references to Wagner are to an actual person, i.e., Richard Wagner. The questions arise, why so many references to Wagner? Moreover, why does Proust give Wagner such a prominent role, even going so far as referencing Wagner both in the early pages and towards the end of the novel, thereby using Wagner as a bookends literary device?

For example, seven pages after the first Wagnerian reference (*Swann's Way*, vol. 1, pp. 136–37), we encounter the second Wagnerian reference. We are at the Verdurins' salon in the opening sentences of the Swann in Love section of *Swann's Way*. The Verdurins are social upstarts and have developed a second-tier salon over which they maintain an iron clad grip. The Verdurins are the consummate social snobs:

> To admit you to the "little nucleus," the "little group," the "little clan" at the Verdurins', one condition sufficed, but that one was indispensable; you must give tacit adherence to a Creed one of

those articles was that the young pianist, whom Mme. Verdurin had taken under her patronage that year, and of whom she said "Really, it oughtn't to be allowed, to **play Wagner** as well as that!" (*SW*, vol. 1, p. 144, emphasis added)

And a few lines later:

If the pianist suggested playing the **Ride of the Valkyries**, or the **Prelude to Tristan**, Mme. Verdurin would protest, not that the music was displeasing to her, but, on the contrary, that it made too violent an impression. "Then you want me to have one of my headaches? You know quite well, it's the same every time he plays that. I know what I'm in for. Tomorrow, when I want to get up-nothing doing! (*SW*, vol. 1, pp. 144-45, emphasis added)

Toward the end of the last book, *The Past Recaptured*, we encounter several references to Wagner: pp. 912, 914–15, 928, and finally on p. 929:

It was the period when there were constant Gotha raids; the air hummed continually with the watchful, noisy vibrations of the French airplanes. But sometimes the siren would rend the air, like the shrieking call of a **Valkyrie**—the only German music heard since the beginning of the war. . . . (*PR*, vol. 2, p. 929, emphasis added)

Despite many direct references to Wagner, the Narrator provides only a handful of places where he discusses Wagner's music at any length. His most extensive discussion occurs in Book 5, *The Captive*, vol. 2, pp. 489–91. The Narrator is sitting at his piano playing Vinteuil's sonata[165] when his mind drifts

---

[165] Vinteuil's "little phrase" sonata, and later septet, plays a vital role in the Narrator's aesthetic development and has more than just a temporal connection to Wagner: "As I played the passage [Vinteuil's sonata], and for all that in it, Vinteuil had been trying to express a fancy which would have been wholly foreign to Wagner, I could not help murmuring 'Tristan' with the smile of an old friend of the family discovering a trace of the grandfather in an intonation, a gesture of the grandson who never set eyes on him." (*C*, vol. 2, p. 489)

to Wagner and to *Tristan* in particular. He begins his discussion on the place of aesthetics in his life:

> Could life console me for the loss of art, was there in art a more profound reality in which our true personality finds an expression that is not afforded it by the activities of life? Every great artist seems indeed so different from all the rest, and gives us so strongly that sensation of individuality for which we seek in vain in our everyday existence. (*C*, vol. 2, p. 489)

Within these very dense few pages, the Narrator focuses on Wagner's music as a means to analyze the joy one experiences in music.[166, 167] He discusses the emotional impact of Wagner's *leitmotifs* (". . . that one would call them the resumption not so much of a musical motive as of an attack of neuralgia"); the way music and the arts enable us to understand and share in others' experiences, i.e., broaden both our temporal and spatial experience of the world. He further expresses amazement at Wagner's ability to capture a particular moment, generalize that moment to other experiences, and link that moment to the

---

[166] A few pages later (*C*, vol. 2, pp. 495–96), the Narrator expands art to include ordinary experience or ordinary objects. The Narrator tells Albertine: "What does it matter that a building is new, if it appears to be old, or even if it does not. All the poetry that the old quarters contain has been squeezed out to the last drop, but if you look at some of the houses that have been built lately for the rich tradesmen, in the new districts, where the stone is all freshly cut and still quite white, don't they seem to rend the torrid air of noon in July, . . . with a cry as harsh as the odour of the cherries waiting for the meal to begin in the darkened dining room, where the prismatic glass knife-rests project a multicolored fire as beautiful as the windows of Chartres?" Also see *WBG*, vol. 1, p. 653: "I tried to find beauty there where I had never imagined before that it could exist, in the most ordinary things, in the profundities of 'still life.'" I believe this is Proust's underlying message to us, that aesthetic experiences are not restricted to the concert hall or a museum or stained glass in an ancient cathedral but are available to us at every moment. Also see *SW*, vol. 1, p. 137: "Then, quite apart from all those literary preoccupations, and without definite attachment to anything, suddenly a roof, a gleam of sunlight reflected from a stone, the smell of a road would make me stop still, to enjoy the special pleasure that each of them gave me, and also because they appeared to be concealing, beneath what my eyes could see, something which they invited me to approach and seize from them, but which despite all my efforts, I never managed to discover."

[167] This discussion of Wagner is a precursor to the Narrator's lengthier and more profound discussion of music, art, the aesthetic experience, vis à vis Vinteuil's sonata and how art defeats time. See *C*, vol. 2, pp. 553–64.

complexity of individuals and the world in which we live.[168] The Narrator argues that originality is essential to being an artist; but then he asks, is originality ultimately a matter of craft?

> Wagner himself was filled with joy, when he discovered in his memory a shepherd's air, incorporated it in his work, gave it its full wealth of meaning. This joy moreover never forsakes him. In him, however great the melancholy of the poet, it is consoled, surpassed— that is to say destroyed, alas, too soon – by the delight of the craftsman. But then, no less than by the similarity I had remarked just now between Vinteuil's phrase and Wagner's, I was troubled by the thought of this Vulcan-like craftsmanship. Could it be this that gave to great artists the illusory appearance of a fundamental originality, incommensurable with any other, the reflection of a more than human reality, actually the result of industrious toil? (C, vol. 2, p. 491)[169]

The Narrator does not answer this question of the relationship between craft, originality, and art. Rather, he chooses to immerse himself in the joy of the music: "Separated from Wagner by the wall of sound, I could hear him exult, invite me to share his joy." (C, vol. 2, p. 491) We are reminded of his "madeleine" moment which he describes as "exquisite pleasure had invaded my senses" and "this all-powerful joy." (SW, vol. 1, p. 34)

So why Wagner? It appears to the Narrator that Wagner's music expressed his individuality and his creations required incredible craftsmanship. In addition, his music stimulated experiences that expanded one's sensitivity to the world by, among other ways, linking those experiences through time. Furthermore, it gave to others the unfiltered experience of joy. In Book 7, The Past Recaptured, vol. 2, pp. 992–1023, the Narrator expands on these themes: "Only by art can we get outside ourselves, know what another sees of his

---

[168] For example, the shepherd's pipe in act 3 of *Tristan* signals that Isolde has not arrived, but also opens the Pandora's box that is Tristan's unconscious.

[169] The Narrator raised the same possibility that "the appearance of real individuality obtained in works of art being due merely to the illusion created by the artist's technical skills" in C, vol. 2, pp. 517–18. We have to wait until the end of the novel to hear the Narrator's understanding of what it is to be an artist.

universe. . . ." (*PR*, vol. 2, p. 1013), "And thinking over again that timeless joy caused by the sound of the spoon or the taste of the madeleine, I said to myself, 'Was that the happiness suggested by the little phrase of the sonata to Swann, who made the mistake of confusing it with the pleasure of love and was unable to find it in artistic creation—that happiness which I came to sense dimly. . . .'" (*PR*, vol. 2 p. 1000)

The purpose of this section was to show that Wagner was a significant influence on Proust. I believe that has been shown. This leads to the question of how Wagner's influence was manifested in the structure of *In Search of Lost Time?* The answer to this question was by employing Wagner's formal elements of *leitmotifs*, endless melody, and *Gesamtkunstwerk*. As always, the devil is in the details.

c. *Leitmotifs*

Wagnerian *leitmotifs* are musical phrases that create a structural coherence within a piece of music. Psychologically, for the listener, they link past and future events. In the article "Wagner and Proust,"[170] Jeffrey Swann quotes Thomas Mann as follows: "'I mean by the use of the leitmotiv, the magic formula that works both ways and links the past with the future, the future with the past. The leitmotiv is the technique employed to preserve the inward unity and abiding presentness of the whole at each moment.'" These musical phrases are "pregnant with meaning."

Leitmotifs also enable the listener to understand more deeply the present moment. To use yet another metaphor, they function both as telescopes and microscopes insofar as they bring the past and the future into focus and simultaneously direct our focus on the psychology engulfing the specific moment.[171] All experience occurs at a moment *in* time, but its significance is revealed *through* time.

---

[170] Jeffrey Swann, "Wagner and Proust," in particular pp. 45–46.

[171] In describing his writing style, the Narrator tells us that, after showing a few friends sketches of his planned novel, "No one understood a word. Even those who were favourable to my conception of the truths which I intended later to carve within the temple, congratulated me on having discovered them with a **microscope** when I had on the contrary, used a **telescope** to perceive things which, it is true, were very small but situated afar off and each of them a world in itself." (*PR*, vol. 2, p. 1118, emphasis added) See Howard Moss, *The Magic Lantern of Marcel Proust*, pp. 27–32. Moss states that Proust is trying to do two things at once, to arrest the moment and to show us the significance of that moment with all its history.

Musically, these recurring themes or *leitmotifs* and their variations and developments add coherency and structure to the musical piece. Musically they can be composed of the same notes that gain significance as the musical work—in this case, opera—unfolds. More often these notes morph through various techniques such as altering their rhythm and tempo, inversion, changing key, moving from major to minor, and using pieces of the motifs to develop new, but related, motifs.

Leitmotifs have a similar function in literature; they create coherence and unity within a piece of writing. In literature, recurring words or phrases that function as *leitmotifs* either can be the same word(s) that take on layers of meaning in different situations or, because of their narrative association, can be different words that have associative significance.[172] We find these different *leitmotific* designs throughout *In Search of*.

In the opening paragraph of *In Search of*, we encounter several central *leitmotifs*: sleep, waking, self-identity, literature, and time:[173] "For a long time I used to go to bed early." "I would try to put away the book. . . ." "Then it [his waking and coming to consciousness] would begin to seem unintelligible, as the thoughts of a former existence must be to a reincarnate spirit;" Three short paragraphs later we find another central *leitmotif*, sex: "Sometimes, too, just as Eve was created from a rib of Adam, so a woman would come into existence while I was sleeping, conceived from some strain in the position of my limbs."[174]

Early in the novel we are introduced to people that Proust describes in such detail that we come to know them both as distinct personalities and as archetypes or universal human types. These characters also have a *leitmotific* function. As these characters move in and out of the novel, they remind us of

---

[172] I believe Proust is speaking about himself when the Narrator states that all great writers seek variety within a sameness: "The true variety is in this abundance of real and unexpected elements, in the branch loaded with blue flowers which thrusts itself forward against all reason, from the spring hedgerow that seemed already overcharged with blossoms, whereas the purely formal imitation of variety (and one might advance the same arguments for all the other qualities of style) is but a barren uniformity. . . ." (*WBG*, vol. 1, p. 420)

[173] Whether time is a *leitmotif* is questionable. I view time as a framework or structure in which *leitmotifs* exist rather than as a *leitmotif* itself. I discuss the status of time in Chapter 5, Conclusion: The Function of Time.

[174] In terms of a recurring pattern, i.e., a *leitmotif*, we learn that as a young man in bed with his mistress, Albertine, as she slept "I had no need to make any movement, I allowed my leg to dangle against hers, like an oar which one allow to trail in the water, imparting to it now and again a gentle oscillation like the intermittent flap given to its wing by a bird asleep in the air." (*C*, vol. 2, p. 427)

the circumstances and surroundings where we previously encountered them. The characters develop, morph, their dynamic and tempo change, and over time their bodies change, yet there is a core element, perhaps captured by nothing more than their name. Their name becomes their ground melody by which we know them, and, by the multilayered associations, we know everyone else in the novel.

In these opening sections, we first meet many of the characters who are associated with *leitmotifs*. These include Swann, Charlus, the Narrator's mother and grandmother, Aunt Léonie, and Françoise. We learn of the composer Vinteuil, and we see through a window his daughter, Mlle. Vinteuil and her friend. We also are introduced to the writer Bergotte, the Duchesse de Guermantes, and M. Legrandin. We learn of other characters indirectly. These include Mme. de Saint-Loup, whom we learn later is Gilberte, and more oblique references, such as to Mme. de Villeparisis's nephew, who we later discover is Robert Saint-Loup.

We meet the tailor and his daughter/niece, who we later learn their names are Jupien and Marie-Antoinette. We also meet a painter, at work in the church, who later we learn is the famous painter, Elstir. We cannot exclude mentioning the "lady in pink" who we later learn is Swann's "unfortunate marriage," i.e., his wife, Odette.[175]

Early in the novel we learn of the Narrator's emotional life. These emotions include unfulfilled desire, conflicting feelings between love and pain (at this early point in the novel, referring to his conflicted feelings for his mother's good night kiss), love and jealousy, snobbery, and recurring disappointment when reality does not correspond to the Narrator's imagined expectation. These emotions become *leitmotifs* as they recur throughout the novel.

The central emotion introduced in the Overture and Combray sections of *Swann's Way* is what I would call an aesthetic experience of the world. The Narrator recalls experiencing "exquisite pleasure," and "all-powerful joy" when he tastes the

---

[175] Determining the age of Proust's characters is difficult for several reasons. However, the age of the people on which they are loosely based can provide a clue. For example, Laure Hayman, on whom Odette primarily is based, was born in 1851, hence twenty years the Narrator's senior. Laure Layman's mother brought her up as a courtesan (Painter, *Marcel Proust: A* Biography, vol. 1, pp. 85–86). Odette was Elstir's model posing as a boy in a painting labeled and dated *Miss Sacripant*, Oct. 1872. If Odette were fifteen, that would make her fourteen years older than the Narrator. One can engage in a lot of fun but futile detective work trying to identify the age of the novel's characters. We should not forget that Proust is writing a fiction and therefore reference to historical characters is only of biographical interest and virtually has nothing to do with the events within the novel.

tea and "short, plump little cakes called "petites madeleines." (*SW*, vol. 1, p. 34) The Narrator also had an aesthetic experience of joy when he completed his first literary creation (*SW*, vol. 1, p. 140),[176] and he described that experience as a "special pleasure, which bore no resemblance to any other, when I caught sight of the twin steeples of Martinsville." (*SW*, vol. 1, p. 138) The Narrator spends the next twenty-two hundred pages trying to recapture and understand the nature of those experiences of joy.

The Narrator introduces a plethora of recurring themes or *leitmotific* ideas. These include: sleeping and waking; consciousness and self-identity;[177] the related concepts of love, desire, possession, obsession, jealously,[178] and disappointment;[179] friendship; social class; essences and permanence; hypocrisy; dying and death;[180] and custom and habit.

Over time, we learn of places and objects that acquire layers of significance during the course of the novel. These include Combray, the stained-glass of Gilbert the Bad, Tansonville, the steeples of Martinville, the Guermantes Hotel in Paris and its environs, railroad stations and platforms, and, of course, the Guermantes Way and Méséglise Way.[181]

---

[176] "I never thought again of this page, but at the moment . . . I found such a sense of happiness, felt that it had so entirely relieved my mind of the obsession of the steeples, and of the mystery which they concealed, that, as though I myself were a hen and had just laid an egg, I began to sing at the top of my voice." The Narrator works on revisions of this early sketch, and it becomes his first publication in the newspaper *Le Figaro*. The "never thought again of this page" is one of the dozens, if not hundreds, of lies the Narrator and others tell without a second thought.

[177] See *CP*, vol. 2, pp. 270–74, for an insightful discussion of the difference between waking and sleeping time or objective and phenomenological time.

[178] The relationship between love and jealousy permeates many of the major relationships: Swann and Odette; Robert Saint-Loup and Rachel; Charlus and Morel; the Narrator with Gilberte and Albertine. Love and jealousy are emotions but also subjects of analysis, hence ideas.

[179] In Book 5, *CP*, vol. 2, p. 293, the Narrator discloses his realization that desire motivates him and not the fulfillment of his desires: ". . . they reminded me that it was my fate to pursue only phantoms, creatures whose reality existed to a great extent in my imagination."

[180] The Narrator provides the reader with many clues regarding his grandmother's illness and pending death. However, only after his grandmother's death does the Narrator and the reader recognize them as clues.

[181] Moss in *The Magic Lantern*, pp. 24–25, points out that the English word "way" like the French "*du côté*" means both a direction or journey and a mode of living. In the Overture and Combray sections of *Swann's Way*, as a child the Narrator observes that the Méséglise Way represents the upper middle class and the Guermantes Way represents the aristocracy. Over time, the Méséglise Way morphs into the idea of love and disappointment and the Guermantes Way morphs into that of Society and superficiality. By the end of the novel the two Ways merge, and the Narrator realizes that the two Ways had always been joined.

The Narrator describes nature, particularly flowers and gardens, hawthorns, and waterlilies. The Narrator discloses several activities, including sex and its many permutations,[182] voyeurism, lying, deceit, dinner parties, and multiple iterations of the narrator's experience tasting the tea and madeleine cake.[183] And there are many recurring words, including Mme. Verdurin's use of the word "bores,"[184] Mme. Guermantes's "wit," and "Mme. Putbus's maid." All of these descriptions, disclosures, memories, and recurring words are *leitmotifs*.

There are hundreds of *leitmotifs* in *In Search of*, all of which warrant closer examination. Somewhat paradoxically, each one of Proust's *leitmotifs* is so pregnant with meaning, the magic formula that works to link the past with the future, the future with the past, so telescopic and microscopic, that thoroughly analyzing one *leitmotif* would unravel the entire novel. Rather than analyzing all of the *leitmotifs* (conceptually not possible) or thoroughly analyzing one *leitmotif* (humanly not possible), we are going to analyze a handful of *leitmotifs* and analyze a few layers of their complexity. We begin with a relatively simple illustration.

Le Figaro. A musical *leitmotif* can have significant impact on the listener even if it is heard only a few times.[185] The same can be true with a literary *leitmotif*. Reference to the newspaper *Le Figaro* occurs only a handful of times, yet *Le Figaro* is a stepping stone in the Narrator's literary ambitions. More significant, from a *leitmotif* perspective, each time *Le Figaro* is mentioned, we are intellectually and emotionally reminded of its early occurrences, and its present usage is enhanced by its history.

---

[182] *In Search of* includes a lot of sex: nocturnal emission, masturbation, prostitution, lesbianism, homosexuality, affairs and adultery, pedophilia, and even sex among flowers and animals, as well as obsession and jealousy that someone else might be having sex with one's lover.

[183] The "petite madeleine" *leitmotif* is repeated in different situations and permutations dozens of times throughout the novel.

[184] In Book 7, *PR*, vol. 2, p. 897, the Narrator observes of Mme. Verdurin that "in proportion as the number of prominent society folk who made overtures to Mme. Verdurin increased, the number of those she call 'bores' decreased. By a kind of magical transformation, every bore who came to call on her or who angled for an invitation suddenly became an agreeable, intelligent person." The word "bore" takes our memory back to our first meeting Mme. Verdurin and her "little clan" in *SW*, vol. 1, p. 144, and all the characters we met in her drawing rooms.

[185] The *leitmotif* "Redemption through Love," also referred to as "In Praise of Brünnhilde" in Wagner's *Ring*, comes to mind. It is only heard twice in its full glory, yet is unforgettable.

In Book 6, the Narrator's mother hands him a copy of the newspaper *Le Figaro*. We read: "I opened the *Figaro* . . . It was my article that had appeared at last!" (SCG, vol. 2, p. 781) This incident harkens back four hundred pages to a seemingly insignificant sentence in which the Narrator expressed disappointment that his article had not been published:

> I rang for Françoise. I opened the *Figaro*, I scanned its columns and made sure that it did not contain an article, or so-called article, which I had sent to the editor, and which was no more than a slightly revised version of the page that had recently come to light, written long ago in Dr. Percepied's carriage as I gazed at the spires of Martinville. (C, vol. 2, pp. 385–86)

The above passage takes us back more than a thousand pages to when the Narrator was returning from a wedding attended by the Duchesse de Guermantes. As he sat in the carriage, he was inspired to write two paragraphs describing the steeples of Martinville. (SW, vol. 1, pp. 138–40) This reference to his adolescent dabbles at writing is significant for at least two reasons. It points back to his early aspirations to become a writer and points forward more than 1,500 pages to his first publication, a minor success. Second, and more important, is his success in conveying his experience of joy, when viewing the steeples of Martinville, into words:

> ". . . an idea came into my mind which had not existed for me a moment earlier, framed itself in words in my head; and the pleasure with which the first sight of them, just now, had filled me was so much enhanced that, overpowered by a sort of intoxication, I could no longer think of anything but them." (SW, vol. 1, p. 139)

The Narrator continues:

> I had finished writing it, I found such a sense of happiness, felt that it had so entirely relieved my mind of the obsession of the steeples and of the mystery which they concealed, that, as though I

myself were a hen and had just laid an egg, I began to sing at the top of my voice. (*SW*, vol. 1, p. 140)

The Narrator's sketch of the steeples, long forgotten by the reader and alluded to once before by the Narrator, comes rushing back, now rich in meaning and significance nearly three thousand pages later. In the closing pages of the novel, as the Narrator contemplates the roles of Françoise and of literature, we are reminded of the Narrator's first public literary endeavor: "... and also because she [Françoise] had lived my life so long that she had developed a sort of instinctive understanding of literary work more correct than that possessed by many intelligent persons and, *a fortiori*, by stupid people. In the same way, years before, when I was writing my article for *Figaro*, whereas the old butler...." (PR, vol 2, p. 1113)

As a *leitmotif*, "*Figaro*" moves the reader back and forth through time and gains significance because each occurrence is enriched by the context of its prior uses.

Combray's Curé. Early in the novel, the Narrator introduces us to a forever nameless and seemingly insignificant player in the novel, Combray's *Curé*, i.e., the parish priest or abbot. (*SW*, vol. 1, p. 48) We learn of the Curé's interest in etymology (*SW*, vol. 1, p. 78), and some thousand pages later we learn that he published the "Curé's guide" to Combray. (*GW*, vol. 1, p. 1102)

Despite the Curé's low profile, he serves two important *leitmotific* functions. First, each time the Curé is mentioned, and always just as a passing glance, the Narrator and the reader are drawn back to the Narrator's childhood in Combray and all its accompanying memories. Discussing the "Curé's guide," the Narrator ponders:

> . . . whether one day Guermantes itself may not appear nothing more than a place-name, save to the archaeologists who, stopping by chance at Combray and standing beneath the window of Gilbert the Bad, have the patience to listen to the account given them by Theodore's successor or to read the Curé's guide? (*GW*, vol. 1, p. 1102)

In Book 4, *Cities of the Plain*, Mme. de Cambremer makes a passing reference to the Curé in response to the Narrator's interest in knowing the origin of certain family names:

> "If these old names interest you," she added, "... the parish priest of a place where I myself have some land, a long way from here, Combray, where the worthy cleric ... is spending his last years in writing a great work upon Combray and its surroundings. I shall send you his pamphlet on the surroundings of Feterne." (*CP*, vol. 2, p. 151)

The second *leitmotific* function of the Curé is to provide a microscopic view into the pedantic Sorbonne professor Brichot.[186] When the Narrator refers to the Curé's book, "I am interested in that priest, and also in etymologies." "Don't put any faith in the ones he gives," replied Brichot, "there is a copy of the book at la Raspelière, which I have glanced through, but without finding anything of any value; it is a mass of error." (*CP*, vol. 2, p. 205) And a few pages later, in response to M. de Cambremer's reference to the Curé's book, Brichot replies: "'I know, I have read it with immense interest,' Brichot replied hypocritically. The satisfaction that his pride received indirectly from this answer made M. de Cambremer laugh long and loud." (*CP*, vol. 2, p. 231)

In spite of Brichot's denunciation, the Curé seems to be given the last word. Near the end of the novel, the Narrator waxes on about the intellectual delight the Curé must have experienced in exploring the etymology of words: "And I admit that, thinking of my reading at Balbec, not far away from Robert, I was greatly impressed-as when, in a French countryside, I came across a trench described by Mme. de Sévigné —or in the Orient, in connection with the siege of Kur-el-Amara (Kut-the-Emir, as we say Vaux-le-Vicomte and Boillend-l'Evêque, as the Curé of Combray would have said if he had extended his thirst for etymology to the Oriental languages...." (*PR*, vol. 2, p. 1077) A name is the

---

[186] This interest in names gives Proust an opportunity for some low brow, yet subtle humor. For example, when discussing the Cambremer's name, the Duchesse de Guermantes and Swann displayed their wit: "'But surely these Cambremers have rather a startling name. It ends just in time but it ends badly!' she said with a laugh. 'It begins no better.' Swann took the point. 'Yes; that double abbreviation!'" (*SW*, vol. 1, p. 262) The joke is that "Cambremers" refers to the word "shit" in three ways. See Patrick Alexander, *Marcel Proust's Search for Lost Time*, p. 224.

carrier of history, of relationships, and of meaning. The humble Combray abbot understood this. (In a bit of Proustian irony, the Curé is never given a name; he forever remains "the Curé.")

The Kiss. A significant *leitmotif* used in *In Search of* is the kiss. The kiss symbolizes desire, frustration, jealousy, betrayal, repressed sexuality, control and domination, and a distortion of the expression of healthy and mature loving. The kiss permeates the Narrator's relationships with both his mother and his mistress, Albertine. Its symbolic meaning as immature control lurks underneath many of the Narrator's real and imagined interactions with other women.

Within the opening pages of *Swann's Way*, we encounter the Narrator as a child waiting in his bedroom for his mother's good night kiss:

> My sole consolation when I went upstairs for the night was that Mamma would come in and kiss me after I was in bed. But this good night lasted for so short a time: she went down again so soon that the moment in which I heard her climb the stairs, and then caught the sound of her garden dress of blue muslin, from which hung little tassels of plaited straw, rustling along the double-doored corridor, was for me a moment of the keenest sorrow. So much did I love that good night that I reached the stage of hoping that it would come as late as possible, so as to prolong the time of respite during which Mamma would not yet have appeared. Sometimes when, after kissing me, she opened the door to go, I longed to call her back, to say to her "Kiss me just once again," but I knew that then she would at once look displeased,.... (SW, vol. 1, p. 10)

A few pages later, the Narrator calculates a way to lure his mother from the dinner table to his bedroom so that he could receive his desired kiss:

> Then, suddenly, my anxiety subsided, a feeling of intense happiness coursed through me, as when a strong medicine begins to take effect and one's pain vanishes: I had formed a resolution to abandon all attempts to go to sleep without seeing Mamma, and had decided to kiss her at all costs, even with the certainty of being in disgrace with her for long afterwards, when she herself came up to

bed. The tranquility which followed my anguish made me extremely alert, no less than my sense of expectation, my thirst for and my fear of danger. (SW, vol. 1, p. 25)

In *Within the Budding Grove*, the Narrator becomes obsessed with Albertine while vacationing in Balbec. Albertine has invited him to her room. The Narrator anticipates sex, but she rejects his advances.

I bent over Albertine to kiss her…. "Stop that, or I'll ring the bell!" cried Albertine, seeing that I was flinging myself upon her to kiss her…. in the state of exaltation in which I was, the round face of Albertine, lighted by an inner flame, like the glass bowl of a lamp, started into such prominence that, copying the rotation of a burning sphere, it seemed to me to be turning, like those faces of Michelangelo which are being swept past in the arrested headlong flight of a whirlwind. I was going to learn the fragrance, the flavour which this strange pink fruit concealed. I heard a sound, precipitous, prolonged, shrill. Albertine had pulled the bell with all her might. (SW, vol. 1, pp. 698-9)

We are reminded of that rejected kiss a thousand pages later in *The Captive*. While living with Albertine, the Narrator recalls his unsatisfying experience with her: "…issuing from the innermost depths of myself, charged with memories and burning with desire, added such a brilliancy, such an intensity of life that its relief seemed to stand out and turn with almost the same magic power as on the day, in the hotel at Balbec, when my vision was clouded by my overpowering desire to kiss her;…." (C, vol. 2, p. 648).

For the Narrator, sexual expression often is imbued with memories of his mother's kiss as well as the saving grace of the Catholic Church and the Holy Eucharist. The Narrator recalls kissing Albertine:

…before leaving me, she used to slide her tongue between my lips like a portion of daily bread, a nourishing food that had the almost sacred character of all flesh upon which the sufferings that we have endured on its account have come in time to confer a sort of spiritual grace, what I at once call to mind in comparison is not the night that Captain de Borodino allowed me to spend in barracks, a favour which cured what was after all only a passing distemper, but the night on which my father sent Mamma to sleep in the little bed by the side of my own. (C, vol 2, p. 384)

References to his mother during sex with Albertine abound: "When it was Albertine's turn to bid me good night, kissing me on either side of my throat, her hair caressed me like a wing of softly bristling feathers. Incomparable as were those two kisses of peace, Albertine slipped into my mouth, making me the gift of her tongue, like a gift of the Holy Spirit, conveyed to me a viaticum,[187] left me with a provision of tranquility almost as precious as when my mother in the evening at Combray used to lay her lips upon my brow." (C, vol 2, p. 431)

In the opening pages of *In Search of*, Proust makes a circuitous reference to "a mother's kiss." The Narrator has been granted his mother's good night kiss, and he is further rewarded by his mother reading to him from George Sand's *François le Champi* (The Country Waif).[188] *François le Champi* is a story about a waif. The waif, François, is taken in by a kind woman, the wife of a brutish miller. The waif calls the woman his mother, and she calls him her son. He longs for his mother's kiss: "Well—it's—it's that you often give Jeannie a kiss and you have never kissed me since the day we were just talking of. And I always take care to keep my face and hands clean because I know you don't care for dirty children, and you are for ever washing Jeannie and combing his hair. But you don't kiss me any the more for that…." The mother responds: "come and kiss me, François," said the miller's wife, taking the child into her lap and kissing his forehead with much emotion. "I was wrong never to think of it, and you deserved more from me. Look—you see how lovingly I kiss you, and now you are quite sure you are no longer a waif, aren't you?"[189]

As a literary *leitmotif*, the kiss functions to move us from its first innocent presentation to underscore the Narrator's lack of mature sexual development.

---

[187] Viaticum is a term used in the Catholic Church for administering the Eucharist to a person who is dying.
[188] SW, vol. 1, p. 30-32. In PR, vol. 7, p. 1004 the Narrator absent mindedly picks up *François le Champi*. *François le Champi* in the Prince de Guermantes's library.
[189] George Sand, *The Country Waif*, translated by Eirene Collis. University of Nebraska Press, Lincoln, 1977, p. 57. The story concludes with the waif, now an adult, and his "mother" getting married to each other.

Referring to *François le Champi* at the end of the novel (PR, vol 7, p. 1004) brings the reader back to Combray and images of the Narrator, as a child, longing for his mother's kiss.[190]

Lying. Lying is one of the oddest *leitmotifs* in *In Search of*. While it may be human nature to occasionally lie, in *In Search of* everyone continually lies for one reason or another, or for no reason at all. We encounter the first instance of lying on page 23 of the Overture to Book 1, *Swann's Way*. The Narrator, as a child, says: "But to give myself one chance of success I lied without hesitation. . . ."

The reason that Proust has everyone lying so often is unclear. Perhaps it has to do with the Narrator's notion of "self." For much of the novel the Narrator discards the notion of a permanent self in favor of multiple selves, each comprised of independent emotional responses to changing circumstances. For example, I am happy this moment and then suddenly I am sad, then I am desirous of a certain food, then I am happy again. Each emotional state is so different from the others that there is a sense that the "self" in one emotional state is different from the "self" in other emotional states.

Lying may be rooted in our being unaware of what motivates our actions. Moreover, because we can have several motivations at any moment, we can believe that we are lying while simultaneously believing that we are not lying. Sometimes we lie by omission and sometimes we lie out of kindness as when the Narrator's grandmother hides her fatal illness from him. Sometimes the lie is to make oneself look more impressive to others, as Block does to impress M. de Norpois about his being on friendly terms with Mme. Swann. (*WBG*, vol. 1, p. 384)[191] Sometimes we lie by reflex, sometimes we lie by calculations, sometimes we lie because lying is part of our nature and we cannot help it. When discussing Albertine and Andrée's lies, the Narrator tells us:

> Falsehood is essential to humanity. It plays as large part perhaps as the quest of pleasure and is moreover commanded by that quest. We lie in order to protect our pleasure or our honor if the disclosure of our pleasure runs counter to our honour. We lie all our

---

[190] Those familiar with Wagner's last opera, *Parsifal*, will recognize the complexity embodied in a mother's kiss.

[191] For a very long stretch of gratuitous lying, see the dinner scene at the Blocks' home, *WBG*, vol. 1, pp. 581–88.

life long, especially indeed, perhaps only, to those people who love us. Such people in fact alone make us fear for our pleasure and desire their esteem. (SCG, vol. 6, p. 810)

Whatever the merits with the Narrator's reasoning, lying is like an ostinato in classical music, a ground rhythm in jazz, or the background radiation in the cosmos. For the Narrator, lying resides at the base of all human interaction. For the reader, it serves as a *leitmotif* linking nearly all the characters of the novel.

There are countless incidences of social lying, such as, asserting that she[192] would never step foot into that woman's house, while longing for an invitation. Another example is when Mme. Verdurin, plotting M. de Charlus's expulsion from her "clan," said: "'I must add that he [M. de Charlus] gives himself airs in my house which I do not at all like'" (C, vol. 2, p. 540), followed a few pages later with "Not that I have anything against Charlus, far from it. He is a pleasant fellow. . . ." (C, vol. 2, p. 549) The Narrator lies to his friend Robert Saint-Loup when he prefers being with the band of girls at Balbec. (WBG, vol. 1, p. 679)

Furthermore, there is lying for no good reason, i.e., when a simple "I have another commitment" would suffice. For example, when Andrée, on first meeting the Narrator, tells him that she has to see her mother when she actually had accepted an invitation to go to a picnic. (WBG, vol. 1, p. 665) Everyone lies and is lying constantly, and perhaps the Narrator is the guiltiest.[193] He even turns lying into a positive trait:

> The lie, the perfect lie, about people whom we know, about
> the relations that we have had with them, about our motives for
> some action, a motive which we express in totally different terms,
> the lie as to what we are, whom we love . . . that lie is one of the

---

[192] The "she" could be almost anyone in the novel, but in this case it is Mme. Bontemps: "Meanwhile Mme. Bontemps, who had been heard a hundred times to declare that nothing would induce her to go to the Verdurins', delighted at being asked to her famous Wednesdays, was planning in her own mind how she could manage to attend as many of them as possible." (WBG, vol. 1, pp. 458–60)

[193] "[A]t that time it frequently occurred that I said things in which there was no vestige of truth. . . . Now untruthfulness and dishonesty were with me, as with most people, called into being in so immediate, so contingent a fashion, and in self-defense, by some particular interest, that my mind, fixed on some lofty ideal, allowed my character, in the darkness below, to set about those urgent, sordid tasks, and did not look down to observe them." (GW, vol. 1, p. 761)

only things in the world that can open a window for us upon what is novel, unknown, that can awaken in us sleeping senses to the contemplation of universes that otherwise we should never have known. (C, vol. 2, p. 530)

The intimate relationship between the Narrator and Albertine is a lengthy exercise in lying to each other: "And so we exchanged our lying speeches." (C, vol. 2, p. 462) In fact, virtually the entirety of Book 5: *The Captive* is one long exercise in mutual lying:

> Albertine blushed. "It is true," she said, "I was not having drawing lessons, I told you a great many lies at first, that I admit. But I never lie to you now." I would so much have liked to know what were the many lies that she had told me at first, but I knew beforehand that her answers would be fresh lies. And so I contented myself with kissing her. I asked her to tell me one only of those lies. She replied: "Oh, well; for instance when I said that the sea air was bad for me." I ceased to insist in the face of this unwillingness to reveal. (C, vol. 2, pp. 504–5)

Lying reaches its apex, but not its last appearance, in the scene when the Narrator tells Albertine that he wants to break up with her. (C, vol. 2, pp. 612–35) They have been living together in the Narrator's home (actually, his mother's home) under a slow burn of mutual torment. The Narrator is driven by his obsession to know whether Albertine has had a lesbian relationship. He is holding her imprisoned in her room as a sadist tortures his captive. She seems to delight in torturing him with her lies. In a sadomasochistic dance, they lie to each other as if lying is part of their intrinsic nature. The Narrator is driven by his need for "despotic possession" (C, vol. 2, p. 637), and Albertine appears to be a compulsive liar who simply cannot help herself.

In Book 6, *The Sweet Cheat Gone*, the Narrator's curiosity is aroused by a group of women. The "fair one" is Gilberte:

> The fair one had a rather more delicate, almost an invalid air, which appealed to me less. It was she nevertheless that was

responsible for my not contenting myself with glancing at them for a moment, but becoming rooted to the ground, staring at them ... I should doubtless have allowed them to disappear as I had allowed so many others, had not (at the moment when they passed by me) the fair one - was it because I was scrutinizing them so closely? - darted a stealthy glance at myself, than, having passed me and turning her head, a second glance which fired my blood. (SCG, vol. 2, p. 777)

A few pages later, Mme. de Guermantes relates Gilberte's version to the Narrator: "and later Mme. de Guermantes informed me that she [Gilberte] had told her, as something very odd and extraordinary, that I had followed her and brushed against her, mistaking her for a prostitute." (SCG, vol. 2, p. 786) The reader simply does not know who to believe. Should we believe the Narrator, Gilberte, or Mme. de Guermantes, or none of them?

This *leitmotific* thread of lying weaves these three characters together in a web that expands outward to include nearly all the characters we have met over the course of the novel. For the reader, the name "Gilberte" brings up memories of her mother, Odette, and her father, Charles Swann, who is the figurehead of the Méséglise Way. Odette reminds us of "the little phrase." The mention of Swann brings up memories of Vinteuil, the Verdurins, Elstir, Bergotte, and Cottard. Mme. de Guermantes recalls for us the huge family comprising the Guermantes Way, including such characters as M. de Charlus, Robert Saint-Loup, Mme. Villeparisis, and associated characters such as Morel and Jupien. Most importantly, we are reminded that the Méséglise Way and Guermantes Way were never that far apart.

Near the end of the novel the Narrator calls into question the veracity of everything he, the Narrator, has been telling us. The reader, therefore, may have been subject to a huge lie. In Book 7, *The Past Recaptured*, the Narrator is at Gilberte's home in Tansonville. He begins to read an account, written by the Goncourt brothers, of an evening at the Verdurins. (PR, vol. 2, pp. 881–87) The Narrator, and the reader, cannot help but notice that there is, at best, a slim resemblance between the Goncourts' account and that given by the Narrator.

Roger Shattuck claims that, in the Narrator's reading of the Goncourts' descriptions of a Verdurins' dinner party, Proust is parodying the Goncourts' "arty journalism."[194] Shattuck further claims that the purpose of this section of the novel is to raise the question of what is the function(s) of literature. The Narrator does not answer this question of function, but he does explain that he is interested in psychological generalizations and not in the actual interaction among the guests:

> Like the geometrician who, stripping things of their perceptible qualities, sees only their linear substratum, what people said escaped me because what interested me was not what they wanted to say, but the way they said it in so far as it revealed their characters or their ludicrous traits; or, rather, there was one thing which had always been the object of my investigations because it gave me a very special pleasure, and that was the point that two human beings had in common. . . . And thus the visible, re-producible charm of people escaped me because I no longer possessed the faculty of confining my attention to it, like the surgeon who, under the glistering whiteness of a woman's abdomen, sees the internal disease gnawing away their. . . . The result was that, when I came to put together all the notes I had been able to make on the guests at a dinner, the pattern of the lines I drew represented a collection of psychological generalizations in which the special interest of the guests' remarks occupied hardly any place. (*PR*, vol. 2, p. 888)

Proust now has taken the *leitmotif* of lying and elevated it to encompass the nature and function of literature. For the Narrator, literature does not describe reality as in a biography or a documentary. Rather, literature, and perhaps all art, aspires to describe the essence of reality. Thus, a particular lie at a particular moment said by particular words is not essential to grasp the reality that people, as part of our nature, lie.

---

[194] Shattuck, *Proust's Way*, p. 77. While Proust might be parodying the Goncourt brothers, he might also be showing that art does not merely describe a historical event, but also explores and discloses the psychology of an individual as that person perceives and understands a real or fictitious event.

Anti-Semitism and the Dreyfus Affair. [195, 196] Anti-Semitism permeates *In Search of,* so much so that it functions as a *leitmotif.* In *In Search of,* anti-Semitism reached its apex during the Dreyfus Affair.

The Dreyfus affair, "which now divided France from end to end" (*GW,* vol. 1, p. 928), had been "latent hitherto, . . . [now] awakened and grown to a positive fury." (*GW,* vol. 1, p. 896) The Dreyfus affair pitted the anti-Dreyfusards, who believed that Dreyfus was guilty of treason, against the Dreyfusards, who believed that Dreyfus was framed. The anti-Dreyfusard position was rooted in deep-seated anti-Semitism:

> [M. de Guermantes]: "By the way, do you know who is a red-hot supporter of Dreyfus? I give you a thousand guesses. My nephew Robert! I can tell you that, at the Jockey, when they heard of his goings on, there was a fine gathering of the clans, a regular hue and cry. And as he's coming up for election next week. . . ." "Of course," broke in the Duchess, "if they're all like Gilbert, who keeps on saying that all the Jews ought to be sent back to Jerusalem." (*GW,* vol. 1, pp. 883–84)

---

[195] France was, and still is, a very Catholic country with anti-Semitic roots that periodically broke ground. During Proust's life, anti-Semitism reached high water levels in the 1890s in what is known as the Dreyfus affair. Alfred Dreyfus (1859–1935), a Jewish captain in the French army, was falsely accused and convicted of passing military secrets to the Germans. (The military secret described the design of a newly developed gun.) His trial and subsequent life-term imprisonment on Devil's Island in 1894 split France into two factions: the government, pro-army, and Catholic anti-Dreyfusards and pro-republican and anticlerical Dreyfusards. Dreyfus was exonerated in a second trial in 1906 and reinstated into the military. In 1898 Émile Zola published his famous article entitled "J'accuse!" ("I Accuse!"), where he attacked the government and military of a cover-up. For his efforts, he was tried, found guilty, sentenced to one year in prison, and fined three thousand francs (the maximum penalty).

[196] Some French Wagnerites were anti-Dreyfusards and some were Dreyfusards. According to Alex Ross, "Circa 1900, anti-Jewishness was not widely considered one of his [Wagner] defining characteristics. . . . Wagner's cultural and political influence gyrated in so many different directions that no one ideology could possess him. Wagnerism was a phenomenon still growing in breadth and complexity." This changed with Houston Stewart Chamberlain (1855–1927). Ross continues, "This remarkable and repellent man, in whom superficial erudition mingled with profound intolerance, is essential to understanding Wagner's fate in the twentieth century. More than any other figure, he forms the bridge between Bayreuth and Nazi Germany." See Alex Ross, *Wagnerism,* pp. 247–49.

During a conversation between the Narrator and Swann, Swann reports that Gilbert, the Prince de Guermantes, would prefer to leave his tooth untreated and to have his house burn down rather than seek the help of a Jew:

> He [Prince de Guermantes] carries it [anti-Semitism] to such a point that when he was in the army and had a frightful toothache he preferred to grin and bear it rather than go to the only dentist in the district, who happened to be a Jew, and later on he allowed a wing of his castle which had caught fire to be burned to the ground, because he would have had to send for extinguishers to the place next door, which belongs to the Rothschilds. (GW, vol. 1, p. 1130)

Gilbert is not an isolated aberration. M. de Charlus opines that Jews were closer to being citizens of Judaea than that of France:

> "[I]t is not a bad idea, if you wish to learn about life," went on M. de Charlus when he had finished questioning me, "to include among your friends an occasional foreigner." I replied that Bloch was French. "Indeed," said M. de Charlus, "I took him to be a Jew." (GW, vol. 1, p. 922)

The anti-Semitism that had "grown to a positive fury" grew from fertile soil. Earlier seeds of anti-Semitism, like the embryonic form of *leitmotifs*,[197] were recognizable but in a seemingly benign form. For example, early in the novel, Marcel brings home a school friend, Block:

> It is true that my grandfather made out that, whenever I formed a strong attachment to any one of my friends, and brought him home with me, that friend was invariably a Jew; to which he would not have objected on principle—indeed his own friend Swann was of Jewish extraction-had he not found that the Jews whom I chose as friends were not usually of the best type. And so I was hardly ever able to bring a new friend home without my grandfather's humming the "O, God of our fathers" from *La Juive* . . . and after a few adroit questions

---

[197] Cooke, *An Introduction to* Der Ring des Nibelungen.

on points of detail, he would call out "On guard! on guard." (*SW*, vol.
1, p. 69)

Anti-Semite assertions were used to create or reestablish old bonds. Mme.
de Gallardon, trying to reestablish relations with her cousin Oriane,[198] the
Princesses de Laumes and the future Duchesse de Guermantes [I include the
speaker's name for clarity]:

> Mme. de Gallardon: "Tell me, have you seen your friend M. Swann?"
> Oriane: "No! my gracious Charles! I never knew he was here. Where
> is he? I must catch his eye."
> Mme. de Gallardon: "It's a funny thing that he should come to old
> Saint-Euverte's. . . ."
> Mme. de Gallardon went on. "Oh, I know the he's very clever,"
> meaning that by very cunning, "but that makes no difference: fancy a
> Jew here, and she the sister and sister-in-law of two Archbishops."
> Oriane: "I am ashamed to confess that I am not in the least shocked,"
> said the Princess des Laumes.
> Gallardon: "I know he's a converted Jew, and all that, and his parent
> and grandparents before him. But they do say that the converted
> ones are worse about their religion than the practicing ones, that it's
> all just a pretense; is that true, d'you think?" (*SW*, vol. 1, p. 257)

At the beach resort in Balbec, the Narrator becomes friends with a group
of young adolescent girls. Albertine, who later becomes the Narrator's lover,
states:

> Often we encountered Bloch's sisters, to whom I was obliged to
> bow since I had dined with their father. My new friends did not
> know them. "I am not allowed to play with Israelites," Albertine
> explained. Her way of pronouncing the word—"Issraelites" instead
> of "Izraelites"—would in itself have sufficed to shew, even if one had

---

[198] See *SW*, vol. 1, p. 257, and *GW*, vol. 1, pp. 1033–37, for explanations of the relationship between the
Parisian Guermantes and Mme. de Gallardon of the provincial Courvoisier line of the family.
Functioning like a *leitmotif*, our memories are returned to the drawing room of Mme. de Villeparisis in
SW, vol. 1, p. 257.

not heard the rest of the sentence, that it was no feeling of friendliness towards the chosen race that inspired these young Frenchwomen brought up in God-fearing homes, and quite ready to believe that the Jews were in the habit of massacring Christian children. (*WBG*, vol. 1, p. 677)

Like the slithering Tarnhelm *leitmotif* in *Götterdämmerung*, the recurring theme of anti-Semitism keeps rearing its ugly head. At one moment, Mme. de Marsantes appears to be the model of kindness, and at the next moment, reveals herself to be a model of bigotry when discussing the Dreyfus retrial. The Narrator tells us that Mme. de Marsantes was reported to be a perfect Christian, yet a few moments later, we hear from her own mouth a different tune:

> She [Mme. de Marsantes] never shrank from kissing a poor woman who was in trouble and would tell her to come up to the castle for a cartload of wood. She was, people said, the perfect Christian. . . . "I did indeed know her at one time," said Mme. de Marsantes. "I confess my faults. But I have decided not to know her any more. It seems she's one of the very worst of them, and makes no attempt to conceal it. Besides, we have all been too trusting, too hospitable. I shall never go near anyone of that race again. While we had old friends, country cousins, people of our own flesh and blood on whom we shut our doors, we threw them open to Jews. And now we see what thanks we get from them." (*GW*, vol. 1, pp. 896–97)[199]

Intelligence is not a shield from bigotry. Below, M. de Charlus, one of the more intelligent characters in the novel, rants over the fact that wealthy Jews seem to always live on streets that have Catholic names:

---

[199] Lest one thinks Mme. de Marsantes represents the Narrator's view, the Narrator provides the reader with his own opinion of Mme. de Marsantes anti-Semitism: "Among the Jews especially there were few whose parents and kinsfolk had not a warmth of heart, a breadth of mind in comparison with which Saint-Loup's mother and the Duc de Guermantes cut the poorest of figures by their sereness, their skin-deep religiosity which denounced only the most open scandals, their apology for a Christianity which led invariably (by the unexpected channel of a purely calculating mind) to an enormously wealthy marriage." (*GW*, vol. 1, p. 1010)

"But a Jew! However, I am not surprised; it comes from a curious instinct for sacrilege, peculiar to that race. As soon as a Jew has enough money to buy a place in the country he always chooses one that is called Priory, Abbey, Minster, Chantry. I had some business once with a Jewish official, guess where he lived: at Pont-l'Évêque. When he came to grief, he had himself transferred to Brittany, to Pont-l'Abbé. When they perform in Holy Week those indecent spectacles that are called 'the Passion,' half the audience are Jews, exulting in the thought that they are going to hang Christ a second time on the Cross, at least in effigy." (*CP*, vol. 2, p. 359)

Lest we think that the reversal of the Dreyfus case would have quieted the anti-Jewish voice, the Narrator tells us:

> But this was the moment when from the effects of the Dreyfus case there had arisen an anti-Semitic movement parallel to a more abundant movement towards the penetration of society by Israelites. The politicians had not been wrong in thinking that the discovery of the judicial error would deal a fatal blow to anti-Semitism. But provisionally at least a social anti-Semitism was on the contrary enhanced and exacerbated by it. (*SCG*, vol. 2, p. 786)

Like a bad song that cannot get out of our heads, the *leitmotif* of anti-Semitism keeps ringing in our ear. It puts an ugly layer of paint on so many of the characters in *In Search of*. However, Proust's characters are so multi-dimensional that a single character trait does not define them, nor totally color our attitude toward them. Nonetheless, the *leitmotif* of anti-Semitism does leave a stain on them.

Death. [200] Death and dying permeate *In Search of Lost Time*. To paraphrase the opening line of Leo Tolstoy's novel *Anna Karenina*, everyone dies, but

---

[200] Malcolm Bowie, *Proust among the Stars*, chapter 7, points out that death bookends *In Search of*. The novel begins with the Narrator facilitating between consciousness and unconsciousness, which Bowie analyzes as between life and death. The novel ends with many of the characters we met in their prime now in a condition of physical and mental decay.

everyone dies in their own way. When learning of the death of Swann, the Narrator tells us:

> The death of Swann had been a crushing blow to me at the time. The death of Swann! Swann, in this phrase, is something more than a noun in the possessive case. I mean by it his own particular death, the death allotted by destiny to the service of Swann. For we all talk of "death" for convenience, but there are almost as many different deaths as there are people. (C, vol. 2, p. 518)

The passage of time mercilessly carries each of us closer to our unique death. Although each death is unique, the experience of death is one we all share. To use musical metaphors, each individual's death is identified by an added note, a change in key, an altered tempo, all parts of the death *leitmotif* in life's musical score. There is, however, a common thread, a *leitmotif*, to nearly all the deaths that occur during this long novel. For the most part, no one cares. In most cases, the recurring sentiment when learning of someone's illness or death is either denial or a social inconvenience best avoided.

M. Dechambre, a member of the Verdurin clan for more than thirty years, has unexpectedly died. M. and Mme. Verdurin do not want to hear about it, not for emotional or sentimental reasons, but because Dechambre is no longer part of the "clan." He is gone and, therefore, to be forgotten:

> "Ah! Poor Dechambre!" he [Brichot] said, but in an undertone, in case Mme. Verdurin was within earshot. "It is terrible," replied M. Verdurin lightly. "So young," Brichot pursued the point. Annoyed at being detained over these futilities, M. Verdurin replied in a hasty tone and with an embittered groan, not of grief but of irritated impatience: "Why yes, of course, but what's to be done about it, it's no use crying over spilt milk, talking about him won't bring him back to life, will it?" and, his civility returning with his joviality: "Come along, my good Brichot, get your things off quickly. We have a bouillabaisse which mustn't be kept waiting." (CP, vol. 2, p. 213)

A few minutes later, upon overhearing people discussing Dechambre:

"What, are you still talking about Dechambre," said M. Verdurin, who had gone on ahead of us, and, seeing that we were not following him, had turned back. "Listen," he said to Brichot, "nothing is gained by exaggeration. The fact of his being dead is no excuse for making him out a genius, which he was not. He played well, I admit, and what is more, he was in his proper element here . . . I will go further, in the interest of his own reputation he has died at the right moment, he is done to a turn, as the demoiselles de Caen, grilled according to the incomparable recipe of Pampilles, are going to be, I hope, unless you keep us standing here all night. . . ." (*CP*, vol. 2, pp. 214–15)

The Duke and Duchess de Guermantes exhibit similar if not worse behavior. They are ready to leave their home to attend the Princesse de Guermantes's ball when they are confronted with two announcements of pending deaths.

First, the Duke learns that his first cousin, Amanien d'Osmond, who has been sick for some time, "had grown suddenly worse" and "was in his last agony." (*GW*, vol. 1, p. 1126) The Duke and Duchess's strategy to avoid this inconvenience is to give the servant the night off so that no announcement of their cousin's death could reach them. The Duke, ranting that no one is inquiring about his health after having eaten too much mutton with béarnaise sauce, continues with: "'However, that doesn't make people come to inquire for me as they do for dear Amanien. We do too much inquiring. It only tires him. We must let him have room to breathe. They're killing the poor fellow by sending round to him all the time.'" (*GW*, vol. 1, p. 1135)

Second, Swann, a longtime friend of the Duke and Duchess, informs them why he cannot travel with them to Italy. "'I shall then have been dead for several months. According to the doctors I consulted last winter, the thing I've got—which may, for that matter, carry me off at any moment-won't in any case leave me more than three or four months to live, and even that is a generous estimate,' replied Swann with a smile, while the footman opened the glazed door of the hall to let the Duchess out." (*GW*, vol. 1, p. 1139)

The Duchess replies:

"What's that you say?" cried the Duchess, stopping for a moment on her way to the carriage, and raising her fine eyes, their melancholy blue clouded by uncertainty. Placed for the first time in her life between two duties as incompatible as getting into her carriage to go out to dinner and shewing pity of a man who was about to die,[201] she could find nothing in the code of conventions that indicated the right line to follow, and, not knowing which to choose, felt it better to make a show of not believing that the latter alternative need be seriously considered, so as to follow the first, which demanded of her at the moment less effort, and thought that the best way of settling the conflict would be to deny that any existed. "You're joking," she said to Swann. (*GW*, vol. 1, p. 1139)

The Duke responds in kind:

And so it was simply from good breeding and good fellowship that, after politely shewing us out, he cried 'from off stage,' in a stentorian voice from the porch to Swann, who was already in the courtyard: 'You, now, don't let yourself be taken in by the doctors' nonsense, damn them. They're donkeys. You're as strong as the Pont Neuf. You'll live to bury us all!' (*GW*, vol. 1, p. 1141)

Soon after Swann's death his widow Odette remarries, and his daughter Gilberte drops "Swann" from her name. Both Odette and Gilberte distance themselves from their association with Swann. Swann does not become part of history; Swann is erased from history.

In some cases, someone's death is a sort of curiosity to explain a change of routine. The Narrator relates a story told to him by a park bathroom employee about a person she had observed for the past eight years. The effect of this person's death on the attendant is no stronger than if someone had removed an indiscriminate shrub:

"For the last eight years, do you follow me, every day God has made, regularly on the stroke of three he's been here always polite,

---

[201] Swann had visited the Duchess almost every day for the past twenty-five years. (*SCG*, vol. 2, p. 790)

never saying one word louder than another, never making any mess; and he stays half an hour and more to read his papers and do his little jobs. Then there was one day he didn't come. I never noticed it at the time, but that evening all of a sudden I said to myself: 'Why, that gentleman never came today; perhaps he's dead!'" (GW, vol. 1, p. 937)

The Narrator's aunt Léonie warranted a few sentences, but no outward expression of sorrow: "during that autumn when we had to come to Combray to settle the division of my aunt Léonie's estate; for she had died at last leaving both parties among her neighbours triumphant in the fact of her demise. . . ." (SW, vol. 1, p. 117)

Princess Sherbatoff, a member of the Russian aristocracy, gets just a clause. "Just as we were about to ring the bell we were overtaken by Saniette who informed us that princess Sherbatoff had died at six o'clock, and added that he had not at first recognized us." (C, vol. 2, p. 536)

M. Verdurin's death is not even mentioned by name. "And as a matter of fact, shortly after her husband's death, Mme. Verdurin had married the penniless old Duc de Duras, who had thereby made her a cousin of the Prince de Guermantes. The old Duc de Duras dies two years later." (PR, vol. 2, p. 1056) This marriage elevated Mme. Verdurin from the bourgeoisie to a low rung on the aristocratic ladder.

The Narrator's good friend and husband of Gilberte, Robert Saint-Loup, died a heroic death at the front line. His death, however, is barely acknowledged by his wife or relatives.

Bergotte, the writer, experienced a personal redemption at his moment of death upon seeing "a little patch of yellow" on Vermeer's *View of Delft*. Bergotte is nearly blind, very poor, and at the point of being forgotten. The Narrator describes Bergotte's death during his visit to a Vermeer exhibition at a local museum:

At last he came to the Vermeer which he remembered as more striking, more different from anything else that he knew, but in which, thanks to the critic's article, he remembered for the first time some small figures in blue, that the ground was pink, and finally the precious substance of the tiny patch of yellow wall. His giddiness increased; he fixed his eyes, like a child upon a yellow butterfly which it is trying to catch, upon the precious little patch of wall. "That is how I ought to have written," he said.

He repeated to himself: "Little patch of yellow wall, with a sloping room, little patch of yellow wall. . . ." A fresh attack beat him down; he rolled from the divan to the floor, as visitors and attendants came hurrying to his assistance. He was dead. (C, vol. 2, p. 509)

Bergotte's death was in a museum surrounded by strangers. Even the papers reported the day of his death incorrectly. However, his public redemption occurred after his death with a resurgence in popularity of his books. He died alone but lives again through his art. "They buried him, but all through the night of mourning, in the lighted windows, his books arranged three by three kept watch like angels with outspread wings and seemed, for him who was no more, the symbol of his resurrection." (C, vol. 2, p. 510)

Albertine, the Narrator's mistress, died in a horse-riding accident. The Narrator receives a telegram informing him of her death: "My poor friend, our little Albertine is no more. . . . " (SCG, vol. 2, p. 716) His response quickly becomes a continuation of his obsessive jealousy, rather than an homage to Albertine's life. Rather than feeling sorrow for her death, much of the Narrator's physical and emotional energies are spent trying to determine whether she had lesbian relations during their relationship. His preference would be to forget her and thereby be unburdened by any residual jealousy. It appears that he did not even attend her funeral. (SCG, vol. 2, p. 777)

We find a glimpse of normal emotions, at least on the theoretical plane, in the case of the famous painter Elstir:

> I had supposed Elstir to be a modest man, but I realized my mistake on seeing his face cloud with melancholy when, in a little speech of thanks, I uttered the word 'fame.' Men who believe that their work will last—as was the case with Elstir—form the habit of placing that work in a period when they themselves will have crumbled into dust. And thus, by obliging them to reflect on their own extinction, the thought of fame saddens them because it is inseparable from the thought of death. (WBG, vol. 1, p. 634)

No person is loved more by the Narrator than his grandmother. However, it takes him almost two years to experience the emotional impact of her death. The Narrator, here speaking as an older man preparing to write his novel, recalls how he, as a young man, missed clues that his grandmother was dying. The Narrator recalls his grandmother returning with some brandy for him:

> My grandmother, who was rather flushed, seemed "put out" about something, and her eyes had a look of weariness and dejection. "I shall leave you alone now, and let you get the good of this improvement," she said, rising suddenly to go. I detained her, however, for a kiss, and could feel on her cold cheek something moist, but did not know whether it was the dampness of the night air through which she had just passed. Next day she did not come to my room until evening, having had, she told me, to go out. (*WBG*, vol. 1, p. 380)

Later, during a casual conversation with his grandmother, the Narrator makes the almost cliché comment that "'I shouldn't be able to live without you.' His grandmother replies: 'But you mustn't speak like that;' her voice was troubled. 'We must harden our hearts more than that, you know. Or what would become of you if I went away on a journey. But I hope that you would be quite sensible and quite happy'." (*WBG*, vol. 1, p. 551)

A bit later, during their stay at the hotel at Balbec:

> When I came back in the afternoon to be alone with her for a little I was told that she was not in the hotel; or else she would shut herself up with Françoise for endless confabulations which I was not permitted to interrupt. (*WBG*, vol. 1, p. 594)

In one of the Narrator's few displays of emotions, other than jealousy, and after the passage of nearly two years, the Narrator emotionally comes to the full awareness of his grandmother's death:

> . . . it was not until this moment, more than a year after her burial, because of that anachronism which so often prevents the calendar of facts from corresponding to that of our feelings, that I became conscious that she was dead. (*CP*, vol. 2, p. 113)

During the Narrator's belated grieving over his grandmother's death,[202] he recalls the hurt he caused her during their earlier visit to Balbec. His grandmother wanted to have a photograph taken of herself to create a lasting image for her grandchild.[203] To hide her illness, she dressed herself in her finest attire:

> When, some days after our dinner with the Blochs, my grandmother told me with a joyful air that Saint-Loup had just been asking her whether before he left Balbec, she would not like him to take a photograph of her, and when I saw that she had put on her nicest dress on purpose, and was hesitating between several of her best hats, I felt a little annoyed by this childishness, which surprised me coming from her. (*WBG*, vol. 1, p. 593)

Much later, the Narrator recalls this scene with regret over his hurtful behavior:

> . . . on the day when Saint-Loup had taken my grandmother's photograph and I, unable to conceal from her what I thought of the ridiculous childishness of the coquetry with which she posed for him, with her wide-brimmed hat, in a flattering half light, had allowed myself to mutter a few inpatient sounding words, which I had perceived from a contraction of her features, had carried, had pieced her; it was I whose heart they were rending now that there was no longer possible, ever again, the consolation of a thousand kisses. (*CP*, vol. 2, p. 115)

---

[202] Her actual death occurs in *GW*, vol. 1, pp. 938–64, and is described in objective medical detail.
[203] Neither the reader nor the Narrator understands the full significance of the photograph until Françoise relates the events to the Narrator. See *CP*, vol. 2, pp. 127–28.

The Narrator recalls when, following his beloved grandmother's stroke on the Champs-Élysées, he sought treatment from a physician known to their family. The physician examined her, but clearly viewed the situation as a social inconvenience. The physician was more concerned with being late for a dinner party than treating his grandmother's medical condition.

Toward the end of *In Search of*, the Narrator is reflecting on the general phenomenon of death, particularly among the elderly:

> And for people of the same age and social standing as the deceased, death had lost much of its weird significance. Moreover, one sent every day to get news of so many people *in articulo mortis*, some of whom had recovered while others had succumbed, that one no longer remembered exactly whether a certain person whom one never had an opportunity to see had gotten well, or had died, of his inflammation of the lungs.... death had become a social formula which described a person approximately and, without indicating by the tone of one's voice that this incident was the end of everything, one would say, "But you forget that So-and so is dead"—in the same way as one would have said, "He has been decorated" (the attribute is different but no more important), "He is a member of the Academy" or—which amounted to the same thing, since it prevented attendance at social functions—"He has gone south for the winter; he has been ordered to the mountains." (PR, vol. 2, p. 1073)

In Search of includes several other scenes of dying and death. Each is unique. However, for the most part, each death shares the common characteristic of being met with social indifference.

Transformation and Metamorphosis. Wagner's *leitmotifs* characteristically evolve, develop, transform, and change into something different but related. The music during Wotan and Loge's descent into Nibelheim at the beginning of scene iii of *Das Rheingold* and two transformation scenes in acts 1 and 3 in *Parsifal* are three of many examples of Wagner's skill at metamorphosing one space and time into another space and time.[204] Proust does something similar, not with music but with characters. Some transform into something better, some into something worse, and some not so much.

Near the end of the novel, after a long absence, the Narrator returns to Society. Here, he observes many of the people he had known for decades. Some he recognizes, but most he does not. The Narrator tells us:

> . . . it seemed to me that the human being can undergo metamorphoses as complete as those of certain insects. I felt as if I were looking into the instructive show case of a natural history museum at the swift and certain evolution of the characteristics of an insect and, before this soft chrysalis, which did not move so much as it vibrated. . . . (*PR*, vol. 2, p. 1032)

Mme. Verdurin, a spiteful and very unpleasant person, rises from the bourgeoisie to the highest of Society, the Faubourg Saint-Germain.[205] Although she undergoes a social transformation insofar as the "social status" of her salon quests are concerned, her character and distasteful behavior are unchanged. She is a very disagreeable person. As a literary *leitmotif*, Mme. Verdurin is easy to identify from start to finish.

Morel is among the slimiest lowlifes within an already contaminated reservoir of characters. Morel is a superb violinist (which may be Proust commenting on the mistake of equating a person's character with their art) but a cruel person, almost to the point of being inhuman. Yet through a twist of fate, after World War I, he was awarded the military medal, the *Croix de Guerre*,[206] despite being forced to return to the front after deserting. The Narrator suggests that this medal could propel Morel into a political career. (*PR*, vol. 2, pp. 891–

---

[204] See Wagner's October 29, 1859, letter to Mathilde Wesendonck, where he says that his greatest skill is in the art of transition: "I should now like to call my most delicate and profound art the art of transition, for the whole fabric of my art is made up of such transitions. . . ." Stewart Spencer and Barry Milligan, *Selected Letters of Richard Wagner*, translated and edited by Stewart Spencer and Barry Millington (New York: W.W. Horton & Co, 1987), p. 475.

[205] At the end of the novel, the Society of the Faubourg Saint-Germain, a relic of a prior age, is morphing either out of existence or into something very different before the Narrator's eyes.

[206] The *Croix de Guerre* medal is given to soldiers who distinguished themselves by acts of heroism.

92) If he were identified by a musical *leitmotif*, his would begin with a sardonic sound and transform into an ironic one.

M. de Charlus transforms, or rather, degenerates throughout the story. Once a larger-than-life character with unequal verbosity and intelligence, the Narrator reports that M. de Charlus passed through World War I in a sadomasochistic brothel. In this brothel M. de Charlus paid fifty francs to be beaten with whips while chained to a bed. M. de Charlus had become unrecognizable, he was a different person. After the war, this proud and articulate person had a stroke resulting in aphasia:

> It may be that he had up till then dyed his hair and now had been ordered to avoid the fatigue involved, but it seemed rather as if his illness, acting like a chemical precipitant, had rendered glisteningly visible all the metal saturating the stands of his hair and beard, which flung it into the air like a geysers of pure silver, giving to the dethroned, aged prince the Shakespearean majesty of a King Lear. (*PR*, vol. 2, p. 986)

Bergotte, an acclaimed and famous writer during his prime years, dies nearly blind and virtually unknown. The Narrator tells us that Bergotte acquired a second fame after his death. As a literary *leitmotif*, Bergotte flowers, withers, and then flowers again. Further examples of significant characters that transform include Berma and Elstir. Berma is the famous actress, who will die in poverty accompanied only by her selfish, pathetic, social-climbing daughter and son-in-law. Elstir is the painter, once the jokester at the Verdurins, who becomes famous, his paintings highly prized.

Odette and M. Vinteuil experience two very different trajectories. Odette emerges almost from nothing. She is introduced to the reader by descriptions rather than by name, and she ends in a similar nameless position, a feeble old lady: "The reason I did not recognize her at once was not that she had changed so much but that she had changed so little." (*PR*, vol. 2, p. 1051) She merely occupies a piece of space and time and then is gone. Odette stands in stark contrast to M. Vinteuil. In the novel, M. Vinteuil is alive for a short time and appears to be as insignificant as the ground on which he treads. M. Vinteuil, however, continues to live beyond his death through his art. Odette morphs into dust; M. Vinteuil morphs into an eternal work of art.

Odette. Early in the Overture section of *Swann's Way*, we learn that, before the Narrator was born, Swann's wife, Odette, had never been invited to the Narrator's parents' house. She is referred to in the Combray community not as "Odette," but as "his unfortunate marriage" (*SW*, vol. 1, pp. 11, 18) and "that wretched wife of his who lives with a certain Monsieur de Charlus, as all Combray knows." (*SW*, vol. 1, p. 26)[207]

In the second chapter of *Swann's Way*, Combray, Odette still remains nameless. The Narrator, at a young age, pays an unexpected visit to his Uncle Adolphe, where Odette is described as a disembodied "woman's voice," with an unknown marital status ("Madame" or "Mademoiselle" ponders the Narrator), and finally as "the lady in pink"[208]: "'I have not met his father, dear,' said the lady in pink, bowing her head slightly. . . .'" (*SW*, vol. 1, p. 58)[209] Early in the next section, Swann in Love, we meet her at the Verdurins as Mme. de Crécy and finally by "her Christian name, Odette." (*SW*, vol. 1, p. 144)

As her character develops, we discover that Odette is a well-employed courtesan who has seduced Swann. Swann is a highly sophisticated person won over by Odette, despite Swann not finding her physically attractive, "having poor taste in music and no interest in the arts, history or anything Swann held in value" (*SW*, vol. 1, p. 188) or possessing in her linguistic arsenal anything more than the commonest courtesan formulas or clichés:

> "Why I have never anything to do. I am always free and I always
> will be free if you want me. At whatever hour of the day or night it

---

[207] Like so much idle gossip, it is unclear whether Charlus and Odette are friends (*WBG*, vol. 1, p. 571) or prior lovers. (*C*, vol. 2, p. 588)

[208] Proust is a master of creating correspondences, or what can be called *leitmotifs*. Soon after the Narrator meets Odette's daughter Gilberte, Gilberte sends the Narrator a "parcel tied with pink bows. . . ." (*SW*, vol. 1, p. 307)

[209] *Leitmotifs* abound in almost every word. Here the "lady in pink" is present in Uncle Adolphe's home (*SW*, vol. 1, p. 58) and on p. 169 we find "Odette had received him [Swann] in a tea-gown of pink silk, which left her neck and arms bare." The "tea-gown of pink silk" reminds us of the Narrator's encounter with "the lady in pink" some fifteen years after the events described in the Swann in Love chapter of *Swann's Way*.

may suit you to see me, just send for me, and I shall be only to delighted to come. Will you do that? Do you know what I should really like—to introduce you to Mme. Verdurin where I go every evening. Just fancy my finding you there, and thinking that it was a little for my sake that you had gone." (*SW*, vol. 1, p. 152)[210]

She is a gold digger *par excellence*.[211] Despite all her superficialities, perhaps because of her superficialities and the techniques of deceit and mendacity, she climbs the social ladder:

Odette had looked on, impassive, at this scene; but when the door had closed behind Saniette, she had forced the normal expression of her face down, as the saying is, by several pegs, so as to bring herself on to the same level of vulgarity as Forcheville; her eyes had sparkled with a malicious smile of congratulations upon his audacity, of ironical pity for the poor wretch who had been its victim; she had darted at him a look of complicity in the crime which so clearly implied: "That's finished him off or I'm very much mistaken. Did you see what a fool he looked?" (*SW*, vol. 1, p. 213)

Once Odette had captured Swann, she could humiliate him at will:

. . . and Swann felt himself suddenly filled with an enormous and unbreakable mass which pressed on the inner walls of his consciousness until he was fain to burst asunder; for Odette had said casually, watching him with a malicious smile: "Forcheville is going for a fine trip at Whitsuntide. He's going to Egypt!" and Swann had at once understood that this meant: "I am going to Egypt at

---

[210] *In Search of* is filled with parallels. For example, Albertine says the same words to Marcel as Odette says to Swann. The pairs Swann/Odette, the Narrator/Albertine, Saint-Loup/Rachel are very close to mirror images. They all share the same traits: the women: flirting, contemporaneous affairs, and lying; the men: jealously, need to possess, their own form of lying, and psychological self-torment. Swann and the Narrator's interest in train timetables illustrate their connection early in the novel. See volume 1, pp. 225 and 295.

[211] Beginning with her first husband, Comte de Crécy, then to the intellectual and wealthy Swann, then to the foolish, yet wealthy boor, Comte de Forcheville, Odette knows how to find and keep herself in the money.

Whitsuntide with Forcheville." And, in fact, if a few days later, Swann began: "about that trip that you told me you were going to take with Forcheville," she would answer carelessly: "yes, my dear boy, we're starting on the 19th; we'll send you a 'view' of the Pyramids." (*SW*, vol. 1, p. 272)

Odette recognizes that she is not getting any younger and decides it is time to marry Swann. The first step in Odette's strategy is to get pregnant. After doing so, she moves in with Swann, blackmails him for more money by threatening to take their child away (Gilberte), and in due course marries Swann. (*SW*, vol. 1, 356f)[212] While Swann's courtship and marriage to Odette resulted in his self-imposed withdrawal from Society, Odette quickly adapts to the lifestyle and social graces of wealthy Society.[213] As Swann continues in his tragic descent, she begins her ascent to social fame as measured by those who attend her dinner parties.

She begins her ascent on a low rung. Responding to a query by the Narrator's mother, M. de Norpois replies:

> "Why, my dear lady, it is a house which (or so it struck me) is especially attractive to gentlemen. There were several married men there last night, but their wives were all, as it happened, unwell, and so had not come with them," replied the Ambassador, with a mordancy sheathed in good humour, casting on each of us a glance the gentleness and discretion of which appeared to be tempering while in reality they deftly intensified its malice. (*SW*, vol. 1, p. 357)

Odette adapts quickly. She changes her hair, her makeup, and her furniture:

---

[212] Why does Swann marry Odette? The Narrator tells us that it was Swann's aim for his daughter, Gilberte, to enter the Guermantes' Society. (*SW*, vol. 1, pp. 360–61)

[213] "[S]o thoroughly had Swann trained her in reserve. She had none the less acquired all the manners of polite society, and however smart, however stately the lady might be, Mme. Swann was invariably a match for her . . . it would have been hard to say, looking at them both, which of the two was the aristocrat." (*SW*, vol. 1, pp. 413)

For since Mme. Swann had picked up from a friend whose opinion she valued the word 'dowdy'-which had opened to her a new horizon because it denoted precisely those things which a few years earlier she had considered 'smart'-all those things had, one after another, followed into retirement the gilded trellis that had served as background to her chrysanthemums, innumerable boxes of sweets from Giroux's. . . . Moreover in the artistic disorder, the studio-like confusion of the rooms, whose walls were still painted in somber colours which made them as different as possible from the white-enameled drawing-rooms in which, a little later, you were to find Mme. Swann installed, the Far East recoiled more and more before the invading forces of the eighteenth century; and the cushions which, to make me "comfortable." Mme. Swann heaped up and buffeted into position behind my back were sprinkled with Louis XV garlands and not, as of old, with Chinese dragons. (*SW*, vol. 1, p. 468)

Odette rises almost to the top of the Faubourg Saint-Germain Society. Over time, all the "smart" people attend her salon, and she is invited to all the "smart" houses, save that of the Oriane, the Duchesse de Guermantes. But unlike Swann, Robert Saint-Loup, and the Narrator, Odette never realizes the vacuity of Society, of her aspirations, and of herself.

After a long absence from the narrative, during which time Odette's two respective husbands, Swann and Forcheville, died, we discover that Odette's daughter, Gilberte, has very little affection or use for her mother. In addition, Odette must now ingratiate herself to Gilberte's husband, Robert Saint-Loup, for money.

As time passes, it becomes clear that she has created nothing and leaves nothing. After speaking with Odette in her twilight years, the Narrator ponders:

> . . . I now thought the minutes spent with her interminable because of the impossibility of finding anything to say to her and so I moved away. Alas, she was not destined to remain long as she then was. Less than three years later, at a reception given by Gilberte, I was to see her, not in her second childhood but a little feeble-minded, no longer able to hide under an expressionless mask what she was thinking—"thinking" is putting it too strongly:

feeling, rather-shaking her head, pursing her lips, shrugging her shoulders at each sensation that came to her, as a drunken man would do, or a child. . . . (*PR*, vol. 2, p. 1054)

Being invited into Society had been Odette's sole focus. And to her credit, she succeeded in her goal, but her goal was vacuous. As a musical *leitmotif*, her story went from major to minor to a single note played very softly. Odette will disappear from history. She offered nothing, she gave nothing, she leaves nothing, and so she becomes nothing. Time devoured her.

We see a different story with M. Vinteuil. In musical terms, Vinteuil's *leitmotif* morphs from minor to major, from soft to loud, from the melancholy key of D minor to the bright C major.

Vinteuil. In the Overture and Combray sections of *Swann's Way*, we learn quite a bit about M. Vinteuil, yet he seems to be an innocuous character; there appears to be nothing special about him.

M. Vinteuil is an elderly neighbor of Swann. (*SW*, vol. 1, p. 19) He condemns Swann for a "most unsuitable marriage." He is very conservative in terms of manners: ". . . M. Vinteuil, who held very strict views on 'the deplorable untidiness' of young people." M. Vinteuil has a problematic daughter who is always accompanied by an older girl "with an evil reputation." We also learn that he died of a broken heart from his wife's death and his daughter's wanton ways. (*SW*, vol. 1, pp. 85–86, 113) Furthermore, he had been the music teacher for the Narrator's grandmother's sisters. In addition, he composed music that he does not play in public.

In these opening pages, we discovered one more seemingly incidental detail about M. Vinteuil. Swann, who was interested in learning the history of a particular piece of music and had been meaning to ask M. Vinteuil whether a relative or someone he knew with the same last name had composed this piece of music. (*SW*, vol. 1, p. 115) Later, while at a party at the Verdurins, Swann was discussing the recent publication of "Vinteuil's" sonata that had caused a great stir among the most advanced school of musicians, but was still unknown to the general public:

"I know someone, quite well, called Vinteuil," said Swann, thinking of the old music-master at Combray who had taught my [the Narrator's] grandmother's sisters.

"Perhaps that's the man!" cried Mme. Verdurin.

"Oh, no!" Swann burst out laughing. "If you had ever seen him for a moment you wouldn't put the question." (*SW*, vol. 1, p. 163)

That piece of music included the famous "little phrase" in the andante movement of the sonata in F sharp for piano and violin. (*SW*, vol. 1, p. 157 and p. 162) The "little phrase" becomes for Swann and Odette "the national anthem of their love." (*SW*, vol. 1, p. 167) For Vinteuil, it is the beginning of his immortalization.

Although Vinteuil never learns of it, that "little phrase" within the sonata had evolved into a septet and had become his instrument to defeat the corrosive effect of time. After his death, his daughter and her friend assembled his unorganized notes and developed the sonata into a septet that was first performed at the Verdurins': "'I understand that an unknown work of Vinteuil is to be performed by excellent artists. . . .' exclaimed Saniette, a member of the Verdurin clan." (*C*, vol. 2, p. 537)

The playing of the septet motivates the Narrator's longest analysis of any work of art. His analysis is a dense ten-page section found in Book 5, *The Captive*, vol. 2, pp. 553–63. We are in the Verdurins' drawing room for a concert of a selection of Vinteuil's unpublished work. The Narrator describes the experience of hearing the septet:

[A]ll of a sudden, I found myself in the midst of this music that was novel to me, right in the heart of Vinteuil's sonata; and, more marvelous than any maiden, the little phrase, enveloped, harnessed in silver, glittering with brilliant efforts of sound, as light and soft as silken scarves, came towards me, recognizable in this new guise. My joy at having found it again was enhanced by the accent, so friendlily familiar, which it adopted in addressing me, so persuasive, so simple, albeit without dimming the shimmering beauty with which it was resplendent. Its intention, however, was this time merely to shew me the way, of the sonata, for this was an unpublished work of Vinteuil in which he had merely amused himself. . . . (C, vol. 2, p. 553)

Within those ten pages, the Narrator bathes us in the joy of experiencing "this new masterpiece," "at once ineffable and piercing." The Narrator contemplates: "One would have said that, reincarnate, the composer lived for all time in his music; one could feel the joy with which he was choosing the colour of some sound, harmonizing it with the rest." (C, vol. 2, p. 556) The Narrator describes the experience as "[I]t was an ineffable joy which seemed to come from paradise . . . a thing that I would never forget." (C, vol. 2, p. 561) The Narrator continues:

> Then this phrase broke up, was transformed, like the little phrase in the sonata, and became the mysterious appeal of the start. . . . In the end the joyous motive was left triumphant; it was no longer an almost anxious appeal addressed to an empty sky, it was an ineffable joy which seemed to come from paradise. . . . (C, vol. 2, p. 561)

We are reminded of the Narrator's descriptions of Wagner's creative spirit: "I could hear him exult, invite me to share his joy, I could hear ring out all the louder the immortally youthful laugh and the hammer-blows of Siegfried. . . ." (C, vol. 2, p. 491); of the joy the Narrator experiences upon tasting the tea and madeleine cake, he waxes: "Whence could it have come to me, this all-powerful joy?" (SW, vol. 1, p. 34)

Unlike Odette, who is dead to those around her and to history even before she dies, Vinteuil, who dies early in the novel, continues to live as art. In an important sense, the name "Vinteuil" transforms from a mortal person to an immortal work of art, in this case, into music.

In *In Search of*, Vinteuil defeats the ravaging onslaught of time in two ways. First, through his music that continues to be played. And second, a statue of him is erected under the patronage of the Minister of Education. (C, vol. 2, p. 564) What matters, the Narrator tells us, is not the person, not his idiosyncrasies, morals, pretentions, or personal foibles, but his art. The disagreeable aspects of a person's life should in no way distract "from the value of life, which produces men of such talent and which is to be found quite as truly in the works of Vinteuil, Elstir, and Bergotte." (PR, vol. 2, p. 890)

The name "Odette" appears throughout the novel. At the end of the novel, when we read her name, we are transported back in time before the Narrator was born, when Odette was Swann's mistress. She went on to have stunning clothes, a beautiful house, and exquisite dinner parties. Through her we recall a great deal of the novel. Yet of her, after her death, all we can say is "So what, who cares?" At best she was a supporting cast member because she left us with nothing that lasted beyond the time she was alive.

The name "Vinteuil" also appears throughout the novel. His reference changes from the person to his music, from decaying flesh and blood to immortal sounds. The first thing that comes to mind when we read or hear "Vinteuil" is not anything about his life or person, but rather the ethereal "little phrase," the music that was "their national anthem of their love." "Vinteuil" is a *leitmotif* like no other. Metaphorically, he begins as a quiet note and gradually transforms into a septet and almost into an orchestra.

This "loss of the person" is characteristic of any great artist or really any world-changing individual. Over time her personal history recedes into historic and cultural memory. First 50 percent, then 90 percent, then nearly 100 percent of the particulars of her life is replaced by her historic significance.[214]

This historic transformation will occur with Wagner. In decades to come, the details of Wagner's life will likely be of scholarly interest alone. The public will forget the name of his first wife (Minna), his connection to Liszt (father-in-law), the name of his second wife (Cosima), his muse for *Tristan and Isolde* (Mathilde Wesendonck), his determination to build the Festspielhaus in Bayreuth, and even his tenuous connection to Hitler (Wagner died before Hitler was born). But Wagner's operas will not be forgotten for as long as orchestras and opera houses exist.

---

[214] The question whether a proper name denotes an object or is a set of descriptions is a central question of twentieth-century philosophy. This question has been analyzed by philosophers of language including Bertrand Russell, Gottlob Frege, Ludwig Wittgenstein, John Searle, and Saul Kripke. The debate is laid out in Kripke's 1980 book *Naming and Necessity*. The Narrator appears to endorse the description concept of the self: "I was not one man only, but the steady advance hour after hour of an army in close formation, in which there appeared, according to the moment, impassioned men, indifferent men, jealous men-jealous men no two of whom were jealous of the same woman." (*SCG*, vol. 2, p. 726) Kripke disagrees with this position. He argues that proper names denote a specific object to which different actual or possible descriptions are ascribed.

d.   Endless Melody[215]

In Search of is almost 1.3 million French words (1,267,069), twice the length of *War and Peace*. It includes exceptionally long sentences, one of which is 958 English words (vol. 2, pp. 13–15) and another is 599 words (vol. 1, p. 6). Two other sentences are over 400 words (477 and 426, respectively). How does Proust hold together these endless sentences?[216] To begin answering this question we need to return to the master, Richard Wagner.

In Wagner's operas, an endless melody is a long segment of continuous music where the listener perceives an endless flow of audibly coherent music. For example, in *Götterdämmerung*, Siegfried's eight-minute "Funeral March" is a long stretch of music that is not a traditional melody as in the Haydn-Mozart tradition. Yet, it has an identifiable unified sound;[217] one needs to hear only a few notes to recognize it as Siegfried's "Funeral March." The musical *leitmotifs*, which constitute Wagner's endless melody, create the coherence within the melody. Each segment flows seamlessly into the next, held together by the threads of *leitmotific* segments.

Proust creates the sense of an "endless melody" through a multitude of literary techniques. The first, and perhaps most obvious to anyone who has made it through to the end of the novel, is when the Narrator decides to write a book, ostensibly the one we just read. Thus, we are asked to embark on this endless journey of rereading the novel we just have finished.

Embedded in this perpetual cycle is Proust's narrative technique of having the protagonist simultaneously speaking in two distinct time periods: the person describing the events in the present tense, as well as describing the events in the

---

[215] For an unmatched example of a literary endless melody see M. de Charlus's encounter with the Narrator in their six-page, one-paragraph exchange (*GW*, vol. 1, pp. 1109–15). It is not an example of stream of consciousness or internal monologue but more like a jazz riff. One is reminded of Wotan's Farewell to Brünnhilde in its intensity and directness at the end of *Die Walküre*, an opera Charlus refers to on p. 1111.

[216] Another Proustian feature is to delay completing a thought. For example, in *GW*, vol. 1, p. 1023, the Narrator informs us "Her friendliness sprang from two causes." We learn the second "cause" seven pages later on p. 1030.

[217] Although many shun labeling *leitmotifs*, labels assist the hearer identify and refer to the particular section of music or "melody." Siegfried's "Funeral March" includes, but is not exhausted by, the following *leitmotifs*: Death chords, suffering, Wälsung, Peace, Sieglinde, Love, Sword, Siegfried, Hero, Brünnhilde, Alberich's Curse, and Tyranny. See Monte Stone, The Ring *Disc.*

past tense. These two perspectives merge into a single *je* or "I."[218] The effect of this doubling technique is to fuse past and present time. This merging can be described either as outside of time or as endlessly in the present moment.

Proust creates another "endless melody" literary technique by providing multiple possible motivations for a person's actions, or explanations for a specific event. Since the Narrator believes we cannot know a person's motivation, he often connects a series of explanations by an "or." The problem, from the reader's perspective, is that the sentence can seem endless. The result is that the reader can lose sight of the subject. Below are three illustrations of this technique; two are easy and the third is more difficult to follow.

First, the two easy illustrations. Here we find a physician examining the Narrator's grandmother. The Narrator provides four possible explanations for the physician's action of looking at his grandmother, instead of "sounding her chest":

> Instead of sounding her chest, fixing on her steadily his wonderful eyes, in which there was perhaps the illusion that he was making a profound scrutiny of his patient, **or** the desire to give her the illusion, which seemed spontaneous but must be mechanically produced, **or** else not to let her see that he was thinking of something quite different, **or** simply to obtain the mastery over her, he began talking about Bergotte. (*GW*, vol. 1, p. 931, emphasis added)

The second illustration is similar in structure, but uses a series of metaphors. The situation takes place toward the end of the novel. The Narrator is trying to recognize an old friend by his laugh:

> When the laugh stopped, I tried to recognize my friend but, **like** Ulysses in the *Odyssey* throwing himself on his mother's dead body **or like** a medium trying in vain to get from an apparition some reply that will identify it, **or like** the visitor at an electrical exhibition who cannot believe that the voice which comes back to him so

---

[218] Roger Shattuck, *Proust's Way: A Field Guide* to In Search of Lost Time, p. 17. Also see pp. 168–69 for a diagram illustrating how, seen from the perspective of the protagonist, his life is comprised of a lot of wasteful empty wanderings, but from the perspective of the Narrator those same wonderings reveal meaningful experiences.

perfectly from the phonograph has not, just the same, been spontaneously uttered by someone else, I was no longer able to recognize my friend. (PR, vol 2, p. 1049, emphasis added)

The third illustration is more complex. M. de Charlus (a homosexual) mistakenly thinks that M. Cottard is sending him sexual signals, signals that M. de Charlus is not interested in receiving. In the following passage, the Narrator, observing this encounter, describes the psychology of an unwanted advance. The problem for the reader is that it is easy to lose sight of the subject being described:

But when they see another man shew a peculiar liking for them, then whether because they fail to realize that this liking is the same as their own, **or** because it annoys them to be reminded that this liking, which they glorify so long as it is they themselves that feel it, is regarded as a vice, **or** from a desire to rehabilitate themselves by a sensational display in circumstances in which it costs them nothing, **or** from a fear of being unmasked which they at once recover as soon as desire no longer leads them blindfold from one imprudence to another, **or** from a rage at being subjected, by the equivocal attitude of another person, to the injury which, by their own attitude, if that other person attracted them, they would not be afraid to inflict on him, the men who do not in the least mind following a young man for miles, never taking their eyes off him in the theater, even if he is with friends, and there is therefore a danger of their compromising him with them, may be heard, if a man who does not attract them merely looks at them to say: "Sir, for what do you take me?" (simply because he takes them for what they are) "I don't understand, no don't attempt to explain, you are quite mistaken," pass if need be from words to blows, and, to a person who knows the imprudent stranger, was indignant: "What, you know that loathsome creature.

He stares at one so! . . . A fine way to behave?" (*CP*, vol. 2, p. 227, emphasis added)[219]

The use of analogies in *In Search of* is another technique used to create the feeling of an endless melody. As a simple example, we find the Narrator at Balbec, the (fictional) beach resort in Normandy, observing a gathering of young girls. The Narrator associates them with a group of birds ready for flight:

> They walked on a little way, then stopped for a moment in the middle of the road, with no thought whether they were impeding the passage of other people, and held a council, a solid body of irregular shape, compact, unusual and shrill, like birds that gather on the ground at the moment of flight. . . . (*WBG*, vol. 1, p. 598)

This next example has a bit more texture. The Narrator describes the scene where Mme. Cottard is being greeted by M. de Charlus. Mme. Cottard, a doctor's wife, is several social layers beneath M. de Charlus. The subject of the sentence—the greeting of Mme. Cottard and M. De Charlus—gets buried beneath several analogies:

> Mme. Cottard, who had been waiting for her husband outside, where M. de Charlus could see her quite well, though he had made no effort to summon her, came in and greeted the Baron, who held out his hand to her as though to a housemaid, without rising from his chair, partly in the manner of a king receiving homage, partly as a snob who does not wish a woman of humble appearance to sit down at his table, partly as an egoist who enjoys being alone with his friends, and does not wish to be bothered. (*CP*, vol. 2, p. 336)

---

[219] There are endless similar illustrations. Here the Narrator excludes the "or" in favor of separate sentences but to the same effect. "Perhaps this was in order that my grandmother might not be saddened by the thought that the sight of her could alarm her daughter. Perhaps from fear of grief so piercing that she dared not face it. Perhaps from reverence, because she did not feel it permissible to herself, without impiety, to remark the trace of any mental weakening on those venerated features. Perhaps to be better able to preserve intact in her memory the image of the true face of my grandmother, radiant with wisdom and goodness." (*GW*, vol. 1, p. 944)

Through the association of ideas, be they historical, artistic, or scientific, a sentence can have the "sound" of an endless melody. But more important, linking ideas semantically through the association of ideas, and syntactically through subordinate clauses, enriches our understanding of the sentence's subject. Layers of analogies and metaphors also invite the reader to increase connections between moments of experience. For example, when we see a group of young people we may think of a "group of birds ready for flight." Likewise, when we see a social snob greeting someone "beneath them," we will think of the imagery in the above passage of Mme. Cottard and M. de Charlus.

Another attribute of endless melody is its growth, not only in time, but in scope. Below are two illustrations of how Proust accomplishes this.

The Combray section in *Swann's Way* (*SW*, vol. 1, p. 37) opens with the Narrator announcing the town of Combray and drawing our attention to one building, the church. The Narrator metamorphoses that little church in a little town into a metaphorical representation of the entire Catholic Church sheltering its flock from dangers across its borders:

> Combray at a distance, from a twenty-mile radius, as we used to see it from the railway when we arrived there every year in Holy Week, was no more than a church epitomizing the town, representing it, speaking of it and for it to the horizon, and as one drew near, gathering close about its long, dark cloak, sheltering from the wind, on the open plain, as a shepherd gathers his sheep, the woolly grey backs of its flocking houses, which a fragment of its mediaeval ramparts enclosed, here and there, in an outline as scrupulously circular as that of a little town in a primitive painting.

The Narrator's depth of associations of one experience, be it sensual or intellectual or emotional, is almost endless. The Narrator, speaking to a telephone switchboard operator, refers to switchboard operators as "the Daughters of the Night, the Messengers of the Word, the Deities without form or feature." (*GW*, vol. 1, p. 812) He is trying to connect with his grandmother:

> We need only, so that the miracle may be accomplished, apply our lips to the magic orifice, and invoke—occasionally for rather longer than seems to us necessary, I admit—the Vigilant Virgins to

whose voices we listen every day without ever coming to know their faces, and who are our Guardian Angels in the dizzy realm of darkness whose portals they so jealously keep; the All Powerful by whose intervention the absent rise up at our side without our being permitted to set eyes on them; the Danaids of the unseen who without ceasing empty, fill, transmit the urns of sound; the ironic Furies who, just as we were murmuring a confidence to a friend in the hope that no one was listening, cry brutally: "I hear you?"; the ever infuriated servants of the Mystery, the umbrageous priestesses of the Invisible, the Young ladies of the Telephone. (GW, vol. 1, p. 810)

In yet another technique, the Narrator's involuntary memory, functioning like a coherent stream of consciousness, creates the structure of an endless melody. The stream of consciousness is coherent because the memories are composed of images that had previously been introduced. This structure of connected memories is similar to the constituent *leitmotifs* in a Wagnerian endless melody.

In the below example, the Narrator smells petrol. This smell generates involuntary memories of his mistress, Albertine. He then continues to remember his childhood bedroom, Balbec, imagining being in an airplane, and fantasizing about having non-committal sex with a passing woman:

> . . . this smell of petrol which, with the smoke from the exhaust of the car, had so often melted into the pale azure, on those scorching days when I used to drive from Saint-Jean de la Baise to Gouville, as it had accompanied me on my excursions during those summer afternoons when I had left Albertine painting, called into blossom now on either side of me, for all that I was lying in my darkened bedroom, cornflowers, poppies, and red clover, intoxicated me like a country scent, not circumscribed and fixed, like that which is spread before the hawthorns and, retained in its unctuous and dense elements, floats with a certain stability before the hedge, but like a scent before which the roads took flight, the sun's face changed, castles came hurrying to meet me, the sky turned pale, force was increased tenfold, a scent which was like a symbol of elastic motion and power, and which revived the desire that I had felt at Balbec, to enter the cage

of steel and crystal, but this time not to go any longer on visits to familiar houses with a woman whom I know too well, but to make love in new places with a woman unknown. (C, vol. 2, p. 667)

Yet another Proustian technique used to create a sense of "endless melody" is through sentences that transport the reader through vast stretches of time, not only by analogy and metaphor, but within the syntax of the sentence. Malcolm Bowie[220] illustrates how the syntax of Proust's sentences often merge past, present, and future time. Bowie does not discuss this feature in terms of *leitmotifs*, but this is exactly how *leitmotifs* function. They create remembrance of the events, people, emotions, and ideas. Bowie uses different words to say as much: "Present reading time is haunted by reading past time."[221]

Proust uses this dynamic temporal syntax design in the first three sentences of the novel. First sentence: "For a long time I used to go to bed early." [The Past but perhaps inclusive of the present] Second sentence: "Sometimes, when I had put out my candle, my eyes would close so quickly that I had not even time to say 'I'm going to sleep.'" [The Past and Present] Third sentence: "And half an hour later the thought that it was time to go to sleep would awaken me;" [The Future].

In Search of is strewed with writing that uses this type of temporal syntax, not only among sentences, but within the same sentence. In the below sentence, the past, present, and future all are jumbled together:

Whatever my disappointment in finding Mlle. Simonet a girl so little different from those that I knew already, [Present/Past] just as my rude awakening when I saw Balbec Church did not prevent me from wishing still to go to Quimperle, Pont-Aven, and Venice, [Past/Future] I comforted myself with the thought that through Albertine at any rate, even if she herself was not all that I had hoped,

---

[220] Bowie, *Proust among the Stars*, chapter 2, "Time." Bowie illustrates how the syntax of Proust's sentences often merge past, present, and future times. Writes Bowie, "Yet this presentation [Proust's time-drama] has as much of a logic of it at the first: the interplay that it creates between the backwards and forward glances of the time-bound individual...begins indeed to resemble a universal key to the understanding of human time. . . ." (p. 43). Also see vol. 1, *WBG*, pp. 643–44 and 646, as examples of mixed time frames. The Conclusion chapter includes a more detailed discussion of the mixing of time frames in *In Search of Lost Time*.

[221] Bowie, *Proust among the Stars*, p. 52.

I might make the acquaintance of her comrades of the little band. [Present/Future] (*WBG*, vol. 1, p. 658)

Proust uses the same technique to move us through "intellectual" space. Continuing to contemplate Albertine, the Narrator ponders the location of a mole on her face:

> I seized the opportunity, while she stood still, to look again and discover once and for all where exactly the little mole was placed. [Present] Then, just as a phrase of Vinteuil which had delighted me in the sonata, and which my recollection allowed to wander from the andante to the finale, until the day when, having the score in my hands, I was able to find it, and to fix it in my memory in its proper place, in the scherzo, [Past] so this mole, which I had visualized now on her cheek, now on her chin, came to rest for ever on her upper lip, just below her nose. [Past/Present and indefinite Future] (*WBG*, vol. 1, p. 659)

As a final illustration of the techniques used by Proust to create an endless melody, and as a segue to the idea of *Gesamtkunstwerk* in a literary work, is the Narrator's description of events in a public space. Public spaces in *In Search of* often include multiple conversations and multiple comings and goings. As a result, these descriptions can become very confusing. For example, toward the close of Book 3, *The Guermantes Way*, the Narrator is in Mme. Guermantes's drawing room during a dinner party. A seven-page paragraph begins with "What a pretty flower, I've never seen one like it. . . ." and ends seven pages later with the sentence: "This utterance shocked me as indicating a misconception of the way in which artistic impressions are formed in our minds, and because it seemed to imply that our eye is in that case simply a recording machine which takes instantaneous photographs." (*GW*, vol. 1, pp. 1084–90)

By my count, this seven-page paragraph includes at least five speakers, twenty people referenced, and topics covered such as painting, botany, insects, marriage, sex, furniture, and literature. Although the paragraph appears to be a cacophony of unrelated topics, they weave together seamlessly, beginning and ending with the topic of art. Also discussed is the role of insects in fertilization.

This diversion into fertilization of flowers, a *leitmotif* itself, is taken up again at the beginning of Book 4, *Cities of the Plain*. In Proust, everything is connected.

e. *Gesamtkunstwerk*

Proust takes Wagner's notion of *Gesamtkunstwerk*, a synthesis of the arts, and explodes it into a multidimensional, multimedia epic on the written page. He weaves into his novel the universe, both the real and the fictional, and miraculously connects them together.[222] To cite just a subset:

- Places: Combray, Paris, Balbec, Venice
- Artists: Bergotte (writer), Elstir (painter), Vinteuil (composer), Berma (actress/theater), Wagner, Debussy, Balzac, Hugo, Ruskin, Racine, Saint-Simon, and the symbolist Maeterlinck
- Architecture: especially churches and cathedrals
- Visual arts: the Paris theater scene
- Fashions and fabrics: detailed descriptions of gowns, hats, and other garments
- Cultural: the Dreyfus affair, the rise and fall of social status
- Homoerotic: homosexuality and lesbianism
- Horticulture and entomology
- Mental states: sleep, love, sexual desire, sexual frustration, jealousy, boredom, betrayal, selfishness, and, of course, different types of memory
- Households: the Swanns, the Verdurins' "little clan," and the Guermantes family

---

[222] Jean-Yves Tadié, a Proust biographer and general editor of the 1987-9 Pléiade edition of *A la recherche du temps perdu* asserts: "*A la recherche du temps perdu* recapitulates the entire literary tradition, from the Bible to Flaubert and Tolstoy, and all literary genres. Proust's novel also espouses the romantic and symbolist dream, shared by Mallarmé and Wagner, of a synthesis of all the arts, painting, music and architecture. Thus are born works which escape the constraints of their time period, their country, their author, and whose glory continues to grow. It has often been said that, if England has Shakespeare, Germany Goethe, Italy Dante, France has no one writer equal to them. The number of critical works devoted to the author of the *Recherche* suggests that France now has, and will have tomorrow, Marcel Proust." David R. Ellison, "Proust and posterity," in *The Cambridge Companion to Proust*, ed. Richard Bales (Cambridge, Cambridge University Press, 2001), p. 200.

Almost any sentence of more than a few words illustrates Proust's ability to weave a multi-spatial, multi-temporal barrage of arts,[223] sciences, sociology, and psychology into that sentence. Taking a random, but short, sentence from Book 2, *Within a Budding Grove*, the sentence describes the Narrator looking at Albertine as she reclines in bed:

> I had a sidelong view of Albertine's cheeks, which often appeared pale, but, seen thus, were flushed with a coursing stream of blood which lighted them up, gave them that dazzling clearness which certain winter mornings have when the stones sparkling in the sun seem blocks of pink granite and radiate joy. (*WBG*, vol. 1, p. 696)

The different "fields" in the above brief sentence include:

- Sidelong view = optics
- Albertine's cheeks = anatomy
- Pale = color
- Streams of blood = hydrodynamics
- Lighted them up = electricity
- Dazzling clearness/winter mornings = climatology
- Pink granite = geology
- Joy = psychology

A more complex example of literary *Gesamtkunstwerk* is illustrated by the phrase "Rachel when from the Lord." In Book 2: *Within a Budding Grove*, the Narrator's friend, Block, takes the narrator to a brothel. There he is offered Rachel, a Jewish prostitute. (*WBG*, vol. 1, p. 439) The Narrator does not have sex with Rachel. He does, however, give her the nickname "Rachel when from

---

[223] For those interested in the many paintings discussed in *In Search of*, see Eric Karpeles, *Paintings in Proust: A Visual Companion to* In Search of Lost Time. "In the novel, over one hundred artists are named, spanning the history of art from the trecento to the twentieth century," p. 10. The book includes 209 illustrations, 199 in color.

the Lord," a reference to Fromental Halévy's 1835 opera *La Juive* ("*The Jewess*"). Rachel does not know of her newly christened name.

Four hundred pages later, the Narrator's aristocratic friend, Robert Saint Loup, introduces the Narrator to his very well-kept mistress and would-be bride, Rachel. (*GW*, vol. 1, p. 827ff) Robert, who a few paragraphs earlier was extoling Rachel's many virtues, refers to her intellect as "there's really something about her that's quite Pythian," i.e., the oracle of Delphi through which Apollo speaks. The Narrator, a bit embarrassed at recognizing Rachel, politely diverts his attention to a garden, which contains pear and cherry blossoms. After discoursing for a few paragraphs about how a person can be seen as so many different things, he comments, "[A]nd indeed, when Robert and I were both looking at her we did not both see her from the same side of the mystery." (*GW*, vol. 1, p. 829) The Narrator draws an analogy with Mary Magdalene "when, in another garden, she saw a human form and thought it was the gardener." (*GW*, vol. 1, p. 829) This is a reference to the risen Jesus mistaken by Mary Magdalene to be a gardener.

From a literary *Gesamtkunstwerk* perspective, there is much to unpack in this little fragment of an episode:

- The Narrator recalls encountering Rachel in a brothel as a twenty-franc prostitute. A reference to memory.
- Rachel now is the mistress and potential wife of someone buying her a thirty-thousand-franc bracelet. A reference to movement between social classes.
- Rachel is a prostitute and Robert's mistress. A reference to sex.
- Pear blossoms symbolize hope for a new couple will be united in marriage while cherry blossoms symbolize the fleeting nature of this relationship. A reference to horticulture and plant symbolism.
- Saint Loup characterizes Rachel as the Pythian. A reference to Greek mythology.
- The Narrator recalls that he gave Rachel a nickname from a character named "Rachel" in an opera named *La Juive*. A reference to music.

- "Rachel" refers to a biblical story in Genesis about a *ménage à trois* between Jacob and Laban's two daughters, Rachel and Leah. A reference to the Hebrew Bible (Genesis).

- *La Juive* takes place in the early 1400s. The opera is about an intolerant Christian who is the father of Rachel. Rachel is believed to have died in a fire but was found near death by the Jewish goldsmith Eleazer. Things do not end well. A reference to social hatred and psychological conflict.

- Mary Magdalene, the sinner who Christ cured, mistakes the risen Christ and angel as two sentries. A reference to the Christian Bible. (John 20:11–18)

Another example of literary *Gesamtkunstwerk* refers to M. de Charlus, who is one of the most colorful characters in *In Search of*. The scene is the mutual seduction between Charlus and Julian, the local tailor, that occurs in the opening pages of *Cities of the Plain*. The Charlus/Julian sexual act was foreshadowed during a dinner party at the Duchesse de Guermantes. At the dinner, guests were discussing Swann's "astonishing" (read "dreadful") marriage to Odette. The dinner-party discussion transitions to the mating practices of plants and insects. The Duchess states: "'Besides, when it comes to that, there was no need to go quite so far. It seems that here, in my own little bit of garden, more odd things happen in broad daylight than at midnight-in the Bois de Boulogne! Only they attract no attention, because among flowers it's all done quite simply, you see a little orange shower, or else a very dusty fly coming to wipe its feet or take a bath before crawling into a flower and that does the trick!'" (*GW*, vol. 1, p. 1085)

The sexual liaison between M. de Charlus and Julian, referred to above, takes place in the Guermantes courtyard. The Narrator, in his voyeuristic position, observes M. de Charlus and Jupien sexually seduce each other:

> Meanwhile, Jupien, shedding at once the humble, honest expression which I had always associated with him, had—in perfect symmetry with the Baron—thrown up his head, given a becoming tilt to his body, placed his hand with a grotesque impertinence on his hip, stuck out his behind, posed himself with the coquetry that the orchid might have adopted on the providential arrival of the bee. (*CP*, vol. 2, pp. 5–6)

In the seven-page seduction scene (*CP*, vol. 2, pp. 3–9), which describes M. de Charlus and Julian's sex act, the Narrator refers to many topics, including geology, botany, genetics, endocrinology, psychology, music, military strategy (during the Boer war), literature, and the Dreyfus affair.

In *In Search of*, any relatively long paragraph or sentence, with its multi-literary, historic, artistic, and scientific references, creates a literary universe for the reader. While a sentence may have a dozen subordinate phrases, each phrase functions to add a richness to the subject of the sentence. Each subject of the sentence becomes a universe unto itself. This richness of experience is the essence of what I believe *In Search of* is all about: any experience can and should encompass a panoramic view of the universe through all its multi-spatial and multi-temporal dimensions. *In Search of* is a literary *Gesamtkunstwerk*; it teaches us that every experience is capable of expanding into its own personal *Gesamtkunstwerk*. Each person's life is a creation of *leitmotifs*, a composition of an endless melody, and a celebration of a *Gesamtkunstwerk*.

CHAPTER 5
Conclusion: The Function of Time

Both *Ulysses* and *In Search of* contain dozens, perhaps hundreds, of literary *leitmotifs*. These *leitmotifs* remind the reader of earlier textual references and thereby enrich the reader's experience of the current moment. Upon subsequent readings, *leitmotifs* also direct the reader both to prior events and future events.

There are other terms or concepts that I call framework terms or concepts. Time is one of those frameworks or structural concepts in both works. Time is not a *leitmotif* because it does not remind the reader of prior or future events. Time is the structure in which *leitmotifs* exist.

For Wagner, Joyce, and Proust, time is not linear but fluid. Events swirl within the stream of time. Events that happen in one moment in time will be retold either directly or from varying perspectives. We have discussed Wagner's musical *leitmotifs* and their function to move us backward and forward through time. Wagner uses a similar tool in his libretti. In Wagner's operas, there is a great deal of repeating or retelling of events. As with musical *leitmotifs*, each time we hear an event's history, our understanding of the overall story is enriched and we gain a new insight into the psychology of the agent retelling the event.

In *Ulysses*, 4:00 p.m. functions as a framework around which other elements acquire their meaning. In episode 4 (Calypso), the jingle of Molly's bed at the beginning of Bloom's day, or the jingle of horse carriages that we hear throughout the day, would be no more than sounds were it not for Molly and Blazes's 4:00 p.m. tryst. Three times Bloom notes that his watch stopped at 4:30 p.m. (episode 13, Nausicaa: 13.547, 13.846, 13.983) Such repetitive information would strike the reader as poor writing were that not the time Molly and Blazes were having sex.

The external story of *Ulysses* travels through objective time. Leopold Bloom's day begins in the morning and each episode follows the standard chronological clock, breakfast at a bit after 8:00 a.m., lunch a bit after 1:00 p.m., and bed after an exhausting day of travels. However, the real action in *Ulysses* occurs within subjective time. We are witness to Bloom's mind, be it his conscious, subconscious, or unconscious mind. Even more significant is that Bloom's thoughts continually time shift between the past, present, and future. At line 58 in episode 4 (Calypso), we hear Bloom's thoughts in the present (their bedstead jingling), the future (he needs to fix the bed), and the past (Molly brought their bed to Dublin from Gibraltar:

> He heard then a warm heavy sign, softer, as she turned over and the loose brass quoits of the bedstead jingled. Must get those settled really. Pity. All the way from Gibraltar. Forgotten any little Spanish she knew. (episode 4, Calypso: 4.58–60)

With little exaggeration, one can select any passage at random and Bloom will be "living" multi-temporally. His subjective time-shifting is his attempt to integrate and understand his past. I previously quoted one of the many passages when he is thinking of Rudy, his son who died in infancy: "If little Rudy had lived. See him grow up. Hear his voice in the house. . . ." (episode 6, Hades, 6.75–78) Below is an example of his thoughts beginning in the present, moving to the future, and ending in the past as he contemplates his dead father:

> Mr Bloom stood at the corner, his eyes wandering over the multicoloured hoardings. Cantrell and Cochrane's Ginger Al (Aromatic). Clery's Summer Sal. No, he's going on straight. Hello. Leah tonight. Mrs Bandmann Palmer. Like to see her again in that. Hamlet she played last night. Male impersonator. Perhaps he was a woman. Why Ophelia committed suicide. Poor papa! How he used to talk of Kate Bateman in that. Outside the Adelphi in London waited all the afternoon to get in. Year before I was born that was: sixtyfive. (episode 5, Lotus Eaters: 6.192–99)

The above selections come early in *Ulysses* and there are countless illustrations of mixed timeframes throughout the novel. A difference between the framework of time in Joyce's *Ulysses* and Proust's *In Search of* is that Joyce is presenting the inner life of a regular person, be it Leopold Bloom, Molly Bloom, or Stephen Dedalus. Like the lives of most people, their self-analysis goes mostly in circles. One gets the feeling that Leopold, Molly, and Stephen are locked in a perpetual cycle, contentedly condemned to repeat June 16, 1904, indefinitely.

Proust's Narrator, on the other hand, is 100 percent self-analysis with specific objectives in mind: to experience Society, to understand the significance of art, and to become a writer. The Narrator's "day" begins several years before his birth and ends some fifty years after his birth. More significant, and hence creating difficulties for readers, Proust's Narrator resides simultaneously in two timeframes: as the present tense Narrator at various stages of his life and as the older Narrator analyzing each of these stages. Roger Shattuck speaks of a doubling of the *je* or "I" as both the character and the narrator: "The double I projects a stereoscopic perspective and creates a narrative relief or depth perception on the events related. This narrative devise arises from Proust's style, from his use of the first-person singular pronoun with two edges on it so that it cuts two ways. We are carried back toward a protagonist growing up and forward toward a mature adult watching his (own) progress."[224] This technique can be very confusing for the reader but is very effective for Proust's goal of merging past and present time by simultaneously describing an event and reflecting on that event.[225]

Proust does not appear to be interested in objective or scientific time as theorized by Newton, Leibniz, Kant, and Einstein. Proust's interest is in subjective, phenomenal, and psychological time. Throughout his retelling of his life, the Narrator discusses the permutations in which our consciousness experiences time. His most sustained discussion occurs in the last book, Book 7: *PR*, particularly in the last chapter, The Princesse de Guermantes Receives. In this closing section, the Narrator flushes out the significance of his petites madeleines experience.

---

[224] Roger Shattuck, *Proust's Way*, p. 17 and 162.

[225] To further complicate matters for the reader, at times Proust has the Narrator step outside the novel to speak about future events and to speak about philosophical, aesthetic, and other theoretical topics. In theatre this is called breaking the fourth wall.

As the Narrator approaches the Princesse de Guermantes's home and waits in the library to enter the concert, the Narrator has several profound experiences. The experiences of stepping on uneven pavement, hearing the sound of a spoon on a plate, or feeling a starched napkin, result in a wholly different kind of memory experience:

> . . . in stepping back, struck my foot against some unevenly cut flagstones, leading to a carriage house. In recovering my balance, I put my foot on a stone that was a little lower than the one next to it; immediately all my discouragement vanished before a feeling of happiness which I had experienced at different moments of my life, at the sight of trees I thought I recognized when driving around Balbec, or the church spires of Martinville, or the savour of a madeleine, dipped in herb tea, or from any other sensations I have mentioned which had seemed to me to be synthesized in the last works of Vinteuil. Just as when I tasted the madeleine, all anxiety as to the future, all intellectual doubt was dispelled. (*PR*, vol. 2, pp. 991–92)

> What happened was that a servant, trying in vain to make no noise, struck a spoon against a plate. The same kind of felicity as I had received from the uneven paving stones now came over me; the sensations were again those of great heat, but entirely different, mingled with the odour of smoke, tempered by the cool fragrance of a forest setting, and I recognized that what seemed to me so delightful was the very row of trees which I had found it wearisome to study and describe and which, in a sort of hallucination, I thought now stood before me as I uncorked the bottle of beer I had with me in the railway carriage, the sound of the spoon striking the plate having given me-until I came to myself again-the illusion of the very similar noise of the hammer of a workman who had made some repairs to a wheel while our train stopped before that little clump of trees. (*PR*, vol. 2, p. 993)

. . . I wiped my mouth with the napkin he had given me; but immediately, like the character in *The Arabian Nights*. . . . The impression was so vivid that the moment I was reliving fused with the real present and, more dazed than on that day when I wondered whether I was really going to be received by the Princesse de Guermantes or was everything going to crash about my head. . . . (PR, vol. 2, p. 993)

The above experiences did not originate by intentionally or intellectually thinking about, or even picturing, the above events. Nor are they like dreams where time sequences are warped and often surreal. The Narrator describes these experiences as reliving the event with all of the accompanying sensations, feelings, and awareness of the original event. The Narrator tells us that these experiences cannot be manufactured by the intellect. Rather, they are triggered by something that brings to conscious awareness the complete or total remembrance in all its rich sensuous detail. The past becomes present. Of these past three epiphanies, the Narrator tells us:

I caught an inkling of this reason why I compared these various happy impressions with one another and found that they had this in common, namely, that I felt them as if they were occurring simultaneously in the present moment and in some distant past, which the sound of the spoon against the plate, or the unevenness of the flagstones, or the peculiar savour of the madeleine even went so far as to make coincide with the present leaving me uncertain in which period I was. In truth, the person within me who was at that moment enjoying this impression enjoyed it in the qualities it possessed which were common to both an earlier day and the present moment, qualities which were independent of all considerations of time; and this person came into play only when, by this process of identifying the past with the present, he could find himself in the only environment in which he could live and enjoy the essence of things, that is to say, entirely outside of time. (PR, vol. 2, p. 995)

At long last, the distinct selves that comprise the multitude of our past experiences are unified into our one self.

The Narrator also provides us with two ways to defeat the corrosive forces of time. One is through creating a public and long-lasting work of art, such as that of Elstir's painting, Berma's performances, Bergotte's books, and Vinteuil's music. The second is by a *remembrance* with such intensity that the memory experience becomes a present experience. This new experience is when past and present merge. The Narrator is under no delusion that works of art last forever or that our experience, no matter how profound, lasts forever. Time in fact destroys history, and with it, works of art. We die, and with our death, so too goes our consciousness. However, while works of art exist and we are alive, we can/should/will feel the connections among experiences, and thereby experience the joy of living.

This lived continuity, whether in works of art or in transcendent experiences, is another expression of the richness embedded within a Wagnerian *leitmotif*. A Wagnerian or literary *leitmotif* is none other than a unifying expression that merges the past, present, and future. This experience will be different for each of us. For me, there are times when I genuinely (re)experience the first time I saw *The Ring*, sitting in the least expensive seats in the top row at the Met. There are other vivid/lived experiences that should only be expressed, if at all, on a psychiatrist's couch. But I believe, as did Proust, that we all have those timeless moments. Admittedly, they are transitory and not within our intellectual control, but they are part of the makeup of human consciousness. Wagner may have been aware of such experiences when he has Siegfried reliving his encounter with Brünnhilde as he dies at the end of act 3, scene ii in *Göttterdämmerung*:

One came to wake you;
his kiss awakes you
and once again he breaks
the bride's bonds:-
and Brünnhilde's joy laughs upon him.-
Ah! Those eyes-
now open for ever!-
Ah, this breath's

enchanted sighing!
Sweet extinction,-
blissful terror-:
Brünnhild' gives me her greeting!

Let us end by giving Leopold and Molly Bloom the last word. Why? For two reasons. First, per their two independent accounts of their eating "the bit of seedcake," they are experiencing a Proustian moment where past and present merge. Second, their accounts illustrate the way Joyce constructs literary *leitmotifs* across the framework time.

Molly's twenty-two-thousand-word stream of consciousness has the intensity for Molly of being all present tense. The below moment comes near the end of her long soliloquy. It is nearing daylight and Molly is reliving the moment she and Leopold kissed in an open field:

> . . . the sun shines for you he said the day we were lying among the rhododendrons on Howth head in the grey tweed suit and his straw hat the day I got him to propose to me yes first I gave him the bit of seedcake out of my mouth and it was leapyear like now yes 16 years ago my God after that long kiss near lost my breath yes he said I was a flower of the mountain yes so we are flowers all a womans body yes that was one true thing he said in his life and the sun shines for you today yes and that is why I liked him because I saw he understood or felt what a woman is and I knew that I could always get round him and I gave him all the pleasure I could leading him on till he asked me to say yes. . . . (episode 18, Penelope: 18. 1571–81)

Earlier in the day, Leopold Bloom is having lunch and his mind wanders to that same open field where he and Molly kissed. We enter Bloom's mind as he slips into a timeless moment in which the past merges with the present with all the sensations and thoughts of a present-tense memory:

> Glowing wine on his palate lingered swallowed. Crushing in the winepress grapes of Burgundy. Sun's heat it is. Seems to a secret touch telling me memory. Touched his sense moistened remembered. Hidden under wild ferns on Howth below us bay

153

sleeping: sky. No sound. The sky. The bay purple by the lion's head. Green by Dumleck. Yellowgreen towards Sutton. Fields of undersea, the lines faint brown in grass, buried cities. Pillowed on my coat she had her hair, earwigs in the heather scrub my hands under her nape, you'll toss me all. O wonder! Coolsoft with ointments her hand touched me, caressed: her eyes upon me did not turn away. Ravished over her I lay, full lips full open, kisser her mouth. Yun. Softly she gave me in my mouth the seedcake warm and chewed. Mawkish pulp her mouth had mumbled sweetsour of her spittle. Joy: I ate it: joy. Young life, her lips that gave me pouting. Soft warm sticky gumjelly lips. Flowers her eyes were, take me, willing eyes. Pebbles fell. She lay still. A goat. No-one. High on Ben Howth rhododendrons a nannygoat walking surefooted, dropping currants. Screened under ferns she laughed warmfolded. Wildly I lay on her, kissed her: eyes, her lips, her stretched neck beating, woman's breasts full in her blouse of nun's veiling, fat nipples upright. Hot I tongued her. She kissed me. I was kissed. All yielding she tossed my hair. Kissed, she kissed me. (episode 8, Lestrygonians: 8.897–916)

Appendix A. Table 1:
References to Wagner in Joyce's *Ulysses*

Counting Wagnerian references is not an easy task in Joyce's writing. Similar to counting *leitmotifs*, counting references is its own sport. In *Joyce and Wagner: A Study of Influence*, Timothy Martin identifies thirty-one Wagnerian references. I identified an additional three references. In Ulysses *Annotated: Notes for James Joyce's* Ulysses, Don Gifford concurred with seven citations and one that was not cited by Martin.

Ulysses Location	Wagnerian References	Timothy Martin Citation	Don Gifford Citation
1.20–23; Telemachus	*Parsifal* (Grail scene)	Mulligan: He added in a preacher's tone: "For this, O dearly beloved, is the genuine Christine: body and soul and blood and ouns. . . ."	
1.23; Telemachus	*Parsifal*, rising of curtain in act 1.	Mulligan: "Slow music, please. Shut your eyes, gents. One moment. A little trouble about those white corpuscles. Silence all."	
2.424–25; Nestor	*The Ring*	Mr. Deasy: "I'd like to break a lance with you, old as I am." (Note: Siegfried breaking Wotan's spear)	
3.16; Proteus	*The Ring*	Stephen: "My ash sword hangs at my side."	
3.289–93; Proteus	*The Ring*	Stephen: "And these, the stoneheaps of dead builders, a warren of weasel rats. Hide gold there. . . ."	

Ulysses Location	Wagnerian References	Timothy Martin Citation	Don Gifford Citation
3.304–5; Proteus	The Ring	Stephen: "Then from the starving cagework city a horde of jerkined dwarfs…"	Reference to the 1331 Dublin famine
3.397–98; Proteus	Flying Dutchman & Tristan and Isolde	Stephen: "He comes, pale vampire, through storm his eyes, his bat sails bloodying the sea, mouth to her mouth's kiss."	Reference to a poem by Douglas Hyde
3.489; Proteus	The Ring	He took the hilt of his ashplant, lunging with it softly. . . .	
7.522–25; Aeolus	Flying Dutchman & Tristan and Isolde	Stephen (poem): "On swift sail flaming from storm and south He comes, pale vampire, Mouth to my mouth"	Reference to a poem by Douglas Hyde
9.295–96; Scylla & Charybdis	The Ring	Stephen looked down… hung on his ashplanthandle over his knee. "My casque and sword."	
9.309		"Our national epic has yet to be written, Dr Sigerson says."	Wagner's Ring and Tristan
9.946–47; Scylla & Charybdis	The Ring	Stephen looked on his hat, his stick, his boots. "Stephanos, my crown. My sword."	
10.813–14; Wandering Rocks	The Ring	Stephen: "Grandfather ape gloating on a stolen hoard." (Note: Albreich and the stolen Rheingold)	Reference to a Yeats's poem

Ulysses Location	**Wagnerian** References	**Timothy Martin** Citation	**Don Gifford** Citation
11.21, 11.590–92; Sirens	*Tristan and Isolde*	A sail! A veil awave upon the waves. A headland, a ship, a sail upon the billows. . . .	Reference to Verdi's *Otello*
11.42–49; 11.1005–8; Sirens	*The Ring*	Bloom: "Low in dark middle earth. Embedded ore. . . . But wait. But hear. Chords dark. Lugugugubrious. Low. In a cave of the dark middle earth. . . ."	Reference to Wagner's *Ring*
12.176-92; Cyclops	*Tristan and Isolde*	List of Irish heroes and heroines of antiquity;... Tristan and Isolde. . . .	References to Irish and English history
12.569; Cyclops	*The Ring*	*Kriegfried Ueberallgemein* (note: Siegfried)	
12.1455; Cyclops	*Tristan and Isolde*	Isolde's tower	Description of the tower
13.1076; Nausicaa	*Tannhäuser*	Bloom: "A star I see. Venus? Can't tell yet."	
13.1077–8; Nausicaa	*Flying Dutchman*	Bloom: "Were those night clouds there all the time? Looks like a phantom ship."	Jewish reference to the *Tract Sabbath*.
14.356; Oxen of the Sun	*Tannhäuser*	Master Dixon: ". . . better they were named Beau Mount..." (Note: reference to Beau Mount = Mount of Venus, i.e., the Venusberg)	"Poetic" for the Mount of Venus
14.1457; Oxen of the Sun	*Die Meistersinger*	Drunken medical students" "Silentium! Get a spurt on. Tension. Proceed to nearest canteen. . . ."	

Ulysses Location	Wagnerian References	Timothy Martin Citation	Don Gifford Citation
15. Circe	*Parsifal*	Suggested that this episode may owe a good deal to act 2 of *Parsifal*	
15.99, 124; Circe	*The Ring*	He flourished his ashplant, shivering the lamp image, shattering light over the world…	
15.1368–70; Circe	Wagner's music of the future and *Flying Dutchman*	Bloom: "That's the music of the future. That's my programme. *Cui bono?* But our buccaneering Vanderdecken in their phantom ship of finance."	Wagner's *Flying Dutchman*
15.1390–91; Circe	*Flying Dutchman*	Bloom: "These flying Dutchmen or lying Dutchmen as they recline in. . . ."	Wagner's *Flying Dutchman*
15.1398–448; Circe	*Die Meistersinger*	Act 4, scene ii, procession into the open meadow. [**my addition,** *Meistersinger*]	
15.3649–53; Circe	*The Ring*	Stephen: Extends his hand to hersmilling and chants to the air of the bloodoath in The Dusk of the Gods. *Hangende Hunger, Fragende Frau, Mach tuns alle kaput.*	*The Ring*

Ulysses Location	Wagnerian References	Timothy Martin Citation	Don Gifford Citation
15.3660	*The Ring*	Lynch: "Sheet lightening courage. The youth who could not shiver and shake." (Note reference to Siegfried's ignorance of fear)	
15.4242–44; Circe	*The Ring*	Stephen: "Nothung!" He lifts his ashplant high with both hands and smashes the chandelier. . . .	
15.4244–45; Circe	*The Ring*	Time's livid final flame leaps and, in the following darkness, ruin of all space, shattered glass and toppling masonry. (Note: in this context, *Götterdämmerung*)	Reference to Blake
15.4646ff; Circe	*The Ring*	Distant Voices: "Dublin's burning! Dublin's burning. O fire, on fire." [**my addition**]	
16.410–12; Eumaeus	*Flying Dutchman*	Why, the sailor replied . . . it might be a matter of ten years. [**my addition**]	
16.859–64; Eumaeus	*Flying Dutchman*	. . . when Michael Gunn was identified with the management of *The Flying Dutchman*...	Possibly Wagner but also a popular play by T. P. Taylor
16.1735–37; Eumaeus	Wagner's music	Wagnerian music, though confessedly grand in its way, was a bit too heavy for Bloom...	Wagner's music

Appendix B. Changing Perspectives:
The Hero, Humor, and Eroticism

The perspective of Western Europeans radically changed between Wagner's Romanticism and Joyce and Proust's Modernism. Among these changes were how heroes, humor, and eroticism were depicted in the arts. These changes can be illustrated by comparing characters in Wagner's operas and those in *Ulysses* and *In Search of*.

1. The Romantic vs. the Modern Hero

According to Simon Williams, the romantic hero, as represented in Wagner's operas, is not a person of ideal or moral stature.[226] Rather, the hero lives outside of conventional morality and generally is not concerned with goodness, virtue, or society's material interests. Romantic heroes are not to be thought of as role models or good citizens, rather, they are asocial. Romantic heroes also tend to be from royal parentage but are born in obscurity and do not know their parents. They often are brought up by a foster parent within the landscape of nature. Heroes are not encumbered by history or their role in it. Hence, they are not burdened by the past. Moreover, heroes do not experience the emotion of fear.

Williams further explains that romantic heroes do have some positive traits, but they are not consciously driven by them. Although heroes enter society as outsiders, they imbue society with their unbounded strength and energy. Moreover, through their vitality, heroes fill a void in society, and we become stronger and more confident human beings because of them.

We find none of the above qualities in the "heroes" of *Ulysses*[227] or *In Search of*. Although Bloom, Stephen, and the Narrator have vastly different personalities, and we would not confuse one with the other, we also would not

---

[226] For a detailed discussion of the Wagnerian romantic hero, as well as the characteristics of the epic and messianic heroes, see Simon Williams, *Wagner and the Romantic Hero*. Also see Simon Williams's "Lecture 2: *Siegfried* – Wagner's Troubled and Troubling Hero," 1:16:39, May 31–June 2, 2013, "Wagner of Washington DC," YouTube, https://www.youtube.com/user/WSWDC.

[227] For a parody of a modern hero in *Ulysses*, see episode 12, Cyclops: 12.150–205.Joyce takes us further down the heroic ladder in Book 2, chapter 3 of *FW*. Here we find the protagonist as a bartender. After he closes the bar, he concludes the evening by drinking the remains in his customers glasses. "He finished by lowering his woolly throat with the wonderful midnight thirst…with the assistance of his venerated tongue, whatever surplus rotgut, sorra much, was left by the lazy lousers… 380:24–381:10.

describe any of them as heroic. Bloom, Stephen, and the Narrator know their parents and are very rooted to their personal and cultural histories. In fact, they are trying to succeed in their respective societies. Bloom works diligently as an advertising salesperson for a local paper and dutifully supports his wife's singing aspirations. Stephen aspires to break free of societal restraints and become a recognized writer. The Narrator seeks to move into the social circles of the rich and famous, i.e., to obtain invitations into Society as well as to become a famous writer. [228]

None of these characters displays any heroic courage. Bloom is aware that he is a cuckold and that he is not going to do anything about it. He ponders divorce several times during the day but concludes just before retiring to bed: "Assassination, never, as two wrongs did not make one right. Duel by combat, no. Divorce, not now." (episode 17, Ithaca: 17.2201–22) Moreover, he is subject to anti-Semitic comments throughout the day, but only once confronts the anti-Semitism and quickly thereafter takes his exit. (episode 12, Cyclops, 12. 1800f)

Stephen is particularly unheroic. He is afraid of water (maybe because water is associated with baptism) and therefore, seldom bathes. He is verbally abused by Buck Mulligan, one of his housemates. He reluctantly, but out of necessity, wears Mulligan's hand-me-down clothes. He is timid in front of his bigoted and ignorant employer, is afraid of dogs, and is pathologically obsessed with the past. He is not an agent, but an observer. He tells us that given the opportunity, he could not save a drowning man because of his cowardice:

> The man that was drowned nine days ago off Maiden's rock.
> They are waiting for him now. The truth, spit it out. I would
> want to. I would try. I am not a strong swimmer. Water cold soft.
> When I put my face into it in the basin at Clonggowes. Can't see!
> Who's behind me? Out quickly, quickly! Do you see the tide
> flowing quickly in on all sides, sheeting the lows of sand quickly,
> shellcocoacoloured? If I had land under my feet. I want his life
> still to be his, mine to be mine. A drowning man. His human eyes
> scream to me out of horror of his death. I. . . . With him together
> down. . . . I could not save her. Waters: bitter death: lost. (episode
> 3, Proteus: 3.322–30)

---

[228] Buck Mulligan speaking of Stephen: "Ten years," he said, chewing and laughing. "He is going to write something in ten years." (episode 10, Wandering Rocks: 10.1089–90) Read the almost orgasmic effect the Narrator experiences when discovering that his article was published in the newspaper *Le Figaro*. (*SCG*, vol. 2, pp. 781–84)

In *In Search of*, the Narrator is no closer to achieving heroic status than Bloom or Stephen in *Ulysses*. Early in *In Search of*, we learn, and are reminded throughout the novel, that the Narrator is a coward, a voyeurist, a liar, and, in his relationship with Albertine, an obsessively compulsive liar:

> And yet, as soon as I heard her "Bathilde! Come in and stop your husband from drinking brandy!" I became at once a man, and did what all we grown men do when face to face with suffering and injustice; I preferred not to see them. . . . (*SW*, vol. 1, p. 10)[229]

> Noiselessly I opened the window and sat down on the foot of my bed; hardly daring to move in case they should hear me from below. . . . I could hear my parents' footsteps as thy went with Swann; and when the rattle of the gate assured me that he had really gone, I crept to the window. (*SW*, vol. 1, pp. 25–26)

> But to give myself one chance of success I lied without hesitation, telling her that it was not in the least myself who had wanted to write to Mamma, but Mamma who, on saying good night to me had begged me not to forget to send her an answer about. . . . (*SW*, vol. 1, p. 23)

All three characters are observers, rather than agents, and none of them adds energy to society: Bloom spends the day avoiding his wife's lover and fails in his business task of acquiring an advertisement for the newspaper; Stephen spends a good part of the day drunk; and the Narrator spends the early part of his life manipulating a good-night kiss from his mother, the next part ingratiating himself to Society, and then enters into a psychologically sadomasochistic relationship with Albertine, which, incidentally, also involves a longing for his mother's kiss.

What if we encountered Bloom, Stephen, and the Narrator in real life, rather than as fictional characters? I suspect we would quickly become bored

---

[229] We are reminded of this scene in *CP*, vol. 2, p. 197, when, as an adult, M. Saniette behaves similarly. Dr. Cottard, a fool of the highest order, is requesting a train porter to expel a peasant who entered the first-class car: "This incident so pained and alarmed Saniette's timid spirit that, as soon as he saw it beginning, fearing already lest, in view of the crowd of peasants on the platform, it should assume the proportions of a rising, he pretended to be suffering from a stomach-ache, and, so that he might not be accused of any share in the responsibility for the doctor's violence, wandered down the corridor, pretending to be looking for what Cottard called the 'water.'"

with Stephen, impatient with Bloom, and mildly disgusted with the Narrator. In contrast, we would likely become mesmerized by the Dutchman, awed by Isolde, fascinated by Kundry, admire the quiet dignity of Hans Sachs, and captivated by the life spirit of Siegfried.

2. A Sense of Humor

Of the Wagner operas, only *Siegfried* and *Die Meistersinger* have happy endings. The lovers (Siegfried/Brünnhilde in *Siegfried*, Walter/Eva in *Die Meistersinger*) overcome many obstacles to their union that were created by the prior generation(s). Siegfried confronts Fafner, Wotan, and magic fire. Walter confronts the Meistersingers and the challenge of creating a master song. While audiences might shed a sentimental tear or two at moments in Wagner's operas, we would be hard pressed to identify a chuckle or laugh in the audience. The only time we might hear a laugh is at Siegfried's *"Das ist kein Mann"* exclamation. This is a highly dramatic scene in the opera, not a comical moment. One does not attend Wagnerian operas for their humor and gaiety.

In contrast to Wagner's characters, the characters in *Ulysses* and *In Search of* are overflowing with highbrow and lowbrow humor. *Ulysses* opens with a humorous scene with Buck Mulligan simulating a black mass. Mulligan uses his shaving tools as a chalice for the sole purpose of annoying the pompous, moody, and once very Catholic Stephen Dedalus. A few pages later (episode 1, Telemachus: 1.584–99), Mulligan sings a sacrilegious ditty. The purpose, once again, is to get under Stephen's sanctimonious skin. The reader cannot help but laugh even at the risk of eternal damnation:

> "I'm the queerest young fellow that ever you heard.
> My mother's a Jew, my father's a bird.
> With Joseph the joiner I cannot agree.
> So here's to disciples and Calvary."

He held up a forefinger of warning.

> "If anyone thinks that I'm not divine
> He'll get no free drinks when I'm making the wine
> But have to drink water and wish it were plain
> That I make when the wine becomes water again."

He tugged swiftly at Stephen's ashplant in farewell and, running forward to a brow of the cliff, fluttered his hands at his sides like fins or wings of one about to rise in the air, and chanted:

"Goodbye, now goodbye! Write down all I said
And tell Tom, Dick and Harry I rose from the dead.
What's bred in the bone cannot fail me to fly
And Olivet's breezy—Goodbye, now, goodbye!"

Bloom is not a comedian, but his meandering thoughts are hilarious. He begins his day by wondering "if it is true if you clip them [cats' whiskers] they can't mouse after. Why? They shine in the dark, perhaps the tips." (episode 4, Calypso: 4.40–41) Both assertions are ungrounded in science. A few lines later (episode 4, Calypso: 4.78), he reasons that black either reflects or refracts heat, but again, he is wrong; black absorbs heat.

Joyce "hides" most of Bloom's mistakes behind his, Joyce's, vast reservoir of knowledge. Therefore, Gifford's Ulysses *Annotated* is crucial to find Bloom's stream of mistakes. For example, Bloom is contemplating the Dead Sea: "A barren land, bare waste. Vulcanic lake, the dead sea: no fish, weedless, sunk deep in the earth. No wind could lift those waves, gray metal, poisonous foggy waters. Brimstone they called it raining down: the cities of the plain: Sodom, Gomorrah, Edom, All dead names." (episode 4, Calypso: 4.219–22) Only a scholar, or a reader of page 75 of Gifford's Ulysses *Annotated*, would know that the Dead Sea was not volcanic in origin and that Edom was not one of the five "cities of the plain" (They were Sodom, Gomorrah, Admah, Zeboiim, and Bela [subsequently Zoar].)

Back to more pedestrian "Bloom" humor, Bloom seriously contemplates whether fish ever get seasick. (episode 13, Nausicaa: 13.1162) He also puzzles over whether statues of gods have anuses:[230]

---

[230] The similarities and differences between Bloom and Stephen are accented throughout *Ulysses*. Bloom contemplates whether statues of gods have anuses whereas Stephen contemplates Eve's navel, or rather her lack of naval. In episode 3, Proteus: 3.41–44, we witness Stephen's stream of consciousness as he ponders Eve's navel: "Spouse and helpmate of Adam Kadmon: Heva, naked Eve. She had no naval. Gaze. Belly without blemish, bulging big, a buckler of taut vellum, no, whiteheaped corn, orient and immortal standing from everlasting to everlasting. Womb of sin." Both Stephen and Bloom contemplate very unusual topics. However, Stephen's contemplations address esoteric questions whereas Bloom's are very pedestrian.

Lovely forms of women sculped Junonian. Immortal lovely. And we stuffing food in one hole and out behind: food, chyle, blood, dung, earth, food: have to feed it like stoking an engine. They have no. Never looked. I'll look today. Keeper won't see. Bend down let something drop. See if she. (episode 8, Lestrygonians: 8.928f)

We learn later that Bloom conducts this empirical investigation. (episode 9, Scylla and Charybdis: 9.609–11, and episode 13, Nausicaa: 13.1215) In the penultimate episode, Bloom laments an "imperfection in a perfect day"—that he was unable "to certify the presence or absence of posterior rectal orifice in the case of Hellenic female divinities." (episode 17, Ithaca: 17.2071–78)

A second "imperfection to a perfect day," and one that has an almost Shakespearian quality, is confusing the name of a raincoat (macintosh) with the name of a person (M'Intosh).[231] The setting: it is around 11:45 a.m. Bloom is at a funeral and is counting the number of attendees. He notices a man in a macintosh, i.e., a full-length waterproof coat, and says to himself:

Now who is that lanky looking galoot over there in the macintosh? Now who is he I'd like to know. Now I'd give a trifle to know who he is. Always someone turns up you never dreamt of. (episode 6, Hades: 6.805-8)

A few lines later, a reporter (Joe Hynes), is tabulating the funeral attendees' names for the evening paper. He asks Bloom if Bloom knows the person in the macintosh raincoat. Joe Hynes asks: "that fellow in the, fellow was over there in the. . . ." to which Bloom interrupts:

- Macintosh. Yes, I saw him, Mr. Bloom said. Where is he now?
- M'Intosh, Hynes said scribbling. I don't know who he is. Is that his name?
He moved away, looking about him.

---

[231] Owens, *Before Daybreak "After the Race" and The Origins of Joyce's Art*, 2010, pp.134–138. Although it is easy just to see the humor in the "macintosh" stream of encounters, Cóilín Owens provides historical context to Mr. M'Intosh. During this period in Irish history, Irish streets were littered with English spies as "observers" (paid local informers) and "carriers" (informers posing as travelers and tourists). Owens argues that Macintosh, first observed by Bloom at Paddy Dignam's funeral (episode 6, Hades), may have been an English spy.

- No, Mr. Bloom began, turning and stopping. I say, Hynes!
Didn't hear. What? Where has he disappeared to? Not a sign.
Well of all the. Has anybody here seen? Kay ee double ell.
Become invisible. Good Lord, what became of him? (episode 6,
Hades: 6.894–901)

Throughout the day, the man in the brown macintosh appears in person, in print, and in thought: 10.1271; 11.1250, 12.1498; 13.1062; 14.1546–53; 15.1558; 15.1663; 15.2308; and 16.1250. Culminating in the early hours of the next day, as Bloom is getting ready for bed, he thinks: "Who was M'Intosh?" (episode 17, Ithaca: 17.2063f)

Joyce is at his linguistic best when he gets on a roll playing with names. For example, in episode 12, Cyclops, beginning at line 1267, Joyce enumerates the guests attending a "fashionable international" wedding. For the next 30 lines he names almost every imaginable tree and then some. For example, attendees include Lady Sylvester Elmshade, Mrs. Barbara Lovebirch, Miss May Hawthorne, Miss Gladys Beech, Miss Bee Honeysuckle, Mrs. Norma Holyoake of Oakholme Regis, etc. The newly married couple, Mr. and Mrs. Wyse Conifer Neaulan will spend a quiet honeymoon in the Black Forest.

The Narrator's humor in *In Search of* generally is more cultured, yet it is equally as hilarious as Bloom's situational quips. While Joyce describes the thoughts of the ordinary person in ordinary terms, Proust describes the thoughts of a highly intellectual and erudite person, i.e., the Narrator. For example, we are at the theater and everyone is looking to see who they recognize:

The Marquis de Palancy, his face bent downwards at the end of his long neck, his round bulging eye glued to the glass of his monocle, was moving with a leisurely displacement through the transparent shade and appeared no more to see the public in the stalls than a fish that drifts past, unconscious of the press of curious gazers, behind the glass wall of an aquarium. Now and again he paused, a venerable wheezing monument, and the audience could not have told whether he was in pain, asleep, swimming, about to spawn, or merely taking breath. (GW, vol. 1, p. 744)

In Search of is, in part, a social satire. In this capacity, Proust uses humor, irony, and ridicule to describe the pretentiousness, snobbery, cruelty, and intellectual sterility present in every social stratum, particularly in the aristocracy. One can either be disgusted or entertained by their superficiality. If you choose the entertainment route, you will spend a lot of time laughing. Perhaps it is best to be both: disgusted and entertained. As one of countless examples, Mme. de Villeparisis invited an unknown middle class gentleman to one of her parties. This integration of different social strata "began gradually to depreciate her in the eyes of the snobs who were in the habit of estimating the smartness of a house by the people whom its mistress excluded rather than by those whom she entertained." (*GW*, vol. 1, p. 849)

Below are several examples of humor in which not knowing the context does not interfere with appreciating the humor.

> Mme. de Guermantes meanwhile had greeted Alix, with apologies for not having been able, that year as in every previous year, to go and see her. "I hear all about you from Madeleine," she added. (*GW*, vol. 1, p. 859)

> "I think you wished to speak to him about the Dreyfus case," she went on, no more considering whether this would suit M. de Norpois than she would have thought of asking leave of the Duchess de Montmorency's portrait before having it lighted up for the historian, or of the tea before pouring it into a cup. (*GW*, vol. 1, p. 874)

> "In fact, it was drolatic," put in M. de Guermantes, whose odd vocabulary enabled people in society to declare that he was no fool and literary people, at the same time, to regard him as a complete imbecile. (*GW*, vol. 1, p 878)

Probably the biggest insult the Narrator can levy against someone is their lack of interest in details. Hence the cutting, i.e., humorous, in Proustian style, comment regarding his father's recently acquired admiration for Mme. de Villeparisis:

> "In fact, he said she kept a School of Wit," my father announced to us, impressed by the vagueness of this expression, which he had indeed come across now and then in volumes of memoirs, but without attaching to it any definite meaning. (*GW*, vol. 1, p. 822)

One of the Narrator's favorite objects of ridicule is Dr. Cottard, a provincial physician trying with all his efforts to climb the social ladder:

> Dr. Cottard was never quite certain of the tone in which he ought to reply to any observation, or whether the speaker was jesting or in earnest. And so, in any event he would embellish all his facial expressions with the offer of a conditional, a provisional smile whose expectant subtlety would exonerate him from the charge of being a simpleton, if the remark addressed to him should turn out to have been facetious. (*SW*, vol. 1, p. 153)

Swann, whose social circle includes the highest levels of aristocratic, nobility, and political French society and beyond, has descended outside the purview of Society to be with Odette at the Verdurins' home. Cottard, having discovered that Swann is "someone," tries to ingratiate himself to Swann:

> But so great and glorious a figure was the President of the French Republic in the eyes of Dr. Cottard that neither the modesty of Swann nor the spite of Mme. Verdurin could ever wholly efface the first impression and he never sat down to dinner with the Verdurins without asking anxiously, "D'you think we shall see M. Swann here this evening? He is a personal friend of M. Grevy's. I suppose that means he's what you'd call a 'gentleman?'" He even went to the length of offering Swann a card of invitation to the Dental Exhibition. "This will let you in, and anyone you take with you," he explained, "but dogs are not admitted. I'm just warning you, you understand, because some friends of mine went there once, who hadn't been told, and there was the devil to pay." (*SW*, vol. 1, p. 166)

The Narrator is not shy in making fun of himself. On one of his first visits, not into Society proper, but a step up the social ladder, he is trying to "figure out the rules":

> Meanwhile we had taken our places at the table. By the side of my plate I found a carnation, the stalk of which was wrapped in silver paper. It embarrassed me less than the envelop that had been handed to me in the hall, which, however, I had completely forgotten. This custom, strange as it was to me,

became more intelligible when I saw all the male guests take up the similar carnations that were lying by their plates and slip them into the buttonholes of their coats. I did as they had done, with the air of spontaneity. . . . On the other side of my plate was a smaller plate, on which was heaped a blackish substance which I had not then known to be caviar. I was ignorant of what was to be done with it but firmly determined not to let it enter my mouth. (*WBG*, vol. 1, pp. 418–19)

He also enjoys pointing out misuses of the French language. For example, the Narrator, after a very nasty reproach to their long-term family servant Françoise: "'[Y]ou have never learned . . . how to pronounce words without making silly blunders'," he realizes that "this reproach was particularly stupid, for those French words which we are so proud of pronouncing accurately are themselves only blunders made by the Gallic lips which mispronounced Latin or Saxon, our language being merely a defective pronunciation of several others." (*C*, vol. 2, p. 99)

I end with an insult by M. de Charlus, perhaps the most colorful character in all of Proust's artistic palate. Charlus is Proust's Falstaff in physical size, slashing verbal skills, waning importance, and in an ignominious end. His verbal tirades have the gymnastic virtuosity of a Charlie Chaplin routine. Charlus loves to hear himself pontificate. Below is an excerpt from his attack on someone's claim to have an aristocratic lineage to the title of "Duke":

"The present Duke, if Duke he can be called, is the third. You may talk to me if you like of people like the Uzes, the La Trémoïlle, the Luynes, who are tenth or fourteenth Dukes, or my brother who is twelfth Duc de Guermantes and seventeenth Prince of Cordova. The Montesquiou are descended from an old family, what would that prove, supposing that it were proved? They have descended so far that they have reached the fourteenth storey below stairs." (*C*, vol. 2, p. 542)

Both *Ulysses* and *In Search of* are filled with humor. Sometimes the humor is easy to miss and can get lost in the serious historical and literary status of these two books. By relaxing your guard against the pretentiousness of "high culture," these two books will give you hours of humorous delight and laughter.

3.   Eroticism

Wagner's operas are highly erotic. I would guess that most men would love to find themselves in Tannhäuser's Venusberg, and I have been told that some women have orgasms during Isolde's Liebestod. Wagner's eroticism ranges from playful, as in the opening scenes of *Die Meistersinger* and act 2 of *Parsifal*, to imaginative, as in Senta's fantasy to redeem the Dutchman, to explicit, as in the closing scenes of act 1 of *Die Walküre* and act 3 of *Siegfried* in *The Ring*.

Wagner's music has been labeled erotic, passionate, orgiastic, indecent, perverse, arousing sexual desire, and having no place in an opera house. A question asked during Wagner's time, and also in our time, was how to distinguish between high art and low art. Another way to state this question is how to articulate the difference between romantic love from "perversity and unnaturalness" and the pornographic.[232]

Charles Baudelaire advocated for Wagner's "high art" status. In "Richard Wagner and *Tannhäuser* in Paris" (1861), Baudelaire was among the first to recognize the erotic nature of Wagner's music as a positive aesthetic achievement. On the other side of the debate is a critique of *Tristan and Isolde* as being no better than "flunkeys covered with reptilian slime" and hysterical females throwing "their pleasure-weary frog-legs into violent convulsions":

> ...the wild Wagnerian corybantic orgy. . . . this lewd caterwauling, scandal-mongering, gun-toting music, with an orchestral accompaniment slapping you in the face. . . . Hence, the secret fascination that makes it the darling of feeble-minded royalty, the plaything of the camarilla, of the court flunkeys covered with reptilian slime, and of the blasé hysterical female court parasites who need this galvanic stimulation by massive instrumental treatment to throw their pleasure-weary frog-legs into violent convulsion.[233]

---

[232] See Laurence Dreyfus, *Wagner and the Erotic Impulse*. In chapter 1, Dreyfus provides an overview of the reaction to Wagner's music in respectable society. For example, "What nineteenth-century critics found appalling in the case of Wagner was the pretense that his music was not designed to titillate or arouse but proposed a philosophy of life" p. 36.

[233] Dreyfus, pp. 34–35, quoted from H. L. Klein's eight-volume *History of Drama* (Leipzig, 1871). For those needing help with some of the terms, "corybantic" means wild frenzied, "caterwauling" means shrill wailing noise like a cat, and "camarilla" means advisors with nefarious purposes.

Convulsing frog legs or not, we encounter an entirely different display of sensuality and sexuality in *Ulysses* and *In Search of.* First, the sex is not subtle. Bloom has been thinking about sex the entire day and finally succumbs to his urges in episode 13: Nausicaa. Written in the style of soft porn, in this episode, both he and Gerty MacDowell mutually masturbate: Bloom, by gazing up a hill at her spreading and rocking her legs; Gerty, by her spreading and rocking legs.

Gerty, gazing down the hill at Bloom, has been fantasizing about "his dark eyes and his pale intellectual face that he was a foreigner, the image of the photo she had of Martin Harvey, the matinee idol" for several pages. Kicking a ball to the children she was babysitting,

> . . . she just lifted her skirt a little but just enough and took good aim and gave the ball a jolly good kick and it went ever so far and the two twins after it down towards the shingle. Pure jealousy of course it was nothing else to draw attention on account of the gentleman opposite looking. She felt a warm flush, a danger signal always with Gerty MacDowell, surging and flaming into her cheeks. Till then they had only exchanged glances. . . . (episode 13, Nausicaa: 13.361–66)

And then, as the evening fireworks display was occurring:

> . . . and she wasn't ashamed and he wasn't either to look in that immodest way like that because he couldn't resist the sight of the wonderous revealment half offered like hose skirtdancers behaving so immodest before gentlemen looking and he kept looking, looking. She would fain have cried to him chokingly, held out her snowy slender arms to him to come, to feel his lips laid on her white brow, the cry of a young girl's love, a little strangled cry, wrung from her, that cry that has rung through the ages. And then a rocket sprang and bang shot blind blank and o! then the Roman candle burst and it was like a sigh of O! and everyone cried O! O! in raptures and it gushed out of it a stream of rain gold hair threads and they shed and ah! They were all greeny dewy stars falling with golden, O so lovely, O, soft, sweet, soft! (episode 13, Nausicaa: 13.730–40)

Bloom, who had been watching with his hands in his pocket:[234]

> Mr. Bloom with careful hand recomposed his wet shirt. O Lord that little imping devil. Begins to feel cold and clammy. Aftereffect not pleasant. Still you have to get rid of it someway. They don't care. Complimented perhaps.... (episode 13, Nausicaa: 13. 851–54)[235]

A bit earlier in the day, Molly, has been having her fling with Blazes Boylan. In episode 18: Penelope, we hear part of her recollections of her afternoon with Blazes:

> . . . when I lit the lamp because he must have come 3 or 4 times with that tremendous big red brute of a thing he has I thought the vein or whatever the dickens they call it was going to burst through his nose is not so big after I took off all of my things with the blinds down after my hours dressing and perfuming and combing it like iron or some kind of a thick crowbar standing all the time he must have eaten oysters I think a few dozen he was in great singing voice no I never in all my life felt anyone had one the size of that to make you feel full up he must have eaten a whole sheep after whats the idea making us like that with a big hole in the middle of us or like a Stallion. . . . (episode 18, Penelope: 18.143–52)

We also learn the when and wherefore of their son Rudy's conception:

> If little Rudy had lived. See him grow up. Hear his voice in the house. Walking beside Molly in an Eton suit. My son. Me in his eyes. Strange feeling it would be. For me. Just a chance. Must have been that morning in Raymond terrace she was at the window watching the two dogs at it by the wall of the cease to do evil. And the sergeant grinning up. She had that cream gown on with the rip she never stitched. Give us a touch, Poldy. God. I'm dying for it. How life begins. (episode 6, Hades: 6.75–81)

---

[234] We learn in episode 15, Circe: 15.3365, that Bloom has a history of masturbating. In a hallucinatory frenzy that takes him back to when he was sixteen, Bloom mutters: "Simply satisfying a need I .... (with pathos) No girl would when I went girling. Too ugly. They wouldn't play...."

[235] Bloom appears to have a history of masturbating outside. See episode 15, Circe, 15.3332-68.

Bloom's sexual expressions often are frustrated, but at least on the surface his sexual desires are within the range of normal. His relationship with Molly, admittedly strained, hopefully will work out with time.

In *In Search of*, the Narrator's sexual expression is stunted; it never developed beyond his early need to possess his mother. As a result, he never develops a mature relationship with a woman.

The Narrator's sexual experience starts out normal enough with nocturnal emissions and adolescent masturbation. On the second page of the book we learn about his early sexual dreams:

> Sometimes, too, just as Eve was created from a rib of Adam, so a woman would come into existence while I was sleeping, conceived from some strain in the position of my limbs. Formed by the appetite that I was on the point of gratifying, she it was, I imagined, who offered me that gratification. (*SW*, vol. 1, p. 4)

And a few pages later he tells us about a room to which he would go to masturbate:

> Intended for a more special and a baser use, this room, from which in the daytime I could see as far as the keep of Roussainville-le-Pin, was for a long time my place of refuge, doubtless because it was the only room whose door I was allowed to lock, whenever my occupation was such as required an inviolable solitude, reading or dreaming, secret tears or paroxysms of desire. (*SW*, vol. 1, p. 10)

The Narrator reminds us of his adolescent habit at the end of Book 6, *The Sweet Cheat Gone*. Gilberte reminds him of an event years ago when they were young, perhaps twelve: "I signaled to you so vulgarly that I am ashamed of it to this day" to which the Narrator later reflects that "Only I had supposed, because of the coarse gesture that accompanied it, that it was a contemptuous gaze because what I longed for it to mean seemed to me to be a thing that little girls did not know about and did only in my imagination, during my hours of solitary desire." (*SCG*, vol. 2, pp. 866–67)

The Narrator's need for self-gratification persists even when Albertine, his mistress, is next door and willing to engage in sexual intercourse:

> I did not send for her at once, especially if it was a fine day. For some moments, knowing that he would make me happier than Albertine, I remained closeted with the little person inside me, hymning the rising sun, of whom I have already spoken. (C, vol. 2, p. 385)[236]

And when he is with Albertine, he masturbates as she sleeps:

> Then, feeling that the tide of her sleep was full, that I should not ground upon reefs of consciousness covered now by the high water of profound slumber, deliberately, I crept without a sound upon the bed, lay down by her side, clasped her waist in one arm, placed my lips upon her cheek and heart, then upon every part of her body in turn laid my free hand, which also was raised like the pearls, by Albertine's breathing; I myself was gently rocked by its regular motion: I had embarked upon the tide of Albertine's sleep. Sometimes it made me taste a pleasure that was less pure. For this I had no need to make any movement, I allowed my leg to dangle against hers, like an oar which one allows to trail in the water, imparting to it now and again a gentle oscillation like the intermittent flap given to its wing by a bird asleep in the air. (C, vol. 2, p. 427)

Now we shift gears into the perverse: the Narrator's voyeurism, his propensity to associating sex with his mother's kiss, and his fondness for young girls, what we call pedophilia.

Early in Book 4: *Cities of the Plain*, the Narrator is looking through a window watching an insect pollinate a plant when he hears Jupien and M. de Charlus enter into a mating courtship mirroring the insect and flower the Narrator is watching. For the next several pages the Narrator describes his exploits in obtaining the best view without calling attention to himself:

> . . . I was greatly annoyed at not being able to hear any more of the conversation between the ex-tailor and the Baron. I then bethought myself of the vacant shop, separated from Jupien's only by a partition that was extremely slender. I had, in order to get to it, merely to go up to our flat, pass through the kitchen, go down

---

[236] See Book 7, *PR*, p. 887, for a continuation of the Narrator's habit for self-gratification when visiting Gilberte, now the Marquise de Saint-Loup.

by the service stair to the cellars, make my way through them across the breadth of the courtyard above, and on coming to the right place underground, where the joiner had, a few months ago, still been storing his timber and where Jupien intended to keep his coal, climb the flight of steps which led to the interior of the shop. Thus the whole of my journey would be made under cover, I should not be seen by anyone. (CP, vol. 2, pp. 7–8)

In the above passage, the Narrator chose to go another way, but his objective was the same: to surreptitiously observe two people having sex.

There is an unhealthy sexual association between the Narrator and his mother, although it is unbeknownst to her. During the Narrator's adult life, the thought of his mother either coming or not coming "upstairs to say good-night to me" (which really involved her goodnight kiss) enters the Narrator's mind so often that it suggests a sexually stunted personality. Even more peculiar, when he is having sex, his thoughts stray to his mother's kiss:

Albertine's throat, which emerged bodily from her nightgown, was strongly build, sunburned, of coarse grain. I kissed her as purely as if I had been kissing my mother to charm away a childish grief which as a child I did not believe that I would ever be able to eradicate from my heart. Albertine left me, in order to go and dress. (CP, vol. 2, p. 373)

I had ceased for a moment to hear these words ringing in my ears while Albertine was with me just now. While I was kissing her, as I used to kiss my mother, at Combray, to calm my anguish. . . . (CP, vol. 2, p. 375)

On other evenings, I undressed, I lay down, and, with Albertine perched on my side of my bed, we resumed our game or our conversation interrupted by kisses ... on one occasion, catching sight of myself in the glass at the moment when I was kissing Albertine and calling her my little girl ... that I felt of keeping Albertine in this way every evening by my side, something that had hitherto been unknown, at least in my amorous existence, if it was not entirely novel in my life ... It was a soothing power the like of which I had not known since the evening at Combray long ago when my mother, stooping over my bed, brought me repose in a kiss. (C, vol. 2, pp. 430–31)

And when planning to pick the moment to break off his relationship with Albertine:[237]

> I must not wait too long, I must be prudent. And yet having waited so long, it would be madness not to wait a few days longer, until an acceptable moment should offer itself, rather than risk seeing her depart with that same sense of revolt which I had felt in the past when Mamma left my bedside without bidding me good night or when she said good-bye to me at the station. (C, vol. 2, p. 656)

We also learn that the Narrator is sexually attracted to young girls. He not only likes to "pick up" young dairy maids, laundresses, and other socially and economically vulnerable girls but also young prostitutes. Conversing with his friend, Robert, about houses of ill repute, Robert says: "'Anyhow, I can take you to some far better ones, full of stunning women.' Hearing me express the desire that he would take me as soon as possible to the ones he knew, which must indeed be far superior to the house to which Block had taken me, he expressed a sincere regret that he could not, on this occasion, as he would have to leave Paris next day. 'It will have to be on my next leave,' he said. 'You'll see, there are young girls there, even,' he added with an air of mystery. 'There is a little Mademoiselle de. . . .'" (CP, p. 69)

Shortly after Albertine leaves him, the Narrator turns to a very young girl:

> Outside the door of Albertine's house I found a poor little girl who gazed at me open-eyed and looked so honest that I asked her whether she would care to come home with me, as I might have taken home a dog with faithful eyes. She seemed pleased by my suggestion. When I got home, I held her for some time on my knee, but very soon her presence by making

---

[237] Albertine's age is unclear when she and the Narrator have their first bedroom encounter: "I was going to learn the fragrance, the flavour which this strange pink fruit concealed. I heard a sound, precipitous, prolonged, shrill. Albertine had pulled the bell with all her might." (WBG, vol. 1, p. 699) Given some textual evidence about the 1989 World's Fair, we can suppose the Narrator to be around seventeen. (WBG, vol. 1, p. 659) We also learned that Albertine was studying for her certificate examination. (WBG, vol. 1, p. 682) In Proust's time, the certificate examination (certificate d'études) was the first examination given to children after compulsory education was instituted. At the time, it was given to children between the age of ten and twelve. This examination no longer exists. I thank Catherine Sandifer for this information. Ms. Sandifer received her MA in British and American literature from the Sorbonne.

me feel too keenly Albertine's absence, became intolerable. And I asked her to go away, giving her first a five-hundred franc note. (SCG, vol. 2, p. 684)

Several pages later the police and the girl's father appear at his door.

Nevertheless, the difficulty of a conviction enabled me to escape with an extremely violent reprimand, while the parents were in the room. But as soon as they had gone, the head of the Sûreté, who had a weakness for little girls, changed his tone and admonished me as one man to another: "Next time you must be more careful. Gad, you can't pick them up as easily as that, or you'll get into trouble. Anyhow, you can find dozens of girls better than that one, and far cheaper." (SCG, vol. 2, p. 694)

The Narrator never outgrows his fetish for young girls. Near the end of the novel, the Narrator, who is now around fifty years of age and ready to write his masterpiece, ponders:

I looked at Gilberte and did not think to myself, "I would like to see her again," but I told her it would always give me pleasure to be invited by her to meet some young girls, but without harbouring the intention of asking anything more of them than to reawaken in me the reveries and sorrows of earlier years-and mayhap, on some unlikely day, a chaste kiss. (PR, vol. 2, p. 1081)

Perhaps we can psychoanalyze the Narrator's need for young girls "in the first bloom of youth" (PR, vol. 2, p. 1080) as an infantile regression to his need for his mother's kiss.

Wagner was a Romantic artist. His portrayals of eroticism, while idealized, pushed social limits. While Wagner's characters engaged in incest (Siegmund and Sieglinde, Siegfried and Brünnhilde) and attempted seduction through memories of a mother's kiss (Kundry and Parsifal), these portrayals were part of an overall uplifting experience for the audience. The characters were intended to provide insight into the human condition by creating empathy, compassion, and the vicarious experience of love. In contrast, Joyce and Proust were Modern artists. In *Ulysses* and *In Search of Lost Time*, the characters engaged in erotic acts for ordinary, mundane, and perverse reasons. In these works, the reader finds that romantic ideals are brought down to earth.

Appendix C. Table 2: Structure of Joyce's *Ulysses*

This schema of the novel *Ulysses* was produced by its author, James Joyce, in 1921 to help his friend, Stuart Gilbert, understand the underlying structure of *Ulysses*. Gilbert published it in 1930 in his book *James Joyce's* Ulysses: *A Study*.[238]

Title	Scene	Hour	Organ	Meaning	Symbol	Art/Science	Technic
Telemachus	The Tower	8:00 a.m.		Dispossessed son	Heir	Theology	Narrative (young)
Nestor	The School	10:00 a.m.		Wisdom of the ancients	Ulster	History	Catechism (personal)
Proteus	The Strand	11:00 a.m.		Primal matter	Tide	Philology	Monologue (male)
Calypso	The House	8:00 a.m.	Kidney	Departing wayfarer	Nymph, vagina	Economics	Narrative (mature)
Lotus Eaters	The Bath	10:00 a.m.	Genitals	Temptation of faith	Drugs, penis	Botany, Chemistry	Narcissism
Hades	The Graveyard	11:00 a.m.	Heart	Descent into nothingness	The past	Religion	Dialogue, narrative
Aeolus	Newspaper	12:00 p.m.	Lungs	Derision of victory	Wind, fame	Rhetoric	Epideictic, tropes
Lestrygonians	The Lunch	1:00 p.m.	Esophagus	Despondency	Food	Architecture	Peristaltic
Scylla and Charybdis	The Library	2:00 p.m.	Brain	Double-edged sword	Hamlet	Literature	Dialectic
Wandering Rocks	The Streets	3:00 p.m.	Blood	Hostile milieu	Homonyms	Mechanics	Shifting labyrinth
Sirens	Concert Room	4:00 p.m.	Ear	Sweet deceit	Female, sounds	Music	*Fuga per canonem*
Cyclops	The Tavern	5:00 p.m.	Muscle, Bone	Egocidal terror	Fanaticism, nation	Politics	Gigantism
Nausicaa	The Rocks	8:00 p.m.	Eye, nose	Projected mirage	Virgin, onanism	Painting	Retrogressive progression
Oxen of the Sun	The Hospital	10:00 p.m.	Womb	Eternal herds	Fertilization, mothers	Medicine	Embryonic development
Circe	The Brothel	12:00 a.m.	Locomotor, apparatus	Man-hating ogress	Whore	Magic	Hallucination
Eumaeus	The Shelter	1:00 a.m.	Nerves	Ambush on home ground	Sailors	Navigation	Narrative (old)
Ithaca	The House	2:00 a.m.	Juices	Armed hope	Comets	Science	Catechism (impersonal)
Penelope	The Bed	∞	Flesh, Fat	The past sleeps	Earth		Monologue (female)

[238] This table is a modified version of "Linati schema for *Ulysses*," *Wikipedia*, last updated December 27, 2019, https://en.wikipedia.org/wiki/Linati_schema_for_Ulysses. I excluded two columns: Color and People. For example, episode 1, Telemachus, the color is gold/white and the people are Telemachus, Mentor, Antinous, Suitors, and Penelope. These people are from Homer's *Odyssey* and are not mentioned by name in Joyce's *Ulysses*. In addition to *Ulysses*, Joyce wrote several other major works. These include *Chamber Music* (1907), *Dubliners* (1914), *A Portrait of the Artist as a Young Man* (1916), *Exiles* (1918) and *Finnegans Wake* (1939).

Appendix D. Tables 3, 4, and 5:
Dates of Composition and Publication

Table 3: Richard Wagner: Mature Operas/Music Dramas[239]

Opera	Date Libretto Completed	Dates of Music Composition	Date Premiered
The Flying Dutchman	1841	1841	1843
Tannhäuser	1843	1843–1845	1845; revised 1861
Lohengrin	1845	1846–1848	1850
Das Rheingold*	1852	1853–1854	1869
Die Walküre*	1852	1854–1856	1870
Tristan und Isolde	1857	1857–1859	1865
Die Meistersinger	1862	1861–1867	1868
Siegfried*	1851	1856–1871	1876
Götterdämmerung*	1848	1871–1874	1876
Parsifal	1877	1877–1882	1882
	* Der Ring des Nibelungen (German); The Ring of the Nibelung		

Table 4: James Joyce: Episodes in Ulysses*[240]

Episode	Date of Completion	Date of Publication in serialized parts in the American avant-garde magazine Little Review
episode 1: Telemachus	November 1917	March 1918
episode 2: Nestor	December 1917	April 1918
episode 3: Proteus	December 1917	May 1918
episode 4: Calypso	March 1918	June 1918
episode 5: Lotus Eaters	April 1918	July 1918

---

[239] This table is a modified version of "Richard Wagner Operatic Works," Wagner Operas, accessed on September 23, 2020, http://www.wagneroperas.com/indexwagneroperas.html.

[240] Ellmann, James Joyce, pp. 440–41.

Episode	Date of Completion	Date of Publication in serialized parts in the American avant-garde magazine *Little Review*
episode 7: Aeolus	August 1918	October 1918
episode 8: Lestrygonians	October 1918	January–March 1919
episode 9: Scylla and Charybdis	February 1919	April–May 1919
episode 10: Wandering Rocks	February 1919	June–July 1919
episode 11: Sirens	June 1919	August 1919–March 1920
episode 12: Cyclops	June 1919	August 1919–March 1920
episode 13: Nausicaa	March 1920	April–August 1920
episode 14: Oven of the Sun	May 1920	September–December 1920
episode 15: Circe	December 1920	September–December 1920
episode 16: Eumaeus	February 1921	September–December 1920
episode 17: Ithaca	October 1921	September–December 1920
episode 18: Penelope	October 1921	September–December 1920
* Published in its entirety in Paris by Sylvia Beach in February 1922.		

Table 5: Marcel Proust: *In Search of Lost Time** [241]

Book	Year of Publication*	Explanation
Swann's Way	1913	
Within a Budding Grove	1919**	Scheduled for October 1914 but delayed due to World War I.
The Guermantes Way	1921	
Cities of the Plain (Sodom and Gomorrah)	1921	
The Captive	1923 posthumously	
The Sweet Cheat Gone (The Fugitive)	1925 posthumously	
The Past Recaptured	1927 posthumously	
* Excluding revisions and proof enrichment, the entire book was completed during the first half of 1918.		
**Awarded the 1919 Goncourt Prize for *WBG*. In September 1920 Proust was awarded the cross of the Legion of Honour.		

[241] Abstracted from *Wikipedia*, "*In Search of Lost Time*," last updated on October 24, 2020, https://en.wikipedia.org/wiki/In_Search_of_Lost_Time.

Appendix E. Glossary of Wagner Operas and Characters Referred to in *Three Pillars of Modern Western Culture*

Wagner wrote 10 major operas that are performed regularly. (See Appendix D, Table 3) Wagner also wrote three early operas (*Die Feen, Das Liebesverbot,* and *Rienzi*) that are rarely performed. Below is a glossary of Wagner operas and characters mentioned in this book. For those interested in a more in-depth glossary of Wagnerian characters, see Jonathan Lewsey, *Who's Who and What's What in Wagner* (Brookfield, Ashgate Publishing Company, 1997).

Alberich. Alberich initiates the story and motivates much of the action of *The Ring.* (See **The Ring of the Nibelung** below.) He is a member of the Nibelungs or dwarf race. In the opening scene of *Das Rheingold,* the first opera of this tetralogy, Alberich is attempting to seduce the Rhine daughters, the guardians of the Rhinegold, when he sees a mound of gold. Upon inquiry, the Rhine daughters inform him that anyone who shapes the gold into a ring will have untold powers, but at the cost of losing the emotion of love. Alberich decides to trade his emotion of love and all that love entails, e.g., friendship, compassion, and kindness, for the power embodied in the gold. He renounces love, takes the gold, and forges the ring. The ring is soon stolen from him by Wotan. (See **Wotan** below.) As a result, Alberich places a nasty curse on the ring: "death to whoever shall wear it," and "each man shall covert its acquisition, but none shall enjoy it to lasting gain." From this point forward, his curse permeates *The Ring.*

Brünnhilde. Brünnhilde is the daughter of Wotan, the king of the gods, and Erda, the primordial earth mother. She appears in the last three operas of *The Ring* tetralogy. (See **The Ring of the Nibelung** below.) Brünnhilde is her father's favorite among the nine Valkyries. Collectively, the role of the Valkyries is to bring dead heroes to Valhalla.

We meet Brünnhilde in *Die Walküre,* the second of *The Ring.* In act 2, she defies her father's orders by defending Siegmund, Wotan's son, against Hunding, the cruel husband of Siegmund's sister, Sieglinde. Her punishment includes losing her god status, thus being transformed into a human, and being put to sleep to be awakened by, and become the property of, the first man to see her. After much pleading by Brünnhilde, Wotan modifies her punishment. He tells Brünnhilde that she will sleep surrounded by fire and will be awoken by a hero. The music tells us the hero will be Siegfried, the son of Siegmund and Sieglinde. Brünnhilde is awakened in act 3 of the third opera, *Siegfried*. She plays a major role in the fourth and final opera, *Götterdämmerung*.

Wotan, Siegfried, and Brünnhilde each are candidates for the status of "the hero of *The Ring*." In some historic periods, the hero label is assigned to Wotan as the embodiment of Schopenhauer's renunciation of the Will. In other historic periods that title is assigned to Siegfried as representing the free spirit of the coming age. Today, that honor often is given to Brünnhilde. Of these three characters, Brünnhilde is the only one aware of the passage of time. Her father, Wotan, is locked in the cultural and moral order of legal contracts. He cannot see his way out of the present that he has created. Siegfried, Wotan's grandchild, has no sense of time. Siegfried lives in the present and outside of history and culture. Brünnhilde knows the role of the past in creating the present and paves the way for a future.

Die Meistersinger von Nürnberg (1867). *Die Meistersinger* takes place in Nuremberg during the sixteenth century, and it is a story about artistic creativity. The story is framed around four people: Walter von Stolzing, an outsider; Eva Pogner, the daughter of a member of the guild of Meistersingers; and Hans Sachs and Sixtus Beckmesser, both members of the Meistersinger guild. Walter, smitten by Eva, learns that to win Eva's hand he first must become a Meistersinger. This entails creating a poem and original music to set the poem. The magnitude of this challenge is compounded by that fact that Walter must create this work of art within a very short time frame and against several covert and overt enemies, one of whom is Beckmesser, who also is interested in Eva. Hans Sachs serves as the metaphorical midwife for the birth of Walter's master song. In the end, love, art, and civic harmony prevail.

Die Walküre (1856). *Die Walküre* is the second opera of *The Ring* tetralogy. In *Das Rheingold*, the first opera of *The Ring*, we are immersed in a universe where love has been bartered for power. In *Die Walküre*, love tries to reassert itself. In act 1, against a background of violence and unhappiness, the love between Siegmund and Sieglinde momentarily flourishes. In acts 2 and 3, all attempts at love fail: the love between Wotan and Fricka (Wotan's wife) is severed, the love between Sieglinde and Siegmund ends in Siegmund's ignoble death and Sieglinde's prospect of a lonely childbirth and death, and Brünnhilde's banishment from Valhalla for disobeying her father, Wotan. We must wait for act 3 of the third opera, *Siegfried*, for love to flourish again, if only momentarily.

Gunther and Hagen. Gunther and Hagen appear in *Göttterdämmerung*, the fourth of *The Ring* tetralogy. Gunther, who is weak and easily manipulated, is the unmarried king of the land of the Gibichungs. Hagen is his stepbrother. Hagen's father is Alberich (see **Alberich** above). Hagen orchestrates much of the action in *Göttterdämmerung*. His plan is to retrieve his father's ring which is now in the possession of Siegfried and Brünnhilde. The ring was taken from his father by Wotan in *Das Rheingold*, the first opera in *The Ring*.

Hans Sachs. Hans Sachs is the humanist and moral backbone in Wagner's opera *Die Meistersinger*. Eva Pogner's father offers his daughter in marriage to the member of the Meistersinger guild who wins the song contest. To win, the suiter must create an original song and melody. Eva loves Walter von Stolzing, but Walter is not a member of the Guild. Hans Sachs, a shoemaker and a member of the Meistersinger guild, serves as the metaphorical midwife and baptizer of Walter's "Prize Song." The Prize Song enables Walter to become a Meistersinger (member of the master singer's guild) and thereby win the hand of Eva Pogner. Hans Sachs exemplifies the humanist tradition of serving the well-being of the community and guiding the community through conflict. He is one of the few Wagnerian characters we would be happy to have as a neighbor.

Hunding. In *Die Walküre*, the second opera of *The Ring* tetralogy, we encounter Hunding, the crude and brutal husband of Sieglinde, the daughter of Wotan. Hunding's home environment for Sieglinde is solitary, poor, nasty, and brutish. This domestic environment is the manifestation of the loveless world created in *Das Rheingold*, the first opera of *The Ring*. Hunding returns home from battle to find the unarmed Siegmund. Hunding learns that Siegmund is a family enemy, and therefore the two must engage in mortal combat the next morning. It is of no interest to Hunding that Siegmund is unarmed.

Kundry. Kundry is among the weirdest characters in the Wagner panoply of characters. She appears in all three acts of Wagner's last opera, *Parsifal*. (**See** *Parsifal* below.) In act 1, she is an unkempt hag. In act 2, she is a seductress, and in act 3, a penitent. *Parsifal* has three main agents: Klingsor, Parsifal, and Kundry. They each made at least one poor decision and are suffering the consequences of that decision. Klingsor castrated himself to quell his sexual desires in a failed attempt at achieving purity. Parsifal killed a swan thereby exhibiting a lack of empathy. Kundry, many lifetimes ago, laughed at Christ as he carried the cross to his crucifixion thereby exhibiting a streak of cruelty. For this act, she is condemned to a karmic series of rebirths from which she desperately longs to escape, i.e., to die. Her most recent reincarnation is in the male monastery, Montsalvat, home to the Knights of the Grail. Here Kundry has two contrasting yearnings. The first, which she detests but is exceptionally good at performing, is sexually seducing the Knights of the Grail. The second, for which she longs to succeed but invariably fails, is to do good. In this instance, her good act is to find the healing ingredient for a wound on Amfortas, the ruler of the Kingdom of the Grail, whom she previously seduced. In act 2, Klingsor, Parsifal, and Kundry have a climactic encounter followed by Kundry's reconciliation and redemption in act 3.

Lohengrin (**1848**). *Lohengrin* is the third of Wagner's mature operas. Elsa, the ward of Friedrich von Telramund and his evil wife, Ortrud, is falsely accused by Telramund of killing her brother Gottfried. Through her silence, Elsa does not deny the charge. The Grail Knight, Lohengrin, answers Elsa's call to defend her by acting as her champion in combat against her accuser, i.e., Telramund. Lohengrin agrees to defend her claim of innocence. He also agrees to become her husband if she swears to never ask him his name or from whence he comes. Ortrud plants seeds of doubt in Elsa as to Lohengrin's background. As a result, Elsa asks Lohengrin those questions, and the opera ends tragically.

 Lohengrin is subject to multiple interpretations. Some of these include (1) the ethereal or divine entering into human history, (2) the non-rational nature of love and the foundation of trust in a love relationship, (3) the plight of the alienated artist, and (4) a rallying cry for German unity. *Lohengrin* was the favorite of King Ludwig II of Bavaria, Richard Wagner's future benefactor.

Mime. We first meet Mime in *Das Rheingold*, the first opera in *The Ring* tetralogy. We learn that Mime is a master gold and silver smith who forged the ring for his brother, Alberich. Mime wants to gain possession of the ring for himself. In the third opera of *The Ring*, *Siegfried*, we learn that Mime acquired Siegmund's broken sword, Nothung, when he finds Sieglinde dying in childbirth. He "adopts" her newborn child, Siegfried. Mime's motivation to raise Siegfried is not from love. Rather, his motivation is to gain possession of the ring by raising Siegfried to kill the current owner of the ring. Mime further plans to kill Siegfried and then take possession of the ring himself. Mime's plan does not work out in Mime's favor; Siegfried acquires the ring and then kills Mime.

 The character Mime also is used as a dramatic device to provide the audience with background information. In *Das Rheingold* he describes the history and current condition of the Nibelungs. In *Siegfried*, he explains the history of what occurred between *Das Rheingold* and *Siegfried*. Through Mime's encounter with Wotan, we learn of the physical and psychological detachment of Wotan. Although Mime does not possess the dramatic stature of many of the characters in *The Ring*, such as Wotan, Alberich, Brünnhilde and Siegfried, he plays an important role in the drama.

Nothung. Nothung (literally "needful") is the name of the magical sword created by Wotan. This sword, a symbol of military power, is designed to help Wotan reacquire the ring he was forced to relinquish at the end of *Das Rheingold*. As the ruler of contracts, Wotan cannot steal it from its present owner. Therefore, he needs someone who is ignorant of the history of the ring and is not bound by the ethics of contracts. This person is Wotan's grandson, Siegfried. He will need a magic weapon to defeat the present owner of the ring, who has now taken the form of a dragon. This magic weapon is the sword, Nothung.

Nothung has a long history in *The Ring*. It was created by Wotan between *Das Rheingold* and *Die Walküre*. Between these two operas, Wotan inserted it into a tree for his son Siegmund to find. In *Die Walküre*, Siegmund extracts it from the tree. Wotan breaks the sword as Siegmund battles Hunding, Sieglinde's legal husband. Brünnhilde retrieves the broken sword and gives it to Sieglinde, Siegmund's sister and declared wife. Mime takes the sword from Sieglinde as she dies giving birth to Siegfried, the son of Siegmund and Sieglinde. Siegfried reforges the sword, uses it as a weapon to kill twice, offers it as a gift, and uses it as a barrier to prevent a perceived infidelity. For an inanimate object, the sword has a very active life.

Parsifal (the opera and the character) (1877). *Parsifal* was the last opera Wagner composed. We first meet Parsifal in act 1. He enters Montsalvat, the castle of the Knights of the Grail, looking for the swan that he had just killed. The brotherhood of the Grail Knights has been in a state of decline ever since the spear that wounded Christ on the cross has been stolen. Gurnemanz, one of the lead knights, suspects that Parsifal might be the person who can restore the spear to Montsalvat. At the end of act 1, it appears that Parsifal will not be Montsalvat's redeemer.

In act 2, Parsifal successfully resists several tempting sexual encounters, the most potent of which comes from Kundry. Parsifal resists Kundry's seduction, and at the end of the act he gains possession of the spear from the evil magician, Klingsor. In act 3, Parsifal returns to Montsalvat with the spear on Good Friday thereby restoring spiritual growth and salvation to Montsalvat. Good Friday commemorates the day that Jesus, through compassion, sacrificed his life to restore salvation to humanity.

Parsifal is a complex opera; at its core, it is a story of a person, Parsifal, learning through and ultimately embodying the human emotion of compassion.

Parsifal begins with Parsifal thoughtlessly killing a swan and concludes with Parsifal gaining compassion for all living things.

Wagner called *Parsifal* a "Festival Play for the Consecration of the Stage" (*Ein Bühnenweihfestspiel*). *Parsifal* often is interpreted as Wagner's homage to Christianity. Many of Wagner's librettos are grounded in myths. For example, *The Ring* is rooted in Teutonic mythology, and *Tristan and Isolde* is based on a Celtic legend. If *Parsifal* is an homage to Christianity, it is to Christianity as mythology. Wagner did not consider myths and mythologies as fantasies or stories meant to entertain. Rather, he understood myths as illustrating core features of the human psyche. Referring to a Christian text as mythology is not to denigrate the text, but rather to elevate it to seriousness and solemnity.[242]

The Flying Dutchman (the opera and character) (1841). The *Flying Dutchman* is the first of Wagner's major operas. The story is relatively simple, but psychologically haunting. It is about a man who made a mistake for which he is cursed. His punishment is that he must keep sailing until the curse is removed through the love of a faithful woman. He comes ashore every seven years seeking this woman. He has a long history of failure to find such a woman. The opera begins as the Dutchman sails into a happy Norwegian fishing village in his continuous quest to find a faithful woman.

Senta, one of the village's young women, is obsessed with the idea of this sad figure. (See **Senta** below.) The townswomen do not disguise their concerns with Senta's obsession. When the Dutchman appears at her father's home, Senta is determined to be his savior. This theme of redemption through love becomes a recurring theme in Wagner's operas.

The Ring of the Nibelung (the opera). The *Ring of the Nibelung* (*The Ring*) is a 16-hour tetralogy written over 28 years, 1848-1876. The framework of *The Ring* is the quest for power and what people will give up for power, such as humanity, community, and love.

Early in the first opera, *Das Rheingold*, we find the Rhine daughters[243] happily swimming around a mound of gold. They tell us that the gold, if shaped into a ring, would give the owner immense power, but the price would be the forfeiture of love. By the end of scene i, this figurative Garden of Eden, has been marred by Alberich's anger at being rebuffed by the Rhine daughters. His anger

---

[242] See Raymond Furness, *Wagner and Literature*, chapter 3: Wagner and Myth. Referring to Jung and Kerényi's analyses of myths, Furness states that myths are "precious psychic revelations" and he describes them as a "re-enactment of certain psychic preoccupations beneath rational thought...." (p. 71)

[243] Rhine daughters are also be referred to as Rhinemaidens. The German word "Rheintöchter" is translated as daughters of the Rhine.

impels him to exchange the emotion of love for the desire of power. Between scenes i and ii, Alberich's brother, Mime, forges the ring for Alberich. Alberich uses this ring's power to amass a horde of gold to facilitate his quest for world domination. In scene ii of *Das Rheingold*, Wotan, the ruler of the world, tries to extract himself from a legal contract. The terms of that contract are that he will finance building Valhalla by using Freia, the goddess of youth and love, as payment. After some negotiation, the contract is amended by substituting Alberich's gold for Freia. Wotan agrees to this change because he plans to take the gold, including the ring, from Alberich to settle his contract. Wotan must relinquish the ring as part of the settlement. Wotan's plan now becomes finding someone to take the ring from its current owner and return it to him.

Wotan's half-baked plan lays the foundation for the next three operas in *The Ring*: *Die Walküre*, *Siegfried*, and *Götterdämmerung*. *Die Walküre* and *Siegfried* portray Wotan's failed attempts to regain the ring. *Götterdämmerung* portrays Alberich's attempt to regain the ring, and it concludes with Brünnhilde burning Valhalla and returning the ring to the Rhine daughters.

In *Die Walküre*, Wotan plans to use two of his children, Siegmund and Sieglinde, to acquire the ring. Wotan's plan is to have Siegmund extract the sword from a tree into which Wotan had previously implanted it. (See **Nothung** above.) Wotan's plan involves Siegmund using that sword to obtain the ring. Act 1 of *Die Walküre* opens by bringing Siegmund and Sieglinde together after having been separated in early childhood. Although Sieglinde is married (see **Hunding** above), Siegmund and Sieglinde fall in love. Despite recognizing each other as brother and sister, Siegmund and Sieglinde become passionate. Their budding love relationship quickly becomes incestuous, and they conceive a child. During act 1, Siegmund extracts the sword. (See **Nothung** above.)

In act 2, Wotan's plan unravels. Wotan instructs Brünnhilde not to defend Siegmund during his battle with Hunding. (See **Siegmund and Sieglinde** below.) Recognizing the love between Siegmund and Sieglinde, Brünnhilde disobeys Wotan. Her disobedience results in Wotan shattering Nothung, the death of Siegmund, and her facilitating the narrow escape of Sieglinde. Brünnhilde also retrieves the broken sword and gives it to Sieglinde. Act 3 focuses on the schism between Wotan and Brünnhilde created by Brünnhilde's disobedience of Wotan. Brünnhilde's punishment is her loss of divinity and banishment from Valhalla. (See **Brünnhilde** above.)

In *Siegfried*, Wotan's plan moves to the son of Siegmund and Sieglinde, Siegfried. Siegfried is raised by Mime. (See **Mime** above.) Siegfried reforges the sword Nothung (See **Nothung** above) and uses it to obtain the ring. He awakens Brünnhilde from her forced slumber, and they pledge their eternal love to each other. Siegfried gives Brünnhilde the ring as a token of his love. During

Siegfried, Wotan comes to realize that the likelihood of his acquiring the ring is becoming remote.

The fourth opera of *The Ring*, *Götterdämmerung*, introduces Hagen (see **Gunther and Hagen** above), Alberich's son. Just as Siegmund and Siegfried were Wotan's instruments to acquire the ring, Hagen is Alberich's instrument to acquire the ring. *Götterdämmerung* is the story of Siegfried's succumbing to the temptations of society. These temptations lead him to betray Brünnhilde. Brünnhilde obtains her revenge on Siegfried by arranging for his murder. *The Ring* concludes with Brünnhilde returning the ring to the Rhine daughters. In doing so, she sets Valhalla on fire thereby destroying the old-world order. The concluding music foretells the ushering in of a new beginning.

The Ring provides many directorial choices. For example, it can be set as an epic beginning with the world's creation and ending with global destruction. *The Ring* can be interpreted in the spirit of Marx's *Communist Manifesto* as the transition from capitalism to socialism or to some other socio-economic system of organization. It also can be interpreted in terms of environmentalism, feminism, or other *-isms*. *The Ring* also can be viewed as a family epic spanning multiple generations, similar to the Greek tragedy of the House of Atreus. The ending leaves open the question of whether the cycle repeats itself or whether we are entering a new age, presumably an age governed by love instead of power.

The ring (the object). The physical object of the ring was created from a mound of undifferentiated gold, known by its eponymous name, Rhinegold. We are told (by the Rhine daughters) that when the gold is transformed into a ring, it bestows untold power onto the owner. The price for forging the gold into a ring is the forfeiture of love and all that is associated with love: friendship, compassion, and empathy. Alberich makes this trade of love for power, but he is robbed of the ring by Wotan. As a result of this robbery, Alberich infuses the ring with two curses: "death to whoever shall wear it," and "each man shall covet its acquisition, but none shall enjoy it to lasting gain."

Senta. Senta and the Dutchman are the central characters of Wagner's first mature opera, *The Flying Dutchman*. (See **The Flying Dutchman** above.) Senta, a young woman, is obsessed with the idea of a man condemned to wander the seas in search of a faithful woman. She fantasizes over a portrait of the Flying Dutchman legend and literally spins tales about him. And then this figure in *corpore* appears on her doorstep. Senta does not hesitate to pledge herself to the Dutchman's redemption. Senta is the first of many Wagnerian heroines who embodies the theme of redemption through love.

By nineteenth century standards Senta is a romantic heroine who will sacrifice everything to redeem her betrothed. By twentieth century standards, Senta is a neurotic woman who is obsessed with the idea of redeeming her man. By late twentieth century standards, Senta is a woman who defines herself totally in terms of a man. Despite her problems, Senta is among the first of many wonderfully complicated Wagnerian characters.

Siegfried. Siegfried is a major character in Wagner's tetralogy, *The Ring*. Siegfried is Wotan's grandson, and his parents are Siegmund and Sieglinde. Siegfried's growth into adulthood is the subject of the third opera of *The Ring*, *Siegfried*. The machinations that lead to Siegfried's death are the subject of *The Ring's* last opera, *Göttterdämmerung*.

Siegfried does several remarkable things during his life. These include reforging Wotan's/Siegmund's sword (see **Nothung** above), killing a dragon, breaking Wotan's spear, conversing with a bird, walking through fire, and winning Brünnhilde's love. Siegfried acquires the ring but is oblivious to its power (see **The ring (the object)** above). He becomes a tool of the Gibichung brothers, Gunther and Hagan. They give Siegfried a potion that leads him to betray Brünnhilde. Siegfried has an ignoble death, yet Brünnhilde vindicates his life with a spectacular funeral.

Wagner discusses the Siegfried character at length in his letter to August Röckel.[244] In this letter he describes Siegfried as "the man of the future" who "must create himself" and is "the most perfect human being because he knows that death is better than a life of fear."[245] The problem for the audience is that Siegfried, as a character, seems one dimensional; he does not appear to develop into a fully integrated person. He acts instinctively in a corrupt world and is easily led astray by societal temptations. Siegfried is more potentiality than actuality, resembling more Aristotle's acorn than an oak tree.

Family relations can become very confusing in *The Ring*. Brünnhilde, Siegmund, and Sieglinde are Wotan's children. Siegmund and Sieglinde are twins, and they are Siegfried's parents. Siegfried's lineage creates a challenging brain teaser. In the 2013 movie "Twilight of the Gods" Siegfried's complex lineage is described sarcastically by Nietzsche as follows: Siegfried is (1) the son of his uncle (Siegmund) and the nephew of his mother (Sieglinde); (2) by virtue of (1) above, his own cousin; (3) the nephew of his wife (Brünnhilde), as well as the son of his aunt (Brünnhilde); (4) by virtue of (3) above, his own uncle by marriage; (5) the son-in-law of his grandfather (Wotan); and (6) the brother-

---

[244] *Selected Letters of Richard Wagner, translated and edited by Stewart Spencer and Barry Millington,* (New York: W.W. Norton & Company), pp. 300-313, particularly 308ff.

[245] *Selected Letters*, pp. 308-9.

in-law of his aunt (Brünnhilde), who also is his sister and his wife. Fortunately, Siegfried is not interested in the past, so he is spared the complexities of his lineage.

Siegmund and Sieglinde. Siegmund and Sieglinde are twins sired by Wotan with a human woman. Their life and role are described in the second opera of *The Ring, Die Walküre* (See *Die Walküre* above.) Wotan fathered the twins for the purpose of regaining the ring for himself. Wotan's plan requires free agents acting independently of his will. Siegmund and Sieglinde are pawns in a game beyond their control or comprehension.

Wotan's plan, somewhat hazy in detail, is for Siegmund to use Wotan's sword to acquire the ring from its current owner and then voluntarily give it to Wotan. Fricka, Wotan's wife and the goddess of marriage, demands Siegmund's death. She makes clear to Wotan the moral and logical shortcomings of his plan. Fricka argues that the twins are guilty of adultery and incest and compels him to defend the marriage contract between Hunding and Sieglinde rather than defend Siegmund. Moreover, she points out that Wotan has orchestrated these events, and therefore they are not free agents.

Three important events occur related to Siegmund. First, Siegmund obtains the sword, christened as Nothung. Second, Siegmund and Sieglinde consummate the relationship that will result in the birth of Siegfried. And third, after Siegmund's sword is broken, Brünnhilde retrieves the broken pieces and gives the pieces to Sieglinde. Siegfried later will reforge these broken pieces in act I of the next opera of *The Ring, Siegfried*.

Tannhäuser (1845). *Tannhäuser* is the second of Wagner's mature operas. Tannhäuser is torn between two different aspects of love: the sensual as represented by lascivious Venus in the Venusberg and spiritual love as represented by saintly Elisabeth in the medieval town of Wartburg. Wagner's orgiastic music in the Venusberg broke the norms of what musically and visually could be portrayed in high art. Through the influence of Baudelaire, *Tannhäuser* set the stage for the French Symbolist movement.

Tristan and Isolde (the opera and the characters) (1859). *Tristan and Isolde* is the musical expression of desire, particularly sexual desire. As background to the opera, Tristan is the nephew of King Mark, the king of Cornwall, and Isolde is an Irish princess. To broker peace between the two waring nations, Isolde is betrothed to King Mark. The opera opens on a ship with Tristan bringing Isolde from Ireland to Cornwall. Tristan and Isolde love each other, but for a multitude of reasons they cannot express their love until the end of act 1.

In this opera, "the day" is contrasted with "the night." The day represents the realm of social obligation and restraint, and the night represents the realm of unrestrained passion and union. The two eponymous protagonists embark on a downward spiral of inseparable longing toward death. *Tristan and Isolde* has had a major influence on the future course of artistic and psychological expression. *Tristan and Isolde's* chromatic music and departure from tonality set the stage for twentieth century musical innovations. The opera's portrayal of the sexual passion set the stage for Freud, and its transcendental portrayal of love and death set the stage for symbolist and decadent artists.

Valhalla. In *The Ring*, Wotan designs Valhalla as the palace from which he will rule the world by enforcing contracts. Between *Das Rheingold* and *Die Walküre*, Valhalla has morphed into a fortress designed to secure his rule against potential usurpers. Planned as a playground for the gods, it became a military fortress populated with dead heroes that Wotan plans to use to defend the gods' rule against Alberich. (See **Alberich** above.) In the fourth opera of *The Ring*, *Götterdämmerung*, Valhalla becomes a funeral pyre using logs from the World Ash Tree.

Valkyries. *The Ring* includes nine very tough and cold-hearted warrior maidens known as Valkyries. Their purpose is to bring dead heroes to Wotan in Valhalla. Brünnhilde (see **Brünnhilde** above) is the lead Valkyrie and the favorite of her father, Wotan. Erda, the earth goddess, is her mother. The Valkyries are Wotan's minions and subject to his will. In act 3 of *Die Walküre*, Brünnhilde disobeys her father, and he punishes her by taking away her Valkyrie status and power.

Wotan. Wotan is the principal god in *The Ring*, and he oversees the current world order. He created the legal structure of binding contracts. These contracts serve as the social and moral glue that keeps chaos from tearing society apart. Of *The Ring's* three major protagonists, Wotan, Brünnhilde, and Siegfried, Wotan is the story's tragic hero because he consciously makes decisions that lead to his downfall.

The Ring has two characters focused on world domination: Alberich and Wotan. (See **Alberich** above.) Alberich wants to acquire world domination, and Wotan wants to retain world domination. Alberich wants power for power's sake, whereas Wotan wants power to provide stability and order to the world. Wagner portrays Alberich as an evil ruler, in the order of Joffrey Baratheon in *The Game of Thrones* or Joseph Stalin. Wagner portrays Wotan as a good ruler, a benevolent monarch, but one with many all too human flaws.

191

Wotan is the most complex personality of the huge list of characters in *The Ring*. He is pompous and arrogant, a husband and adulterer, a terrible father, short-tempered and malicious, a wrangler and conniver, a strategist but a poor one. By the end of the saga, he is dejected and resigned to his own death. He has gotten himself so twisted up in his own machinations that when he withdraws from the world in the third opera, *Siegfried*, it is less of a choice than a realization that he is at count nine in a ten-count boxing match.

Appendix F. Philosophical Influences

Wagner, Joyce, and Proust were very well read, including in philosophy. Each of these artists was significantly influenced by specific philosophers, and this influence impacted their respective artistic works. It is not necessary to be familiar with their philosophical interests to enjoy their works. However, just as familiarity with their biographies adds a dimension of appreciation, an awareness of their philosophical interests adds another dimension of appreciation of their artistic creations.

Richard Wagner was principally influenced by the German philosophers Ludwig Feuerbach (1804-1872) and Arthur Schopenhauer (1788-1860). Feuerbach deconstructed Christian theology into an anthropological framework and fundamentally rejected traditional metaphysics in favor of secular humanism. Whereas Feuerbach brings speculative metaphysics down to earth, Schopenhauer returns to speculative metaphysics by resurrecting Kant's concept of the noumena and reinterpreting it into his concept of the Will. Schopenhauer aims to explain how the physical world came into being, but without employing any religious underpinnings. Schopenhauer's philosophy, while rooted in Kant's phenomenon-noumenon distinction,[246] rejected Kant's epistemological theory that we cannot know anything about the noumenon. Schopenhauer argued that we can know about the noumenal realm, and that it is undifferentiated energy and blind impulse (the noumenal Will). Schopenhauer's ideas influenced *Tristan and Isolde*, *Parsifal*, and a draft libretto of the ending of *The Ring*. An early draft of *The Ring*, commonly identified as the Feuerbach ending, concludes with love and human liberation as the outcome. Wagner changed this ending to what is commonly known as the Schopenhauer ending in which Brünnhilde sings of the negation of the Will. Wagner ultimately rejected both of these endings and opted to conclude *The Ring* with pure music. Arguably, this is a very Schopenhauerian statement since Schopenhauer argued that music was an expression of the Will.

James Joyce was influenced by Plato (428-348 BCE), Aristotle (384-322 BCE), Thomas Aquinas (1225-1274), Giambattista Vico (1668-1744) and George Berkeley (1685-1753). Joyce incorporated ideas from these thinkers into his novels as ideas to either accept, reject, or modify. Joyce used Plato's and

---

[246] Phenomenal reality includes objects in space and time and subject to the framework of causation. Noumenal reality includes objects not in space or time.

Aristotle's ideas of form and substance, reason and experience, mysticism and realism, and potentiality and actuality. He used Aquinas's concept of the Christian Trinity in terms of paternity (God the Father and God the Son) and developed an aesthetic theory of the artist as both creator and created. Joyce used Berkeley's argument that all that exists is the mind and that to exist is to be perceived ("esse est percipi") by a mind. Joyce used this idea of the mind as the artist who synthesizes experience. The opening of episode 3: Proteus in *Ulysses* is an homage to Berkeley. In this episode, Stephen is debating within himself different theories of reality: "Open your eyes now. I will. One moment. Has all vanished since? If I open and am for ever in the black adiaphane." (episode 3, 3.26-27)

Vico, an early philosopher of history, provided Joyce with a theory of universal history of human development and civil society. Vico's theory is rooted in the cyclical concepts of birth, development, pinnacle, decline, collapse, and rebirth; and he used this pattern to explain the rise and fall of civilizations. Vico argued that this pattern was as rigid as the laws of natural science. Vico's explanation in terms of cycles, in contrast to the Christian explanation of divine teleology and eschatology, provided Joyce with the foundation for his cyclical theory of human history and the rise and fall of civilizations. The cycles of birth, development, death, and rebirth continue, only the individuals differ. This pattern is captured by the phrase "there is nothing new under the sun." For example, Leopold Bloom is a modern-day reenactment of Homer's Odysseus. Likewise, *Finnegans Wake* is the retelling of human history's births, marriages, burials, and rebirths at both the micro and macro levels.

Marcel Proust was influenced by Henri Bergson (1859-1941). Specifically, he was influenced by Bergson's analysis of consciousness, memory, and the depth and complexity of our psychological experiences. Bergson analyzed the nature of consciousness. Unlike physical objects, the content of consciousness does not exist in space. Feelings, memories, and all that is encompassed in what we call subjective or psychological experience, cannot be laid out side by side or mapped onto a Cartesian grid as quantities. Bergson argued that subjective experience is not a series of successive moments, but rather moments that simultaneously spread forward and backward through time. Objects of consciousness have duration, not location. As a result, psychological phenomena can occur simultaneously and be integrated onto and into each other. For example, Friday's experiences include Thursday's experiences, not in terms of sequence, but rather as Thursday's experiences being layered upon Friday's experiences. Learning something about you on Thursday intrinsically informs my experience of you on Friday.

The experience of remembering is not isolated from the experiences preceding and following that act of remembering. For example, if I meet someone on Friday, and we meet again the following Wednesday, I bring to the second meeting my experiences/memory of our prior meeting. Those experiences on Wednesday are colored by my experiences from the prior Friday. Wednesday's experiences are not pristine, but are infused with the past Friday's experiences, those either of memory or of imagination. In *Time and Free Will*, Bergson writes: "Thus I said that several conscious states are organized into a whole, permeate one another, gradually gain a richer content...." (p. 122) Hence, an experience is enriched by both future experiences and memories of past experiences. Life is retained in memory. Throughout *In Search of*, Proust weaves the insight that memories are woven:

> From the sound of the rain I recaptured the scent of the lilacs at Combray, from the shifting of the sun's rays on the balcony the pigeons in the Champs-Elysées, from the muffling of all noise in the heat of the morning hours, the cool taste of cherries,.... (SCG, vol 2, p. 718)

Bibliography

Select Bibliography for James Joyce

Attridge, Derek, ed. *The Cambridge Companion to James Joyce*. Cambridge Companion to Literature. Cambridge: Cambridge University Press, 1990.

Blissett, William. "James Joyce in the Smithy of His Soul." In *James Joyce Today: Essays on the Major Works*, edited by Thomas F. Staley, 96–134. Bloomington: Indiana University Press, 1966.

Ellmann, Richard. *James Joyce*. Oxford: Oxford University Press, 1983.

Gifford, Don, and Seidman, Robert J. Ulysses *Annotated: Notes for James Joyce's* Ulysses. Berkeley: University of California Press, 1974.

Gilbert, Stuart. *James Joyce's* Ulysses: *A Study*. New York: Vintage Books, 1955.

Joyce, James. *Ulysses*. Edited by Hans Gabler. New York: Vintage Books, 1986.

Martin, Timothy. *Joyce and Wagner: A Study of Influence*. Cambridge: Cambridge University Press, 1991.

McCarthy, Jack, and Ross, Danis. *Joyce's Dublin: A Walking Guide to* Ulysses. New York: St. Martin's Press, 1986.

Owens, Cóilín. *Before Daybreak "After the Race" and The Origins of Joyce's Art*. Gainsville: University Press of Florida, 2010.

Select Bibliography for Marcel Proust

Alexander, Patrick. *Marcel Proust's Search for Lost Time: A Reader's Guide to* The Remembrance of Things Past. New York: Vintage Books, 2007.

Bales, Richard, ed. *The Cambridge Companion to Proust*. Cambridge Companion to Literature. Cambridge: Cambridge University Press, 2001.

Bergson, Henri. *Time and Free Will: An Essay on the Immediate Data of Consciousness*. New York: The Macmillan Co, 1910.

Bowie, Malcolm. *Proust among the Stars*. New York: Columbia University Press, 1998.

Carter, William C. *Marcel Proust: A Life.* New Haven: Yale University Press, 2000.

Karpeles, Eric. *Paintings in Proust: A Visual Companion to* In Search of Lost Time. London: Thames & Hudson, 2008.

Moss, Howard. *The Magic Lantern of Marcel Proust.* Philadelphia: Paul Dry Books, 2012.

Nattiez, Jean-Jacques. *Proust as Musician.* Translated by Derrick Puffett. Cambridge: Cambridge University Press, 1989.

Painter, George D. *Marcel Proust: A Biography.* London: Pimlico, 1996.

Proust, Marcel. *Remembrance of Things Past.* Translated by C. K. Scott Moncrieff and Frederick A. Blossom. Two volumes. New York: Random House, 1934.

Shattuck, Roger. *Proust's Way: A Field Guide to* In Search of Lost Time. New York: W. W. Norton & Company, 2000.

Swann, Jeffrey. "Wagner and Proust." *The Wagner Journal* 12, no. 2: 34–55 (2018).

Select Bibliography for Richard Wagner

Bribitzer-Stull, Matthew. *Understanding the Leitmotif: From Wagner to Hollywood Film Music.* Cambridge: Cambridge University Press, 2015.

Carr, Jonathan. *The Wagner Clan: The Saga of Germany's Most Illustrious and Infamous Family.* New York: Atlantic Monthly Press, 2007.

Cooke, Deryck. *An Introduction to* Der Ring des Nibelungen. Decca, The Classic Sound (2 CDs), 1967.

Cooke, Deryck. *I Saw the World End: A Study of Wagner's* Ring. London: Oxford University Press, 1979.

Dreyfus, Laurence. *Wagner and the Erotic Impulse.* Cambridge: Harvard University Press, 2010.

Hamann, Brigitte. *Winifred Wagner: A Life at the Heart of Hitler's Bayreuth.* Translated by Alan Bance. Orlando: Harcourt, Inc., 2005.

Hilmes, Oliver. *Cosima Wagner: The Lady of Bayreuth.* Translated by Stewart Spencer. New Haven: Yale University Press, 2010.

Holman, J. K. *Wagner's* Ring: *A Listener's Companion & Concordance.* Portland: Amadeus Press, 1998.

Lewis, Pericles. *Modernism, Nationalism, and the Novel.* Cambridge: Cambridge University Press, 2000.

Newman, Ernest. *The Life of Richard Wagner*, in four volumes. New York: Alfred A. Knopf, 1933–1946.

Nietzsche, Friedrich. *The Case of Wagner in Basic Writings of Nietzsche.* Translated by Walter Kaufmann. New York: The Modern Library, 1968.

Quenoy, Paul du. *Wagner and the French Muse: Music, Society, and Nation in Modern France.* Palo Alto: Academia Press, 2011.

Schopenhauer, Arthur. *The World as Will and Representation.* Translated by E. F. J. Payne. New York: Over Publications, 1958.

Spotts, Frederic. *Bayreuth: A History of the Wagner Festival.* New Haven: Yale University Press, 1994.

Stone, Monte. The Ring *Disc: An Interactive Guide to Wagner's Ring.* 1999.

Wagner, Richard. *Richard Wagner Prose Works.* Translated by William Ashton Ellis. Multi-volumes. Lincoln: University of Nebraska Press, 1995.

Selected Letters of Richard Wagner. Translated and edited by Stewart Spencer and Barry Millington. New York: W. W. Norton & Company, 1988.

Wagner Society of Washington, DC, YouTube.

Williams, Simon. *Richard Wagner and Festival Theatre.* Westport: Praeger, 1994.

Williams, Simon. *Wagner and the Romantic Hero.* Cambridge: Cambridge University Press, 2004.

Select Bibliography for Romanticism to Modernism and "Wagnermania"

Furness, Raymond. *Wagner and Literature.* Manchester: Manchester University Press, 1982.

Horowitz, Joseph, *Wagner Nights: An American History.* Berkeley: University of California Press, 1994.

Martin, Stoddard. *Wagner to "The Waste Land": A Study of the Relationship of Wagner to English Literature.* Totowa: Barnes & Noble Books, 1982.

O'Connor, Charles A., III. *The Great War and the Death of God.* Washington, DC: New Academia Publishing, 2014.

Rasula, Jed. *History of a Shiver: The Sublime Impudence of Modernism.* Oxford: Oxford University Press, 2016.

Ross, Alex. *Wagnerism: Art and Politics in the Shadow of Music.* New York: Farrar, Straus and Giroux, 2020.

198